AN ENGLISH GOVERNESS IN THE GREAT WAR

An English

Governess in the

Great War

THE SECRET BRUSSELS DIARY

OF MARY THORP

Sophie De Schaepdrijver
and Tammy M. Proctor

OXFORD
UNIVERSITY PRESS

OXFORD
UNIVERSITY PRESS

Oxford University Press is a department of the University of Oxford. It furthers
the University's objective of excellence in research, scholarship, and education
by publishing worldwide. Oxford is a registered trade mark of Oxford University
Press in the UK and certain other countries.

Published in the United States of America by Oxford University Press
198 Madison Avenue, New York, NY 10016, United States of America.

Library of Congress Cataloging-in-Publication Data
Names: Thorp, Mary, 1864–1945, author. | De Schaepdrijver, Sophie, 1961– editor. |
Proctor, Tammy M., 1968– editor.
Title: An English governess in the Great War : the secret Brussels diary of Mary Thorp /
[edited by] Sophie De Schaepdrijver and Tammy M. Proctor.
Description: New York, NY : Oxford University Press, 2017. | Includes bibliographical references.
Identifiers: LCCN 2016045081 | ISBN 9780190276706 (hardback)
Subjects: LCSH: Thorp, Mary, 1864–1945—Diaries. |
World War, 1914–1918—Personal narratives, British. |
English—Belgium—Brussels—Diaries. | Governesses—Belgium—Brussels—Diaries. |
World War, 1914–1918—Social aspects—Belgium—Brussels. |
Civilians in war—Belgium—Brussels—History—20th century. |
Brussels (Belgium)—Biography. | BISAC: HISTORY / Military / World War I. |
HISTORY / Europe / Western.
Classification: LCC D640 .T57 2017 | DDC 940.3493/32092 [B] —dc23
LC record available at https://lccn.loc.gov/2016045081

1 3 5 7 9 8 6 4 2

Printed by Sheridan Books, Inc., United States of America

CONTENTS

AN ENGLISH GOVERNESS IN THE GREAT WAR

Introduction

This is the diary of Mary Thorp, an English governess living in German-occupied Brussels during World War I. Though she disparaged her diary as a mere chronicle of "local gossip and 'side-shows' of the War," it lucidly observed civilian life under military occupation. It did so anonymously and in secret: Thorp did not leave her name in the manuscript, and she hid it because keeping a diary in wartime Brussels was dangerous. Her diary documents the daily indignities of living under enemy control, and it offers a personal story. As a foreigner and an educated woman in between classes, Thorp was alert to dimensions of life during occupation that might have escaped others.

Living under occupation was a war experience pertaining to neither battlefront nor home front. Across Europe, occupying armies controlled populations in an atmosphere made up of parts coercion, parts wary cohabitation. This existence was a slog: civilians were cut off from the outside world, they lived under constant surveillance, and many struggled to survive as economies stagnated. Some civilians kept diaries as a way to remind themselves that their lives were not on hiatus.

Mary Thorp was one of them. Keeping a diary was her way to try to make sense of the war and to express where she stood: what she hoped for, whom she felt responsible for, and what she felt to be her calling. She was painfully attuned to the war's events; it is no coincidence that she started her diary in September 1916, a time of hope for the success of the Somme offensive. At the same time, it was exceptional for a civilian to start a diary in that month; most of the civilians who kept diaries in wartime Belgium started at war's outbreak, a time of dramatic events and great exaltation. That Thorp kept writing until January 1919 was unusual as well; many diaries lost momentum well before the Armistice.

Over thirty months, she kept up the (almost) daily discipline of making entries in tidy notebooks—five in all—covering both everyday and exceptional events; she chronicled what she saw around her as well as the echoes of global affairs. In one and the same sentence she could report on discussions in the *Reichstag* and deplore the dearth of potatoes. But then in a war diary, potatoes are never just potatoes. One could put the blame for their scarcity on civilian profiteering, as some diarists did; or one could, like Thorp, blame the occupying army. Either way the price of potatoes was a fundamentally political matter.

The diary's length, the time period it covers, and its richness of themes all give it particular value to historians interested in the history of the First World War "from below." We had both used the diary in our research and wanted to see it published. But who was the author? Because Thorp did not identify herself, the notebooks were deposited at the In Flanders Fields Museum in Ieper in 1989 as an "anonymous woman's diary." We needed to find the woman who wrote with such a clear sense of herself and her world. We had two clues: her employers' names and their Brussels address. The Brussels population registers listed the inhabitants; among them was an English governess named Mary Thorp. Could she be our diarist? On we went to the foreigners' registers. We found Thorp's entry form. It bore her signature—in the same hand as the diary entries. We had found her! From that point on, records in Brussels, Bruges, London, Antwerp, and elsewhere allowed us to reconstruct her story, starting with the bare bones, then filling in details. The greatest of fortunes led us to the family archive of Thorp's employers, containing her governess notebooks, pictures of the family homes, and, a precious find, photos of Thorp herself.

So, who was Mary Thorp? She was born into a lower-middle-class family in London on January 1, 1864, the first child of Thomas Thorp and Annette née Townshend. The family lived in London until the early 1870s and then relocated to Bruges, Belgium, where her parents lived until their deaths. Mary's complicated family background had a profound effect on her sense of her place in the world. Her father, who was born in 1816, married Mary Townshend, Annette's elder sister, in 1835. They lived in Marylebone, London. Local chronicles show Thomas Thorp to have been a respected citizen.[1] As a self-employed cab proprietor, he would have identified either as respectable working class or lower middle class. The couple's three eldest sons held skilled working-class jobs as a cab driver, a smith, and a house-painter/decorator.

Thomas Thorp's occupation left a trace in his daughter's war diary many years later, when she pitied small business owners whose workhorses were taken by the German army. "It breaks my heart," she wrote.[2] Her father made a living from the horse-drawn cabriolets (light carriages) nicknamed "cabs" that dominated the

London streets by the 1850s. A cab proprietor's business rose and fell on the health of his horses, whose average working life was only two or three years. Thorp probably managed and drove a single cab only, making his business precarious. The neighborhoods surrounding the major rail and road networks were spider-webbed with small streets known as "mews" that held combination homes and stables for those employed in horse trades. The Thorp family lived in a series of such houses near the Marylebone Road.

The Thorps may well have relocated to Belgium in 1873 because of personal and financial difficulties. The 1850s were a hard decade for them: their youngest child died, as did Mrs. Thorp's parents. In addition, Thorp's business failed, and he was confined to the Marylebone workhouse for debt in 1856.[3] While he was listed again as a "cab proprietor" in the 1861 census, other difficulties arose. His wife Mary died, and he married her sister Annette in September 1863. This was a problematic marriage in a legal sense. While many Victorian widowers relied on their single sisters-in-law to come and keep house for them, they were forbidden from marrying them by the 1835 Deceased Wife's Sister Act, which could annul such marriages years after the fact, rendering children illegitimate and disinherited. Yet historians have found that the law did not actually stop such marriages; many widowers preferred to break the law rather than live outside of marriage, especially if there was a sexual relationship—as there was in this case. Annette Townshend came to live with her brother-in-law to take care of his young children. The two were married in September 1863, and Mary Theresa Agnes Thorp, our diarist, was born on January 1, 1864.[4]

The marriage put a strain on the family. In early 1865, Thomas Thorp brought suit against one of his sons from his first marriage, Thomas Jr., regarding an unpaid loan. Tensions ran high: when, in 1864, Annette Thorp had asked for the money back, her stepdaughter-in-law had called her a prostitute. The account stated, "There had been some family disagreements, and the present claim was an afterthought." Thomas Jr. and his wife accused his father of not really being married to his stepmother, forcing them to produce their marriage certificate. In the end, the judge ordered Thomas Jr. to pay 1£ 10s and for the two parties to split court costs. As he left court, Thomas Jr. declared, "I will see my father d[amne]d first before I will shake hands with him."[5]

It was true that another one of Thomas Thorp's elder sons, William, continued to live with them[6] and remained in touch with his stepsister for many decades afterward, as Mary Thorp's diary shows; still, the family had fractured over Thomas's remarriage, which may have been another reason to leave the country in February 1873, to live first in Ostend and then in Bruges.[7] By then, they had three children: Mary's sister, Georgina, was born around 1866 and her brother Richard, "Dick," arrived in 1870. A fourth child, Leonard, was born in Bruges in 1874. Apart from financial uncertainty, age (Thomas was fifty-seven), and family difficulties, one reason for the move may have been employment: Annette listed her occupation as a "teacher" in the Bruges population registers.

Bruges, a handsome yet low-cost city, was a logical choice. Its English-speaking colony had its own shops, churches, schools, and community organizations. By 1869, there were about 1,200 British residents (out of a total population of 50,000). An 1895 guide called Bruges "an inexpensive place of residence" that offered high-quality and affordable education.[8] The author assured his English readers that even with poor French language skills, they would find a welcoming atmosphere. (They clearly were not expected to know Flemish.) In short, the Thorps found a thriving expatriate community with first-rate educational and cultural opportunities at a fraction of the cost of life in London.

As a result of her parents' move, Mary spent most of her life in Belgium. She did travel: she resided with a well-to-do maternal aunt and uncle in London around 1881 and visited cousins in the United States in 1893. And she corresponded with family and friends around the world, especially with her maternal relatives, the Townshends. They were her direct link to the educated middle class: her grandfather John Townshend ran successful businesses in London. His sons worked in law and medicine and several of his daughters married well-to-do men. Mary and Annette were exceptions. Still, Annette's daughter, Mary, kept in close touch with her Townshend cousins. In 1893, she visited her cousin Mary "May" Townshend Rennard in New York, the daughter of her maternal uncle John, a jurist who had done very well for himself in the United States.[9] May married John C. Rennard, an electrical engineer.[10] The family was well connected in New York circles.[11] A son, John Townshend Rennard, married the daughter of former New York City mayor William Gaynor. He served in the US Army in the First World War; Mary noted it in her diary, remembering him as a toddler from her New York visit.

Mary's family background informed her view of her place in the world. Her wealthy and well-connected relatives gave her a sense of herself as solidly middle class and linked her to the wider world. In addition, she was, as her writings show, a well-educated woman; her French, for one thing, was superb. Yet at the same time, given her immediate family's more precarious social status, she put this education to use not as an affluent woman managing her own household but as an employee in the homes of the wealthy.

Like many other well-educated middle-class young women, Mary Thorp turned to teaching to make ends meet. In 1911 Britain, one of every three working women was employed in domestic service. Governesses were only a small part of this group, but their numbers rose by the end of the century because the middle class grew and governesses remained cheaper than boarding school fees. Organizations placed governesses in respectable households; books gave advice. Emily Peart's *A Book for Governesses* (1869) advised keeping a distance from actual servants: "Have as little to do with them as possible; treat them with invariable politeness."[12] Thorp, as her diary clearly shows, did not see herself as part of the domestic help at all; she referred to them as "our servants." This aloof stance carried the risk of isolation, especially in the suspicion-ridden circumstances of wartime: as she noted in her diary, many employers were afraid their servants would report them to the German military police. Thorp did not think of herself as a servant because she had not come to her work from a poor background. Typically, well-bred young ladies became governesses when their other options were exhausted, often because their fathers had died. Even in the respectable middle classes, limited savings and an absent safety net, paltry or no widows' pensions, and the absence of life insurance spelled poverty.

Thorp took her first job as a governess in December 1887, one month before her twenty-fourth birthday. It was a time of crisis for the family. Earlier that year, her younger sister had died from complications of childbirth, leaving her two young children with their twenty-three-year-old father. He was addicted to drink and incapable of caring for them, so the children went to live with Thorp's mother. Thorp's father died in March 1888 and may have needed expensive medical care before that. All in all, circumstances seem to have propelled Thorp to make her own living. But she was either luckier or better connected than other young governesses; records indicate that she worked only for well-to-do families. Her English birth, her education, and her familiarity with Belgium (including fluent French) helped: governesses of English, Swiss, or German background were in great demand in Belgium.

Governesses assumed control of boys' and girls' education from the ages of seven or eight years. Employing a governess, especially a foreign one, conferred prestige. It could be a lonely life, as governesses were often isolated as "workers between two worlds."[13] Thorp took her first job in the region of Ghent. After that, by early 1888, she was ensconced with the Boulez family in Waregem near Bruges; she was to maintain very fond ties with them, as her diary shows.[14] By 1910, she was working for one of the wealthiest families in Belgium, the Wittoucks.

In May 1910, Thorp moved into the Wittoucks' grand townhouse in Brussels, where she worked with their three boys, Paul (Pavlick), Michael (Micha), and Serge, aged ten, eight, and six, respectively. Her employers were Madame Wittouck, born Catherine de Medem, a Russian aristocrat,[15] and Paul Wittouck, owner of one of the largest sugar refineries in Europe in the town of Tienen (Tirlemont). An American journalist who interviewed him in November 1907 in his Brussels "palatial home" described him as "the king of beet-sugar." He found Mr. Wittouck perfectly affable but unwilling to grant permission to visit the Tienen factory. The journalist went anyway to find the plant heavily guarded. Though Paul Wittouck declined to disclose how much he had invested, feeling it to be "a typical American question," it was clear that the Wittoucks were extremely wealthy.[16]

Their residences were decorated with the requisite Old Master paintings, and they were among the very few Belgians to own a car. In his wartime journal, US Minister Brand Whitlock mentioned them often.[17] In January 1915, he attended a party chez Wittouck; the lady of the house, "despite the fact that a war is on, and that social functions are not being given, wore an elaborate heliotrope satin gown with roses on her corsage and at her knees, and sat there on the [car] fender smoking a cigarette with another in her fingers when that had been smoked up. Much of her silk stockings showing and her long shoes. Her husband is a country man, very rich, and son of an ouvrier [laborer]."[18] In reality, Paul Wittouck was not a country laborer's son at all; the family had been Brussels patricians since the mid-eighteenth century. Paul's brother and business partner, Frantz, married an Austrian woman;[19] the family was, then, quite cosmopolitan. But Whitlock presumably took his cue from Madame Wittouck, who was aware of her status as an aristocrat.[20] She certainly propelled the household to the center of Brussels social life; the Wittoucks were written up more than once in the Paris high society press.[21]

The family maintained two homes. Their town residence was the so-called Hôtel Wittouck on the chic Boulevard de Waterloo, an 1875 urban palace with two carriage entrances and various salons decorated in different styles.[22] In April 1910, the month Thorp came to work for the Wittoucks, they acquired a summer residence called La Fougeraie (Fern Meadows). This was a somewhat nondescript modern château in the elegant suburb of Uccle; Paul Wittouck commissioned the French architect Louis Süe to completely rebuild it in Louis XVI style. A prestigious landscape designer remodeled the expansive grounds. With the family, Mary Thorp spent summers in La Fougeraie, the rest of the year in Brussels.

In spite of her more modest pedigree, Thorp appeared to fit well in this world because of her education, her international connections, and her social confidence. She made close friends among upper-middle-class and aristocratic Belgian women. She was at ease in cosmopolitan circles; during the war, the diplomats she met at the Wittoucks' house clearly appreciated her conversation. She moved with facility between the elevated world of formal dinners and the domestic world of sick children and schoolbooks.

In this domestic world, she was an authority. Her teaching notes, which the family has kept to this day, show her to be a demanding and dedicated educator. They also show that she was often disapproving of what she saw as the boys' lack of diligence. Her hopes were highest for the second boy, Micha. She counted on him to show his two brothers a good example; "he, at least, understands that dissipation only bears bad fruit," she wrote in May 1914. According to family lore, if Micha seems to have been Miss Thorp's favorite, the eldest, nicknamed "Pavlick" ("little Paul" in Russian), was his mother's favorite. But he did not find much favor with his governess. "When will I be able to give him a favorable report!" she scolded in November 1913. Pavlick refused to speak to her in English during their lessons. He paid no attention, his homework was sloppy, his desk untidy—"he lazes about on every score."[23] What irked Thorp most about her eldest pupil was what she saw as his entitled attitude and lack of politeness. He was, she noted, especially rude to the German teacher, to the point of mocking her attire. "How I wish for him to become a fundamentally thoughtful person [she used the term *générosité d'âme*, a staple of moral injunctions] and to rid himself of his selfishness," she wrote in May 1914.[24] That she was not afraid to report her disapproval to her employers shows she did not feel a need to ingratiate herself. She was appointed as a transmitter of values and acted as one.

Many indicators point to Thorp's valued position in the Wittouck household. The Wittoucks' grandson, Éric, was born after Thorp's death, but he recounts his father's description of Thorp as "une maîtresse femme" [roughly, "a woman in charge"].[25] Her central position in the household was obvious; at the death of her employer, Paul Wittouck, she wrote, "We are in the greatest grief. Our best friend has gone."[26] When Madame Wittouck died, in 1928, Thorp was still registered as living with the family. She herself died in Uccle, close to the Fougeraie, in 1945; in all probability, upon retirement the family had provided her with a pension and a residence.

Thorp's wartime dinners with the Wittoucks and their guests made for many conversations with people from the Belgian elite as well as with diplomats, which she recorded. She was, as her entries show, as well-informed as a civilian under occupation could be. She also engaged in those activities that were open to civilians under occupation: she volunteered in a wartime charity for the impoverished lower middle class, a cause probably dear to her because of her own background, but also a cause that women of the Belgian elite (including Madame Wittouck) took on with especial zeal. Another connection she shared with those around her was faith: though christened Anglican, Thorp had at some point become a devout Catholic. A June 1911 photo shows her dispensing catechism to her charges: she is enthroned—the term is not excessive—amid the three boys, meekly arrayed around her in their sailors' costumes. This image once more shows Thorp's *maîtresse femme* status in the household—a pillar, not a servant. When it came to something as crucial to this household as religious education, Thorp was entrusted with it, and she acquitted herself of the task with her customary vigor. Her faith provided solace in wartime. The cyclical celebrations of the Roman Catholic calendar gave rhythm to years that otherwise would have seemed hopelessly lost. And throughout her diary, but even more so in moments of despair, she called for divine intercession.

Remaining active was a form of solace, too, as she sometimes remarked to herself. She was steeped in the concrete details of life: for one thing, she did the arduous rounds of shops for the boys' wardrobes, which brought her face to face with the soaring prices of scarce goods. In short, her position straddled the world of leisure and work. She herself was aware of her closeness to the affluent and their rich tables, and she made a point of redistributing her riches by taking rare treats like sugar or butter to impoverished friends. On occasion, the family's privileged status emerged in non sequiturs: in one June 1917 entry, Thorp worried first about Russia's flagging war effort and then about the Wittouck boys' dwindling supply of tennis balls— apparently a rare commodity in wartime.

But this positioning between worlds also made her vulnerable. As a British national, the German occupation authorities classified Thorp as an enemy alien. She had to check in regularly with the military registration office, and she suffered the sequestration of her life savings by the Germans, which made her even more dependent on her employers. This vulnerable position only added to her strong sense of Englishness. She was particularly proud of those British institutions that provided help to British expatriates in occupied Belgium (among whom she had close friends). Thorp's sense of self as an Englishwoman, then, was key: an element of her identity possibly even more important than her religious belief, her education, her social class, and her attitude toward her profession.

Importantly, she saw herself as someone who had a duty to fulfill abroad. "If I were in England," she wrote at some point, "how glad I should be to volunteer for the civil service, in such great need just now; still I feel I did my duty in remaining at my post & trying to make good men of the three boys—they are still in great need of guidance, moral & other."[27] While, in fact, there was little for her in England and her livelihood was in Brussels, the sentiment squared with her sense of self as someone who had *chosen* her path and was no less English for it.

Thorp's understanding of Englishness comes through with special clarity in her interactions with her nephew and godson, Richard "Dick" Dodson, a civilian internee at Ruhleben camp outside Berlin. Dodson was held there because, though born and raised in Belgium and married to a Belgian national, he was classified "English" during the war; his parents had been English, and his birth was registered as a foreign one. Thorp spent much of her diary worrying about Dick and his sister, Edith, who by the end of the war was working for the American Red Cross in France. Edith and Dick led very different but equally dangerous wartime existences. Edith crossed the submarine-infested Atlantic, while Dick was interned. Thorp sent letters and parcels to Dick and to his family in Antwerp, and she asked neutral diplomats to intervene to make his life in the camp a little easier.

It seems likely that Thorp saw herself in loco parentis for these two, who lost their mother, Georgina, at a very young age. Mary's sister, two years her junior, had married another English expatriate born in Bruges, Richard Raikes Dodson, around 1885. He appears to have tried to care for the children initially, but this was not a success. He was repeatedly arrested for being drunk and disorderly. The Bruges police described him as having "sunk very low," for all that he was extremely fond of his children. Before long, Edith and her little brother came to live with Annette Thorp, their grandmother.[28] Richard Jr. left for work in Antwerp in 1906, and Edith joined her father in Brussels when her grandmother died in 1910.[29] Annette's death left Thorp as the responsible family member; moreover, she was Dick's godmother. She extended her care and concern to the Dodson family more broadly; her diary records visits with Dick's aunt, Ellen Rinquet, and her husband, Ernest.[30]

Thorp, then, went out of her way to look after others: her direct and extended family, her friends, the charity cases in her care. She maintained her network and she volunteered her time even as she took her work as an educator very seriously. Her diary gives the impression of a woman who found purpose in working for and with others. She set aside time to keep the diary that allowed her to make sense of the war, of its "side-show," and of her own role. But at other times she was in motion. Thorp's diary shows a woman at home between worlds who, though grieving over the miseries of war, had faith in her own ability to negotiate whatever life might bring her.

NOTES

1. *Bell's New Weekly Messenger*, February 13, 1848.
2. MT (Mary Thorp), (diary entry for) January 25, 1917.
3. Thorp admission to workhouse January 25, 1856; London Workhouse Admission and Discharge Records 1659–1930; *Perry's Bankrupt Gazette*, November 13, 1858.
4. Kensington marriage register, September 1863, v. 1a, p. 96; Kensington birth register, January–March 1864, v. 1a, p. 79; Belgium, State Archives, Foreigners' file 470286 (Mary Thorp).
5. *Marylebone Mercury*, March 25, 1865.
6. 1871 UK census entry, Kensington District, Kensington Town, 9 Lancaster Mews.
7. Belgium, State Archives, Foreigners' file 470286 (Mary Thorp).
8. William Reed-Lewis, *Bruges: An English Guide* (Bruges: English Printing Works, 1895), 5–6.
9. Obituary, *New York Times*, August 12, 1911.
10. Obituary, *New York Times*, March 7, 1945.
11. *New York Times*, April 29, 1919, and December 19, 1933.
12. Quoted in Trev Broughton and Ruth Symes, eds., *The Governess: An Anthology* (New York: St. Martin's, 1997), 28–29, 107.
13. Valérie Piette, *Domestiques et servantes: Des vies sous condition* (Bruxelles: Académie Royale de Belgique, 2000), 455.
14. The Boulezes were wealthy landowners. Thorp's friend Dame Anna Boulez, an avid horsewoman, launched the Waregem thoroughbred race, which remains Belgium's Ascot to this day.
15. The de (or von) Medems, an aristocratic family originally from lower Saxony, established in the Baltic since the sixteenth century, came to prominence in the eighteenth century. Some branches of the family were in the service of the Habsburgs, others in royal Prussian service, others in the service of the tsarist state. Catherine de Medem was a descendant of the "Russian" Medems. Her forebear General Count I. F. de Medem had played a major (and brutal) role in Russia's eighteenth-century imperial expansion.
16. Samuel G. Ruegg, "Tirlemont and Beet-Sugar in Belgium," *Louisiana Planter and Sugar Manufacturer* 54, no. 7 (1915): 110–111.
17. The United States did not yet have an embassy in Belgium so Whitlock was the "minister" in charge of the US Legation.
18. January 27, 1915, journal entry; Box 2 Journals; Brand Whitlock Papers, Library of Congress.
19. Frantz Wittouck, a younger brother of Thorp's employer Paul Wittouck, with whom he had purchased the Tirlemont sugar refinery in 1894, died shortly before the war. His widow, Albertine Brandeis, was the daughter of Heinrich Brandeis, scion of a Viennese Jewish banking family. Albertine Brandeis's widowed mother, Margarethe, lived with her daughter in Brussels until her death in 1915. The Wittouck-Brandeis mansion was exactly opposite that of the Wittouck-de Medems, on avenue de la Toison d'Or (Mr. Éric Wittouck, correspondence, January 16, 2016). The Wittouck-Brandeis family also owned a country house near Brussels, Villa Les Bouleaux (also known as Villa Wittouck) at Tervuren, a focal point of Brussels musical life. These Wittoucks had three children: Jean, b. 1901; Élisabeth, b. 1903; and Marie-Thérèse, b. 1905.
20. In the family, the Wittouck-de Medem marriage is remembered as a social mismatch. The couple met when Catherine de Medem was vacationing at Karlsbad with her father in 1897; family lore has it that she had vowed not to return from that holiday without a fiancé, given that her younger sister had already gotten engaged. The couple were indeed engaged very shortly afterward. They were married in August 1898. Mr. Éric Wittouck, personal communication, March 8, 2016.
21. In 1910, for instance, the Paris *Le Gaulois*, a periodical known for its chronicle of high society, reported a soirée with a performance by Parisian singers and actors at the mansion

of "Madame Paul Wittouck, née Baroness de Medem." *Le Gaulois: politique et littéraire*, May 31, 1910.

22. Mr. Éric Wittouck, correspondence, January 16, 2016. The house was sold in 1985 and became derelict. Completely gutted today, with only the façade remaining, it serves as the Brussels "flagship store" of the Abercrombie & Fitch clothing chain. "L'hôtel Wittouck attend ses protecteurs," *La Libre Belgique*, December 13, 2005.

23. According to Mr. Éric Wittouck, her verdict on Paul's lack of drive was prescient: Paul Wittouck Jr. would never work a day in his life.

24. *Bulletin enfants 1913–1914*, manuscript notebook, Mr. Éric Wittouck personal archive, with thanks. Pavlick as the personal favorite of Madame Wittouck and his nonworking lifestyle. Mr. Éric Wittouck, personal communication, March 8, 2016.

25. Mr. Éric Wittouck, personal communication, July 24, 2015.

26. MT, November 12, 1917.

27. MT, March 6, 1917.

28. Belgium, State Archives, Foreigners' file 510766 (Richard Dodson Sr. and Jr.).

29. Belgium, State Archives, Foreigners' file 510766 (Richard Dodson Sr. and Jr.) and 2344455 (Edith Dodson); New York Naturalization Records, 1936 (Richard Sr.) and 1938 (Edith). The two immigrated to the United States in 1911. Richard Dodson Sr. died in 1947 (USA), and Edith died in New York in September 1970 (US Social Security Death Index).

30. West Flanders Civil Registers, Bruges. Charlotte Hélène "Ellen" Dodson (b. April 10, 1872) married Ernest Antoine Désiré Rinquet.

Life in an Occupied City: Brussels

On July 12, 1916, the German governor-general of occupied Belgium warned the populace that "it is forbidden to celebrate the Belgian national holiday in any way." Violators faced six months in prison or a 20,000-mark fine.[1] It was in the midst of such restrictions that Mary Thorp kept a secret diary. Observing life in Brussels, Europe's largest occupied city, gave her diary a particular urgency.

Before the war, Brussels was a growing and thriving capital city, with some 750,000 inhabitants, or 1 out of 10 Belgians. It was not a metropolis, but it stood at the heart of a constellation of other large and midsize cities. Unlike France, Belgium was not divided between capital city and provinces: many in Belgium's upper classes lived in other cities, which had their own circles of prestige.

Still, Brussels was a locus of ambition, where enterprise, banking, political energy, social-reform thinking, and the arts converged—as did the colonial spoils that paid for much of the city's elegance, so attractive to visitors. "What boulevards, what parks, what palaces, what galleries, what cafés, and above all what restaurants!" wrote the English novelist Arnold Bennett in 1914, looking back on his first visit to the city twenty years earlier.[2] Next to the chic boulevards with apartment buildings built in the 1870s in the manner of France's Haussmann, a style more specific to Brussels had emerged in the 1890s: Art Nouveau. Its sinuous lines suited the city's steep inclines; and most of the residential buildings were single-family homes, reflecting the Belgian middle classes' dislike of apartments. This preference drove many out of the central city, transforming villages into city districts. But even as Brussels spread outward, Belgium's fierce particularism ensured that all boroughs kept their own municipal government; there was no burgomaster (mayor) of Greater Brussels. Brussels had no large factories yet was Belgium's most important manufacturing city because of a plethora of small businesses—machine-building workshops, bronze foundries, breweries, carton factories, and so on. It also, of course, had an energetic service sector with many jobs for women, which, though often badly paid and precarious, still promised independence. Mary Thorp's own professional opportunity emerged from a convergence of destinies possible only in a city like Brussels: the union of Belgium's "king of sugar" and a Russian noblewoman of Baltic descent had produced three boys in need of the firm guidance that only an English governess with a command of the French language could give.

The war cut deeply into the life of this city. Brussels, so tightly connected to the outside world, was suddenly shut off. The war paralyzed manufacturing and the service sector. Struggling middle-class families could no longer afford to pay their servants. At the same time, Brussels offered a vision of abundance to unsuspecting visitors. Theaters, cinemas, cafés, restaurants, and bars sprang up all over the city. Yet this booming entertainment sector was, in a way, an outgrowth of misery and corruption. Sucking on cheap sweets on an empty stomach, people congregated in warm cinemas to flee their unheated lodgings. While bona fide business languished, entertainment venues catered to the middlemen who made money dealing with the German army. They also catered to German troops, for whom Brussels was a rest and recreation center, and to German officials, their families, and their secretarial staffs.

Brussels had a specific position in this war. It was not, like Ypres, situated in the firing line. While bombs occasionally fell on Brussels, it was not targeted by Allied bombing and shelling as were Ostend and Bruges. Nor had Brussels suffered at the hands of the invading army, like Leuven (Louvain) and other "martyred" towns. In short, Belgium's capital city found itself in the lee of war's direct and extreme violence. But this position did not preclude other forms of violence. The city experienced curfews, fines, arrests, executions of resisters, and deportation of forced laborers.

As the capital city of a country whose invasion was internationally decried, Brussels held another specific position. It was a front in the battle for legitimacy between the military occupying regime and the civilians. In the first year of the occupation, October 1914 to October 1915, patriotic outrage over enemy occupation had been most intense. Thorp's diary still echoes this outrage, partly because she moved in those circles where the sentiment was strongest. Her diary demonstrates the resilience of this patriotic culture and how it had a practical dimension, expressing itself in charity. But her diary also documents the strains on this collective effort as the occupation wore on.

On September 15, 1916, Mary Thorp finally started the diary she had been want-ing to keep since the start of the war. She had been, in her words, "dissuaded from doing so, because it was considered dangerous; a Jesuit father was shot during the tragic Louvain days of August 1914, for having written a few impressions."[3] As she started writing, Belgium had been under military occupation for two years, and the "tragic days"—the invasion armies' massacres of civilians, which claimed a total of 5,500 victims from August through October 1914—had long given way to a regime of measured coercion. Most of Belgium, except for the northwestern corner where the 1914 German advance had been halted and where Belgian and British forces held the line, was under German occupation. The German military had made conquered Belgium into a hinterland for its front. The areas closest to the front and the coast, comprising one-third of occupied Belgium, were under exclusively military control; this region was known as the Étape (staging area).[4] The other two-thirds of occupied Belgium were under a more mixed civilian-military occupation regime. That region, called the Government-General, was ruled by a German governor-general who resided in Brussels. Three elderly aristocratic Prussian career officers served in this function: Field Marshal Colmar von der Goltz from September through November 1914; General Moritz von Bissing, from December 1914 until his death in spring 1917; and General Ludwig von Falkenhausen. The governor-general was not an official of the German state: he answered only to the German emperor in his capacity as "su-preme war lord." This means that the governor-general's authority was essentially military in nature. But he was assisted by a civilian administration (*Zivilverwaltung*), which answered to the German government, and which, though always subordinate to military priorities (or what was defined as such), possessed real power.

As Thorp started her diary, Belgium's second governor-general, seventy-two-year-old Moritz von Bissing, had consolidated control. This energetic conservative was keen on establishing durable German rule in Belgium. On his watch, a grow-ing force of German occupation officials strove to manage ever-widening aspects of civilian life in an effort to base German authority on more than just military power. His Political Department worked with especial energy to anchor the occupa-tion regime's authority. It was headed by Oscar baron von der Lancken Wakenitz, a brilliant, polyglot diplomat; "some people here say he is practically the governor of Belgium," wrote Thorp.[5]

Conversely, Belgian authority shrank. The Belgian government had gone into vol-untary exile in the autumn of 1914, as had King Albert, who commanded the Belgian army. Cabinet ministries either closed down or were reduced to routine tasks. Only local authority still functioned fully. Town governments were the ones that had to interact with the occupation regime to tend to the population's needs. This required a complicated dance with a power that relished throwing its weight around but also needed the local authorities as indispensable intermediaries—for brute force would have led to inertia and possibly riots. To forestall civilian resistance, the occupation regime greatly restricted civilians' mobility. By and large, civilians were stuck in their own town or village, and even the shortest trip outside of municipal boundaries required a permit. Thorp, for one, was able to leave greater Brussels only once, in the summer of 1917, for a day's visit to relatives in Antwerp.

Men of military age had to register weekly at the Meldeamt (registration office) to demonstrate they had not attempted to join the Belgian army. Civilians found the landscape of their daily lives suddenly crisscrossed with a web of borders, checkpoints, and no-go zones. The boundary between the Government-General and the Étape was an actual border, very heavily guarded. On the other side lay an occupation regime much harsher still, as Thorp often remarked. Many of her friends lived in those parts; she commented on the lack of communication between Government-General and Étape, on the even greater restrictions under which people in the Étape lived, and on how they were in permanent danger of losing their homes if these were in the path of war operations.

Another harsh military frontier was the previously porous border with the neutral Netherlands. In the summer of 1916, a German engineer corps put the last touches on an electric fence that completely sealed off the Dutch-Belgian border—the first such wall in history. To deter civilians from trying to cross it, the occupation authorities circulated grisly pictures of electrocuted corpses. In June 1917, Thorp reported on the deaths of two acquaintances who had tried to cross the wire. Only one was subsequently confirmed, that of a fifty-five-year-old industrialist from Liège who had been denied a passport to travel to the Netherlands to check on his business interests abroad and had tried to cross the wire by crawling through a barrel. Thorp's employers experienced restrictions themselves. Madame Wittouck requested a passport for Holland in June 1918 but was "flatly refused."[6] The Wittouck boys were denied permission to ride their bikes to school.

Still, the Wittoucks retained advantages that others in occupied Belgium did not have. Madame Wittouck's "fine new Minerva motor car," requisitioned in early October 1918, was "quietly sent home" after two weeks.[7] It was true that she had been forbidden from driving it during the war. No sooner was the ban lifted than Madame Wittouck ordered her driver to cross a roadblock, telling the German sentry that she refused to put up with any further nonsense. He merely shrugged. Things could have gotten out of hand, but German soldiers, even as military authority was crumbling, remained deferential to the car-driving set; they were not "Russian Bolchevists," as Madame Wittouck remarked.[8]

The flow of information was as restricted as the flow of people. Civilians could not correspond with the front. Other armies communicated with their home fronts through millions of letters a week, but the men in the Belgian army were entirely cut off from their families and friends. News of loved ones from the front had to be acquired by roundabout ways. As correspondence with the Étape was particularly arduous, Thorp had the greatest of difficulties in communicating with her friend Valérie in heavily occupied Ghent; "to think we are losing three years of the happiness of friendship! it means so much at our, & especially her age."[9] Civilians could barely correspond with Allied or neutral countries—even those civilians with good contacts in the diplomatic world. Thorp's modest request to send her photo to friends in England via the US diplomatic pouch was rejected. In March 1917, Madame Wittouck tried in vain to send a telegram to Petrograd via the Spanish envoy, to find out whether it was true that her brother-in-law had been murdered in Russia.

Inside the Government-General, communication was likewise stifled. Civilians had to send their letters in open envelopes through the mail; sixty-five German censorship offices across the territory inspected them. To accommodate the censors, the only languages allowed were French, Flemish, and German. Mail was slow as a result: Thorp's messages from her nephew Dick at Ruhleben camp near Berlin arrived in Brussels the next day, but it took up to twelve days to forward them to his wife in Antwerp. People caught carrying even private messages were severely punished. In August 1916, Madame Wittouck had to spend a night in prison and was fined 300 marks for carrying two letters from the Liège region to Brussels. And, of course, civilians could not use telephones.

Public information was as restricted as private communication. In December 1914, the Government-General's Press Office had decreed that all printed matter not expressly authorized by the Governor-General was banned.[10] In protest, most Belgian newspapers stopped publishing. Allied newspapers and magazines did not reach occupied Belgium, save for the odd smuggled copy. Neutral newspapers did enter the Government-General, the papers from the Netherlands especially. The Brussels bourgeoisie (which, before the war, did not usually read Dutch) avidly perused these dailies for signs of liberation. The educated also read German papers, including the socialist *Vorwärts*, for signs of war-weariness. Such fare occasionally, as Thorp noted, led German soldiers and Belgian civilians to blame Germany's military leadership in unison.

In response to the Belgian press strike, the occupation government had launched its own newspapers, such as the ostensibly "native" Brussels daily *La Belgique*. Next to local news, updates on rules and schedules, job ads, and other necessary information, these new papers offered curated news from the fronts, as well as reports and editorials that suggested the durability of German rule. They also belittled expressions of patriotism. In late November 1916, for instance, an editorial deplored the curfew imposed on Brussels after churchgoers had sung the national hymn, and claimed—possibly correctly—that an ever-growing number of *bruxellois* blamed the demonstrators for making their fellow citizens' lives even harder. It was true that the curfew was particularly hard on Brussels' nightlife and on the people who depended on it for their income.[11] Thorp, who had rejoiced over the hymn-singing and scoffed at the curfew, thought it a "horrid article."[12] But she did read *La Belgique*, as did many others, for the public were starved for news. And even the censored papers could not keep major developments such as the US entry into war from civilians.[13] Still, even such news could be editorialized into insignificance. The Brussels journalist Charles Tytgat (who, like Thorp, started a diary in the late summer of 1916) observed how many civilians failed to understand the importance of the American entry into war because the censored press assured them that the United States had already spent most of its resources in helping the Allies, and to no avail.[14] In November 1918, after liberation, memories of the censored press's steady drip of disheartenment would lead furious crowds to set fire to newspaper stalls.

The need to counteract this disheartenment generated an underground press with periodicals such as *La Libre Belgique*, whose title, "*Free Belgium,*" was a rebuke to *La Belgique*. These periodicals sought to keep up civilians' spirits by assuring them that a regime built on military might was doomed to end. Most professed a patriotism rooted in religious faith, not unlike Thorp's. But she seldom mentioned the clandestine press; because of persecution by the German police, it was at a low ebb when she started her diary. Thorp, then, pieced together war news from those papers that reached her. But the Wittoucks' circle of diplomats, especially those from the US Legation and the Spanish and Dutch embassies, also provided important information. Less-well-connected civilians had to make do with the censored papers as well as the German posters in the streets bearing decrees, announcements, military news—and, from time to time, printed on a threatening red background, the news that resisters had been executed.

Repression was central to the occupation regime's quest for order. A vast police apparatus dealt with various forms of civilian resistance. In greater Brussels, the Military Police was 1,000 men strong by 1917, not counting the hundreds of military patrolling the railway stations and tracks. In addition, the Political Police, using Belgian, Dutch, and French informers, infiltrated networks of civilian resistance. Some of these networks specialized in helping trapped British soldiers and Belgian army volunteers escape into the neutral Netherlands so they could join their armies. The English nurse Edith Cavell, executed in Brussels in October 1915, belonged to such a network. Another type of resistance was espionage: thousands of men and women collected information on the German troops for the benefit of Allied armies.

In reaction, the occupation regime took ever more energetic measures to clear the German army's hinterland of civilian resistance. In 1916, the German police services dismantled one network after another by arresting and interrogating hundreds of people on the slightest suspicion. These actions found an echo in Thorp's chronicle. To make suspects talk, the police kept them in solitary confinement; Thorp heard stories. Military tribunals then handed out fines, prison sentences, and, for some, the death penalty. As the military governor of Brussels stated in 1916, the safety of the German army required "unrelenting action."[15]

This included repressing subversion among the Germans' own troops, as well as, of course, punishing civilians for insulting the German army. In 1915, for instance, Thorp's friend Mary d'Alcantara, a thirty-year-old aristocrat from Ghent, had been fined 80 marks over a disparaging remark. She denied the occupying army her money and took the alternative punishment of ten days in prison. As the occupation wore on, fines rose vertiginously. In January 1917, the director of a Brussels department store was fined 10,000 marks for selling toy German soldiers in a posture of surrender. These heavy fines show that, next to order, the occupation regime had another priority: that of siphoning off occupied Belgium's resources for the German war effort.

The invasion of Belgium had brought random requisitions and all-out plunder, but these were soon followed by an orderly system of exploitation. From December 1914, the occupied country had to pay a monthly war tax of 40 million francs, which was twenty times the sum total of all taxes yielded by the prewar Belgian economy. In addition, civilians had to pay heavily for all manner of permits; and heavy fines for even minor infringements regularly hit municipalities, institutions, businesses, and private citizens. In November 1916, for instance, a Mass in two Brussels churches ended on a chorus of the Belgian national anthem; to retaliate, the military governor imposed a curfew and a fine of up to 10,000 marks for trespassers.

As Thorp started her diary, exploitation took a turn for the worse. In November 1916, against von Bissing's protests, the Prussian minister of war (an appointee of the new German leadership under Hindenburg and Ludendorff) increased the monthly tax from 40 to 50 million francs. The German army massively stepped up its requisitioning of valuable goods.

The seizing of private households' copper utensils crossed a line: private homes were no longer safe. Some requisitioning parties ransacked houses and drilled through walls. Others were more reticent: the men who came for the copper chez Wittouck were, Thorp wrote, apologetic. Still, they took not only freestanding copper items but fixtures too, such as the kitchen boilers. For Thorp, as for other civilians, the vexation of seeing one's home opened up and one's possessions carted away was compounded by the grief of knowing the metal would be used against Belgian and Allied soldiers. To boot, in May 1917, the monthly tax rose to 60 million francs, and, soon after, the German army requisitioned wool mattresses and pillows. The loss of bedding compounded malnourished civilians' misery, especially among sick and old people too poor to heat their lodgings—for coal was in ever-shorter supply. Belgium's coal mines still produced enough to cover domestic needs, but the German military seized a large part of production in both direct and indirect ways. Its Kohlenzentrale (Coal Central) was ostensibly organized to prevent a black market in coal and to make sure it would reach those who needed it most. In reality, the relief services received only a small part of the coal; most went to the German army to operate its own black market or to use in rewarding civilians willing to cooperate.

The Coal Central was not unique: an entire system of "Centrals" placed Belgian resources under German jurisdiction. These Centrals tallied, seized, and distributed local produce. Belgium's own modest grain harvest as well as its more abundant yield of potatoes, beet sugar, fruit, dairy, vegetable oils, and other goods were now channeled by the Zuckerzentrale, the Ölzentrale, the Obstzentrale, and so on. Centrals also seized stocks of fabrics, leather (a military necessity), and other resources. The Centrals allowed the Government-General to control domestic distribution, to export goods to neutral countries, to ship goods on which there was no ban (such as vegetables) to Germany, and, for contraband goods, to create black-market schemes with complicit Belgian producers and middlemen to circumvent the ban and siphon them off to the German army or home front. Only a small proportion of native goods made it to the relief services, or, at extortionate prices, the market. Meanwhile, in the Étape, the military did not even bother with Centrals but continued to seize domestic goods outright.

Meanwhile, Belgium's industrial equipment was being dismantled. A decree of February 1917 placed Belgium's ailing industries under complete German control. Unless firms agreed to work for the occupation army, which most did not, their equipment was seized. Machines, boilers, furnaces, and other equipment were taken apart and shipped to Germany; factory halls were demolished. Earlier that winter, Thorp had feared for the sugar refineries, too. While their disappearance would not have displeased sugar manufacturers in Germany, Belgium's sugar refineries, like other food-processing industries, remained relatively unharmed because it was not in the occupying army's interest to dismantle them. But other industries suffered. The military, in accord with Germany's heavy-industry interest group, overrode the arguments of the ailing von Bissing (he died in mid-April 1917) that a reasonably prosperous protectorate was more in Germany's interest.

It was not the first time Germany's Supreme Command and industrial lobbies had the better of the governor-general. By fall 1916 they had managed to push through a measure that von Bissing condemned as "unworthy of a civilized state,"[16] namely, the deportation and forced labor of working-class men. Starting in the Étape, by and by the deportations reached the Government-General and drew nearer to Brussels. In mid-October 1916, Thorp wrote of the general fear that the Germans wanted to "[empty] Belgium of all able bodied men."[17] On November 17, Brand Whitlock noted that "Brussels is in terror; the net closes in."[18]

The municipal authorities played for time by refusing to hand in the lists of unemployed men, invoking constitutional liberties. The military retaliated by fining or arresting municipal employees and seizing lists of relief beneficiaries. And local authorities could only stall. The deportations in greater Brussels started in late January 1917. Of the 8,000 civilians ordered to report for work, many did not show up. Others did, fearing that the punishment would be even harsher than the work or hoping to be selected out. Over four days, in the bitter cold, the Brussels South railway station was the theater of grim, brief selections. The sick were generally spared, as were men older than fifty-five and adolescent boys. In the end, the military loaded 1,400 men on trains bound for holding-camps in Germany. Those who had signed a work contract under duress were sent on to factories, mines, and farms. Those who had not remained in the camps to be beaten and starved into compliance. Thorp feared for her eldest charge, Pavlick. She had little reason to fear, for the deportations hit the working class almost exclusively; it was no coincidence that more than half of the Brussels deportees came from one industrial borough.

But although the deportations did not concern the social class of Thorp's employers, they were more of a reality in her own circle. In Antwerp, her nephew's wife, Sidonie, witnessed her stepfather being taken away in November 1916. The family's food parcels were pilfered en route. Thorp, through her diplomatic acquaintances, took steps on his behalf. He was freed in late March 1917. By then, the deportations had been halted anyway, in response to the global outcry. (At least, they ceased in the Government-General; in the Étape, where perceived "military necessity" trumped all, they continued until the very last days of the war.) But many men returned in a terrible state. Of the 120,000 men taken from both the Government-General and the Étape, 2,500 died during deportation and a large number shortly thereafter; many remained invalids for the rest of their lives.

This horror played out against the backdrop of deepening material misery, a recurring theme in Thorp's diary. Time and again she observed the staggering cost of everyday goods and their shoddy quality. She had to pay cutthroat prices for footwear containing only token bits of leather. Soap was prohibitively expensive yet mere "muck": "when shall I get my good Pears soap again!"[19] And things were much worse in poor households, where, she noted, the lack of soap and washcloths led to an epidemic of skin disease, and where ill-clad people were freezing to death in unheated rooms. For all the material hardships she herself experienced, she was keenly aware that she wrote from the relative comfort of the Wittoucks' well-provisioned household. In June 1917, Thorp noted that while she herself was better off for having lost weight since late 1915 ("tant mieux for me," she joked), others were wasting away.[20]

Most people relied on the "Alimentation," subsidized food stores where civilians could obtain staples such as rice, beans, canned meat, and flour. These food stores were part of an international effort to help the civilians of the occupied territories behind the Western Front survive the war. This extraordinary effort, sustained over fifty months, was one of the first global humanitarian actions in history. Yet it had started small. At war's outbreak, Belgium had faced famine. The most densely populated country in the world at the time, with a population the size of Canada's on territory no larger than Maryland's, it imported three-quarters of its food. But food imports were in disarray. In response, an ad hoc committee of businesspeople in Brussels, working with local government and enlisting the protection of neutral diplomats, began purchasing food abroad. The German military pledged not to seize it so as to avoid food riots. An emissary from this committee, sent to London to purchase grain, contacted a business acquaintance and London-based mining entrepreneur: Herbert Hoover, the future US president. Hoover put together what would become the Commission for Relief in Belgium (CRB), a volunteer group of private citizens from the United States tasked with purchasing food, raising funds, overseeing shipping, and liaising with the Brussels committee. In the meantime, the Belgian government in exile had earmarked 25 million francs a month to pay for the imported food. This was complemented by worldwide donations in cash to "Brave

Little Belgium." These, however, were to dwindle considerably, forcing the Belgian government in early 1917 to increase its monthly outlay on food relief to 37.5 million.

To safeguard the goods from the German army, the CRB imported them under the protection of neutral diplomats from the United States, Spain, and the Netherlands. Thorp knew several of these neutral "dips" (as she called them). These men found themselves playing a crucial role in the relief effort and, beyond it, the championing of the occupied civilians' interests. Civilians often exaggerated the extent of their influence with the occupation regime. In late September 1916, for instance, Thorp wrote that the neutral diplomats were investigating a bombing that had killed ten people in Brussels. The Germans blamed Allied planes; civilians blamed German anti-aircraft guns.[21] People in Brussels told each other that US Minister Brand Whitlock had confounded von Bissing by presenting him with shards of German flak shells. In reality, neither Whitlock nor his Spanish counterpart, the Marquis de Villalobar, planned to intervene in a matter that was very much out of their hands; and Whitlock in his private diary wrote scathingly of civilians' naiveté in blaming only Germany for the air-raid victims—"Such children as they are!"[22]

Whitlock, a prolific writer who would, in 1919, publish a well-regarded memoir of his years in wartime Belgium, was a major presence in wartime Belgium. Thorp, who thought highly of him, probably met him in 1915 when he was a frequent guest at the Wittouck house; but her 1916–1919 diary does not mention a single conversation. Her relationship with Whitlock, then, was a distant one, but she was friendly with his assistant, Albert Ruddock, as she was with Maurits Willem Radinck Van Vollenhoven, counsel at the Dutch legation, and the Spanish envoy Don Rodrigo de Saavedra y Vinent, Marquis of Villalobar. She mentioned both men frequently. She particularly admired Villalobar, a diplomat of long aristocratic pedigree whose savvy and wit had allowed him to build a brilliant career in spite of severe physical handicaps. Before she knew Villalobar, Thorp scathingly called him "the diminutive grandee" and thought that he tried to take all the credit for the relief work. But over the course of 1917, the marquis drew closer to the Wittoucks. Thorp and Villalobar sparred amicably over politics, and she came to share his wish for a negotiated peace.

Inside occupied Belgium, the CRB had a local counterpart that distributed the imported goods. This was the National Committee for Relief and Victualling (Comité National de Secours et d'Alimentation; hereafter Comité), chaired by the energetic Belgian financier Émile Francqui; like Hoover, he was a rich and well-connected man with a brisk executive outlook. Thorp, who called Francqui "the alimentation man," approved of his work, though she frowned on his having married his niece.[23]

The Comité was a remarkable organization. An ad hoc, unincorporated entity that did not exist on paper so as to evade German control, it employed some 125,000 agents across Belgium. It rationed out the nonperishable food brought in under CRB auspices in warehouses known, fondly, as "the American stores." The Comité also purchased Belgian-grown food to sell and tussled with the German "Centrals" in the process. The destitute had access to relief goods at little or no cost; others were charged higher prices. With the proceeds, complemented by donations, the Comité operated soup kitchens, provided schoolchildren with lunches, and furnished nourishing meals to pregnant or breastfeeding women. The organization also distributed coal, clothing, blankets, and other necessities, and offered cash relief to the needy. This redistributive system required an intricate administrative machinery.

The result was a vastly altered landscape of consumption. In the cities, especially, all but the affluent now had to meet their daily needs through a regimented system of provisioning. In the words of the Stanford scholar Frank Angell, whom Hoover had sent to Belgium to observe the workings of the Comité, "the status of Belgium under the occupation as far as food supply was concerned was that of a socialistic state administered by a native committee which determined [the] degrees of want and need of the inhabitants."[24] But this "socialistic state" operated in a social landscape marked by class differences. People of the middle classes, however impoverished, were reluctant to openly request relief. These new poor met with deep sympathies among the purveyors of relief. Officers' wives received help in cash, not in kind. Penurious middle-class people could take meals in *restaurants économiques* (budget restaurants), which spared them the humiliation of the bread line. The petite bourgeoisie was considered to be particularly deserving and particularly hard hit by the war. Whitlock expressed the thought of many in the Belgian elite when he wrote in his memoir that "the very poor ... were as well nourished as they had been in former times, perhaps better, or at least more regularly and scientifically nourished"—whereas deeper hardship befell those "too proud to expose their condition to the world."[25] That the poor did not have it worse than before the war was a somewhat callous and certainly incorrect statement: by April 1917, working-class Belgians were reduced to some 350 grams of food per person per day (most of it bad bread), plus half a liter of relief-issue soup. But it was true that, among the middle classes, the vast majority were barely better off. The journalist Charles Tytgat described how, by April 1917, his household too had to make do with the 350 grams per person per day the warehouses offered: 300 grams of bread (about the size of a baguette), the rest made up of dried beans, lard, and noodles with no meat or cheese. This insubstantial diet sapped away at people's resistance: "The old die in great numbers, as do children."[26] Tytgat himself died shortly after the war, age forty-seven.

Tytgat and his household were prime examples of the deserving "new poor." In 1914, German censorship had led Tytgat and his colleagues to shut down their newspaper in protest. They received some help from a charity designed to assist artists and writers who refused to write under occupation. The general mood of warm concern for the people known as the *pauvres honteux* (poor but proud) inspired the relief organization to which Thorp devoted a great deal of her considerable energies: the Assistance Discrète (Discreet Relief). Unlike most of the Comité's offices, which were overwhelmingly staffed by men, the Assistance Discrète was a largely female organization. Launched and led by Marie Haps, a Brussels financier's wife who after the war would make a name as a champion of women's education, it was backed by many aristocratic and middle-class Brussels ladies. Madame Wittouck and her sister-in-law were among them, as well as Paul Wittouck's sister, Emilie. Thorp, together with many of her acquaintances in Brussels, was among the hundreds of volunteers. The Assistance, then, was a constituent element in the wartime lives of women of the Brussels elite and of some working women who were both close to this elite and personally aware of the precariousness of middle-class status, like Thorp.

The Assistance was given funding from the Comité, but it also received private donations. Fundraisers further sharpened the Assistance's profile as an initiative of the patriotic Brussels elite. Charity events were one of the few permissible forms of entertainment left, since it befitted patriots not to go out in wartime. Not that these charity events were simply genteel affairs: there was a robust pragmatism about them. At the Assistance's Easter 1918 charity bazaar, for instance, Thorp planned to offer cats for sale at the flower stall. She had noticed that mice proliferated because people had started to eat cats, and she concluded that people were not looking for flowers so much as for things that were useful or "eatable." She did not specify whether the cats were to be employed or consumed.[27] Other volunteer work offered a similar combination of pragmatic female energy and patriotism: the volunteers who went to market to purchase food for the care packages, wrote Angell, lugged the goods to the Assistance's distributing room "by sheer force of feminine muscle which two years before had known no harder work than was involved in wielding a . . . tennis raquet."[28] He did not mention that, under the occupation, young women of the respectable classes were not *allowed* to wield tennis rackets; patriotic opinion considered women's sports unseemly while young men were risking life and limb at the front. In this respect, too, then, charitable work channeled thwarted energies. "Women seem to have found themselves," Whitlock observed; "they *work*, from patriotic motives, but they work."[29]

As befitted its title, the Assistance distributed aid discreetly. One chronicle explained how respectable housewives who did not want to present themselves at the soup kitchens had their shopping bags filled, anonymously, at the Assistance, where "ladies who remain unseen . . . offer mothers who would be mortified at being recognized . . . all they need to make a nourishing soup in the privacy of their own home."[30]

Volunteers also delivered packages at home—small parcels of modest goods such as sardines or oatmeal. Thorp made house calls to the old and to the sick; she provided medication and referred them to the doctors who volunteered for the Assistance. What she saw on those house calls upset her greatly.

Thorp also volunteered for another largely female initiative, the Union Patriotique des Femmes Belges (Belgian Women's Patriotic Union). Launched at the start of the war by two prominent suffragists, Jane Brigode and Louise Van den Plas, the Union engaged in modest job creation programs for women, such as providing service personnel for soup kitchens, sewing work for officers' wives, and orders for lace-workers.

The Union was steeped in ideas of middle-class respectability, as was the Assistance. Both charities sought to foster what Angell called a "commendable spirit of pride" and frowned on people whom they considered overly disposed to live in "a state of willing dependence."[31] Thorp, who valued self-sufficiency while remaining aware of situations in which even the pluckiest needed help, would have found this outlook appealing. She, at any rate, did her bit to contribute to the core mission that the organizers of civilian relief in occupied Belgium had set themselves: not just to fight starvation, but to defiantly uphold the fabric of civil society, class distinctions included. In Thorp's actions, then, the ideological and practical work of war merged.

Meanwhile, the occupation authorities worked to discredit Belgian relief efforts. Thorp's diary offers a telling vignette. She strove to provide the needy people in her care with sugar, considered a basic foodstuff: the notion of "empty calories" did not yet exist. Her employer, Paul Wittouck, owned Belgium's largest beet sugar manufacturing plant, but he could not tap freely into its product, although the manager occasionally let the family have a modest amount of sugar. Thorp went to the German Sugar Central (Zuckerzentrale) to request sugar direct from the Tienen factory to distribute to her friends and charity charges. The official politely informed her that all the sugar had to go through the Central, but did suggest that with a doctor's certificate she could force the relief warehouse to sell her sugar for her invalid charges; if this failed, she should appeal to the German district administrator. For good measure, he blamed the dearth of sugar on Belgian hoarding. This vignette shows that the Centrals served to muscle in on relief efforts and, if possible, discredit them vis-à-vis civilians.

This obstructionism stemmed from the occupation regime's mistrust of the Comité. "We must not hide the fact," wrote von der Lancken in a report to Berlin in late July 1916, "that the influence of the [Comité] on the Belgian population is sizeable. . . . The common opposition of all Belgians vis-à-vis the Germans is concentrated in the [Comité]. In other occupied enemy countries, political forces concentrate in secret societies; here, they are channeled by an organism born of economic distress, which the occupying power has had to tolerate to avoid catastrophe."[32]

In the absence of the Belgian government, the Comité represented the ongoing legitimacy of the Belgian state. Material matters—food, health, (re)distribution—could make or break a state's credit in wartime; the Comité's leaders knew that their organization's practical function had deeply political implications. The tussle over food control shows that occupied Belgium was the theater of a standoff over the question of legitimacy.

This standoff was clearly enunciated in the pastoral letter "Endurance and Patriotism," issued by Belgium's Cardinal Mercier in January 1915: "The Power which has invaded our soil and temporarily occupies most of it . . . is not a legitimate authority. In your heart of hearts you owe it neither respect, nor loyalty, nor obedience."[33] In response to this open challenge to the legitimacy of his rule, von Bissing had briefly considered arresting the cardinal, but could not risk Germany's further discredit in world public opinion. The pursuit of legitimacy had to proceed through subtler ways: the repression of dissenting opinion (as voiced by citizens less well known than Mercier); collective punishments (fines, curfews) for patriotic demonstrations. Extolling the benefits of German governance was part of this policy. From June 15 through October 15, 1916, for instance, at an amusement site in Brussels, the occupation authorities ran an exhibition on social security and national health in Germany.[34]

Von Bissing's Political Department, headed by von der Lancken, endeavored to foster the Government-General's legitimacy through press policies, church policies, scrutiny of the Comité, and sifting through Belgian ministerial archives in search of material that would discredit the prewar Belgian state. The Political Department was particularly active in addressing Flemish linguistic grievances. Flemish (Dutch) was the mother-tongue of a slight majority of Belgians. Flemish had been declared legally equal to French at the turn of the century, but French remained the language of Belgium's elites. Almost all of the Belgians Thorp knew, including those who lived in Flanders, spoke only French. This linguistic hierarchy had long been contested by the lively ensemble of cultural and political associations known as the Flemish Movement. Its major goal, in the prewar years, had been a Flemish-language university in the city of Ghent. The "Flemish question," then, seemed a self-evident wedge issue for an occupation government keen on discrediting the prewar Belgian state and on ingratiating itself with a part of the occupied population. Moreover, like all colonial regimes, German occupation administrations on both the Western and the Eastern fronts viewed conquered populations through an ethnic lens.

And so the occupation authorities had from 1915 set about to work on the "Flemish question," at first by small touches such as placing Flemish before French on posters. They launched a set of Flemish newspapers. Outrage over the invasion was too widespread for the policy to attract followers even among Flemish Movement leaders, but it swayed some radicalized students and rank-and-file militants. In the next stage, the "Flemish policy" widened its appeal with the launching of an all-Flemish university in Ghent in fall 1916. But this new university's credit suffered from the heavy-handed measures enacted against those who rejected it. Moreover, the Von-Bissing-University (as critics called it) was located in the particularly heavily occupied city of Ghent in the Étape, and its grand opening coincided with the first deportations of forced laborers from Ghent. This unfortunate coincidence exemplified how the shift toward extreme exploitation, so deplored by von Bissing, was bound to doom his legitimizing drive.

By and by, those Flemish militants willing to work with the occupation authorities grew more radical. They called themselves "activists" to claim that they actively pursued the Flemish agenda, unlike the majority of Flemish militants (whom they dismissed as "passivists"). By and by, the "activists" embraced the goals of those in Germany and in the occupation administration who wanted to break up the Belgian state. In February 1917, a self-appointed "Council of Flanders" issued a manifesto calling for "national liberation." It did so anonymously, for the "activist" position was unpopular. It became even more so when the underground press reported that on March 3, a delegation of this council had traveled to Berlin to meet Chancellor von Bethmann Hollweg, a visit widely decried as sycophantic. A group of leading Flemish authors wrote an open letter to von Bissing to deny that "the unknown body that calls itself Council of Flanders" spoke in their name.[35] Thorp too was indignant, calling the Berlin delegation "mad idiots" for going along with the Germans' "game" of divide and conquer. "Fortunately," she wrote, "they don't represent all the Flemish people."[36]

Radicalization came to a head in January 1918 when the Council of Flanders declared Flemish independence. This, in turn, galvanized civilians into protest at a time when more and more people, exhausted by hardship, had started to turn in upon themselves. In Brussels, a crowd assembled in front of City Hall in hopes of being able to jeer the "activists" who had come to read the declaration of independence. The activists did not appear, "so all the people who were out to 'counter-manifest' were deprived of their sport," as Thorp wrote. Still, the crowd "made the usual noise." Sixteen-year-old Micha Wittouck was there, together with his cousin Jean.[37] A German police agent stopped them; a lengthy interrogation ensued, with threats of prison. Eventually, the boys were each fined the enormous sum of three thousand marks. Citing this incident, the Germans denied Madame Wittouck a passport for the Netherlands in June 1918.

Thorp and her circle, though in no way involved in active resistance, adhered to the dicta of patriotic culture. This entailed keeping as much distance from the Germans as possible. As Thorp observed, in the winter of 1916–1917 the Brussels municipalities had the ice on ponds and lakes broken up to prevent the Government-General from snapping photos of happily skating Germans and Belgians "to make the world believe we are on good terms with them in every day life."[38] But for all her wish to maintain patriotic distance, Thorp disapproved of her friend Ellen Rinquet's snarling at a German officer who was only "trying to be commonly polite" by helping her get on the tram.[39] And she was touched by German soldiers' piety, observing some of them praying devoutly at a church in her neighborhood.

If faith was a realm of possible conciliation, it was also a realm of patriotic resolve. Catholic culture was a locus of defiance. Cardinal Mercier's January 1915 denial of legitimacy to the occupation regime made him, Thorp wrote, "the most popular Belgian after the King."[40] The underground press and resistance networks hailed much more often from Catholic circles than from Liberal or Socialist ones. (These were the three main political "families" of Belgium.) Church services offered occasions to protest the regime: in November 1916, for instance, Mercier condemned forced labor from the pulpit; and he praised those priests who, out of solidarity with men threatened with deportation, refused to have their identity papers stamped to mark them as exempt from forced labor.

Thorp was on excellent terms with other energetic ecclesiastics, such as the Reverend Théophile Reyn, the superior of the Congregation of Labor Chaplains, tasked by Mercier to create a vocational school in Brussels with funds from Belgium's wealthy; the Wittoucks contributed. Her diary is punctuated with events that merge the religious and the patriotic. For instance, she attended funerals for fallen soldiers, where the Belgian national anthem was defiantly played on the organ. In fact, her public resistance always took place in a religious setting.

Thorp's view on the occupation regime was that of all patriotically minded civilians: she denied it legitimacy. At the same time, her view of the war differed slightly from that of occupied Belgians because of her nationality. Even after living abroad for so many years, she still felt English. And the war deepened this feeling. She envisioned herself as a proud Englishwoman in Brussels:

> Isie & I were standing in a very overcrowded tram. A gentleman got up to give us his seat, saying: Madams, had I heard immediately you were English, I should have offered you my seat immediately. I thanked him for "his homage to my country." I know all the decent Belgians (those who do mind about their country not being germanised) have a proper feeling for all they owe to England.[41]

The relief effort, too, cemented national differences. The Comité offered British nationals food relief, but cash benefits came from the British Relief Fund. Specific forms of aid contributed to Thorp's sense of Englishness. She hoarded sugar and strained off tea from her teapot to save for Englishwomen desperate for their tea fix. Keeping up with the war's events further deepened Thorp's sense of communion with the English. She recalled her intense grief over the June 1916 death at sea of British Field Marshal Horatio Herbert Kitchener, and after the downing of an Allied airplane, she dreamed of the escaped pilot, automatically, if erroneously, imagining him to be English.

She applauded the English culture and care that surrounded her nephew Dick Dodson amid the hardship of his internment at Ruhleben, a former racetrack near Berlin. In describing Dick's life in Ruhleben, Thorp touched on what it meant to be English. Some issues pertinent in her own life appeared as commentary about Dick's situation. She discussed the reproduction of a mini-England in the camp—or as she called it, "a bit of England in Germany."[42] She was thrilled to learn in January 1917 that Dick was getting regular parcels from the British government. Thorp delighted in the "Britishness" of the photographs, camp magazines, and accounts she received from Dick. The camp theatricals were English literary standbys such as *The Mikado* and *The Merry Wives of Windsor*. Thorp appreciated the stoic humor, considered typically British, inherent in calling the *Mikado* production *Makeado* (make-do), a comment on conditions in the camp. Landmarks in the camp received familiar English names such as Trafalgar Square. The internees even held an election, demonstrating the basics of British parliamentary procedure. All of this reassured Thorp that

English national identity stood up as sturdily to the stress of imprisonment as it stood up to expatriate life. After war's end, Thorp would disapprove of her nephew's doomed attempt to establish himself in London, as opposed to taking *her* path—that of remaining "staunchly British" while living in Belgium. For Thorp, being British in Belgium showed fortitude and loyalty; plus, she wanted him near her.

In addition to caring for her nephew and supporting British expatriates in Brussels, Thorp also campaigned to provide an English presence at funerals for English soldiers who died in the hospital near her home. She saw herself as a surrogate for those in England who could not attend the funeral or visit the gravesite. England, then, still meant "home" for her. This sense of belonging led her to resolutely take the British side with regard to the conduct of war. In addition, small touches show Thorp's unquestioned imperial outlook. Her unflagging indignation about the German invasion coexisted comfortably with satisfaction at the prospect of seeing Britain and Russia share the spoils of the Ottoman Empire. Like so many of her contemporaries, Thorp was in no doubt that her belligerents' cause was divinely sanctioned.

The value of Thorp's diary, then, lies in its stalwart attempt to make sense of the war as it manifested itself in the cramped "side-show" of civilian life under occupation. Thorp relied on echoes from the outside world, on her own observations, on her network of friends, on her framework of moral and political references, and on what she deprecatingly called "gossip" to grasp what was happening and define what she ought to think about it. Her diary shows this ever-renewed effort; it gives a sense of time passing and of an ordinary civilian "seeing it through," with all that entailed in terms of doubts, fears, moral judgment, and expectations. From the winter of 1916–1917, she reflected on the possibility of a negotiated peace to end the bloodshed. At the same time, she strove to convince herself of the unacceptability of a peace that left Germany with some of the war's spoils in Europe. As a result, she was torn between, on the one hand, a stern fight-to-the-finish stance, and, on the other hand, horror at the sheer cost of war, especially its effect on civilians which she saw firsthand. This tension was never far from the surface in her writing: in apparent non sequiturs, she shifted seamlessly from talking about the international situation to grieving over war's destruction. She despaired of ever being able to make sense of it all.

As the war dragged on, Thorp's writing testified to the heavy weight of precious time passing, never to return: time taken, for instance, from her friendship with her beloved Val, who at only fifty kilometers' distance was as remote as if she had lived across an ocean. From time to time, she set little markers, projecting herself backward or forward in time: "Three times the roses have faded since we lost our dear liberty!!!" she wrote in October 1916.[43] The start of new notebooks or of a new year prompted her to look forward. She had embarked on her first notebook expecting it to be the only volume of her war diary, but the war outran its pages. In March 1917, she began her second notebook, one with a "startling" red cover. She had not chosen the color deliberately—but it did, she wrote, suggest "how much blood must be shed before I come to the end." She hoped that once she had filled that second notebook, which she expected to do in the summer of 1917, the war would be nearing its end.[44] But there was to be a third notebook, and a fourth. And a fifth, which she started in October 1918. She entitled it "The Book of Peace!!!" But its first entry reflects her anxiety and keen awareness of peace's high cost.[45]

Throughout, her diary returned to the war's great, intractable question: a compromise peace versus a peace that would bring a possibly pyrrhic victory. Meanwhile, the everyday became ever more political, generating a plethora of questions about fairness and sacrifice; in entry after entry, therefore, apparently banal observations are shot through with moral judgment. The questions which confronted the entire belligerent world are, then, as urgently and sharply formulated in this "side-show gossip" as they are in any of the war's theaters.

NOTES

1. Avis no. 516, 12 July 1916; Box 3795; Oorlogsaffiches 1914–1918. Stadsarchief Leuven.

2. Arnold Bennett, "The Return," in Hall Caine, ed., *King Albert's Book. A Tribute to the Belgian King and People from Representative Men and Women throughout the World* (London: Daily Telegraph, 1914), 37–39.

3. MT (Mary Thorp), (diary entry for) September 15, 1916.

4. Behind the actual operations zones (Operationsgebiet) of the German Fourth and Sixth Armies on the northernmost part of the Western Front lay their military staging areas (Etappengebiet or Étape). On the coast, the Ostend-Bruges-Zeebrugge triangle became a base under exclusive control of the German navy; this was the Naval Zone (Marinegebiet). But we will refer to all of these military zones taken together as the Étape, which was the term most often used, including by Thorp.

5. MT, January 11, 1918.

6. MT, June 23, 1918.

7. MT, October 25, 1918. That the car was requisitioned this late may also indicate some privilege.

8. MT, November 10, 1918.

9. MT, January 31, 1917; see also October 28, 1916.

10. Decree of October 13, 1914, followed by a November 4, 1914, order. Printed matter included photos and sheet music. The ban extended to public representations: lectures, plays, poetry readings, and so on. Charles H. Huberich and Alexander Nicol-Speyer, eds., *Deutsche Gesetzgebung für die Okkupierten Gebiete Belgiens* (The Hague: Martinus Nijhoff, 1915–1918), 1:21–2; Von Köhler, *Staatsverwaltung*, 25–27; Jacques Pirenne and Maurice Vauthier, *La législation et l'administration allemandes en Belgique* (Paris-New Haven, n.d. [1925]), 138–140; Arthur Boghaert-Vaché, *La presse pendant l'occupation* (Brussels: Brian Hill, 1919), 17–24. In August 1916, a decree expressly reminded civilians of the ban on sheet music (Avis no. 559, August 29, 1916).

11. "Bon sens," *La Belgique*, November 1916, 2.

12. MT, November 30, 1916.

13. MT, April 5, 1917.

14. Charles Tytgat, *Bruxelles sous la botte allemande, de la déclaration de guerre de la Roumanie à la délivrance. Journal d'un journaliste* (Brussels: Imprimerie scientifique Charles Bulens & Cie, 1919), 282–283 (April 9, 1917).

15. De Schaepdrijver, *Gabrielle Petit*, 85–92, 115–118.

16. Jens Thiel, *Menschenbassin Belgien. Anwerbung, Deportation und Zwangsarbeit im Ersten Weltkrieg* (Essen: Klartext Verlag, 2007), 105.

17. MT, October 19, 1916.

18. Allan Nevins, ed., *The Letters and Journal of Brand Whitlock* (New York: D. Appleton Century Company, 1936), 323 (November 17, 1916).

19. MT, February 24, 1917.

20. MT, June 9, 1917.

21. MT, September 28, 1916.

22. Nevins, *The Letters and Journal of Brand Whitlock*, 298–299 (September 29—October 1, 1916).

23. MT, August 9, 1918.

24. Hoover Institution Archives, Stanford, California, Frank Angell Papers, Box 3, typescript, "The Belgians under the German Occupation," n.d. (written in late 1916 and slightly revised in December 1918), 163.

25. Brand Whitlock, *Belgium: A Personal Narrative*, vol. 1 (New York: D. Appleton and Company, 1919), 519–520.

26. Tytgat, *Bruxelles sous la botte*, 285–290 (April 17, 1917).

27. MT, February 12, 1918.

28. Angell, "The Belgians," 152.

29. Nevins, *The Letters and Journal of Brand Whitlock*, 287 (August 17, 1916).

30. Louis Gille, Alphonse Ooms, and Paul Delandsheere, *Cinquante mois d'occupation allemande* (Brussels: Albert Dewit, 1919), 2:312 (September 24, 1916).

31. Angell (referring to the Assistance), "The Belgians," 147.

32. Michaël Amara and Hubert Roland, eds., *Gouverner en Belgique occupée: Oscar von der Lancken-Wakenitz—Rapports d'activité 1915–1918. Édition critique* (Frankfurt: P.I.E.-Peter Lang, 2004), 217.

33. Fernand Mayence, *La correspondance de S.E. le Cardinal Mercier avec le gouvernement-général allemand pendant l'occupation 1914–1918* (Brussels: Albert Dewit; Paris: Gabalda, 1919), 462–463.

34. MT, October 21, 1916.

35. Sophie De Schaepdrijver, *La Belgique et la Première Guerre Mondiale* (Frankfurt: P.I.E.-Peter Lang, 2004), 260–261.

36. MT, March 5, 1917. See also March 11, 1917.

37. Jean Wittouck, b. 1901, son of the late Frantz and of Albertine Brandeis.

38. MT, February 1, 1917.

39. MT, October 14, 1916.

40. MT, November 18, 1916.

41. MT, May 20, 1918.

42. MT, July 2, 1917.

43. MT, October 24, 1916.

44. MT, March 1, 1917, preface to Book 2.

45. MT, October 14, 1918.

Mary Thorp with her charges, the three Wittouck boys, in June 1911. Although the caption on the back reads, "The catechism lesson given by Miss Thorp," the book she is holding is not a catechism but the children's book Noted Horses *and* Noted Dogs. *Still, the formal photograph shows Thorp's role as educator on the occasion of one boy's first communion.* PHOTOGRAPH FROM FAMILY ALBUM IN POSSESSION OF MR. ÉRIC WITTOUCK. USED WITH PERMISSION

A recent photograph of the Wittouck family's formerly elegant townhouse on the Boulevard de Waterloo in Brussels (before the building was gutted and refitted as a clothing store). The imposing nature of the residence suggests the comfort of Mary Thorp's life, even during wartime. PHOTO BY TAMMY PROCTOR

La Fougeraie (Fern Meadows), the Wittoucks' summer home in Uccle, outside Brussels, built in fashionable neo–Louis XVI style. The picture was probably taken in 1913, when the house was just finished. PHOTOGRAPH FROM FAMILY ALBUM IN POSSESSION OF MR. ÉRIC WITTOUCK. USED WITH PERMISSION

Bal costume du 17 mars 1912

Pavlick en pêcheur Napolitain

Catherine de Medem, the wife of Paul Wittouck, about 1910. Mary Thorp's employer was a Russian aristocrat; her husband was a wealthy Belgian entrepreneur. The couple met at the spa resort of Marienbad; family lore has it that she had vowed to return from that holiday with a fiancé. The couple were engaged very shortly afterward and married in August 1898.

Pavlick Wittouck dressed as a "Neapolitan fisherman," March 1912. The photo albums show the Wittoucks' predilection for costume balls, common among the Belgian elite at the time. In the diary, Mary Thorp writes of attending many formal dinners and receptions.

Mary Thorp with members of the Wittouck family on the steps of the Uccle mansion about 1910. She stands between Madame Wittouck's mother and Paul Wittouck. Though small and blurry, the snapshot, probably taken by Madame Wittouck, shows Thorp's status as a pillar of the household. PHOTOGRAPH FROM FAMILY ALBUM IN POSSESSION OF MR. ÉRIC WITTOUCK. USED WITH PERMISSION

Mary Thorp presides over Pavlick and Serge's sickroom in early 1911. The caption, probably written by Madame Wittouck, reads, "Miss Thorp and Sister Basile, the two home nurses." Both boys had suffered double ear infections in February–March 1911, and little Serge had undergone a trepanning (a hole drilled in the skull). PHOTOGRAPH FROM FAMILY ALBUM IN POSSESSION OF MR. ÉRIC WITTOUCK. USED WITH PERMISSION

"Miss Thorp's" summer schoolhouse for the three Wittouck boys on the grounds of La Fougeraie, c. 1911. This schoolhouse supplemented the schoolroom at the Brussels residence. Thorp's possession of special spaces for her work reinforced her status in the household. PHOTOGRAPH FROM ALBUM IN POSSESSION OF MR. ÉRIC WITTOUCK. USED WITH PERMISSION

Bekanntmachung | Bekendmaking | Avis

1. Ein Belgier, welcher sich neben gewerbsmässigem Brief- und Personenschmuggel gegen Bezahlung damit befasste, feindliche Spionageagenten über die Grenze zu befördern und auch selbst Spionageberichte über Bewegungen deutscher Truppen in Belgien über die Grenze nach Holland brachte, wurde vom Feldgericht des Gouvernements der Festung Antwerpen wegen Kriegsverrats, begangen durch Spionage, zum Tode verurteilt.

2. Ein belgischer Soldat, welcher sich bis jetzt in Zivil unangemeldet in Belgien aufhielt und sich gegen Bezahlung im Auftrage eines englischen Kommandanten damit befasste, wehrfähige Belgier über die Grenze nach Holland zu bringen, um sie dem feindlichen Heere und der feindlichen Heeresindustrie zuzuführen, wurde durch Urteil des Feldgerichts des Gouvernements Brüssel wegen Kriegsverrats, begangen durch Zuführung von Mannschaften an den Feind, zum Tode verurteilt. Er ist geständig, mehrere Hundert solcher Belgier über die Grenze gebracht zu haben.

Beide Urteile wurden am 8. 9. 16 bezw. 14. 9. 16 durch Erschiessen vollstreckt.

Ich bringe dies hiermit zur Kenntnis der Bevölkerung des ganzen mir unterstellten Gebietes.

Brüssel, den 14. September 1916. [Bestätk. — S. 574.]

Der General-Gouverneur in Belgien,
Freiherr VON BISSING,
Generaloberst.

G. G. IIIa. 14296.

---

1. Een Belg, die voor beroep had tegen betaling brieven en personen over de grens te smokkelen en, die bovendien vijandelijke verspiedingsagenten en ook zelf verspiedingsberichten over Duitsche troepenbewegingen in België naar Nederland overbracht, werd door den Veldkrijgsraad van het gouvernement der vesting Antwerpen wegens krijgsverraad, bestaande in verspieding, ter dood veroordeeld.

2. Een Belgisch soldaat, die tot nu toe, zonder zich te hebben aangemeld, als burger gekleed in België verbleef en, tegen betaling in opdracht van een Engelschen kommandant, weerbare Belgen naar Nederland overbracht voor dienstneming in het vijandelijk leger of in de vijandelijke legernijverheid, werd, bij vonnis van den Veldkrijgsraad van het gouvernement te Brussel wegens krijgsverraad, bestaande in het toevoeren van manschappen naar den vijand, ter dood veroordeeld. Hij heeft bekend verscheidene honderden weerbare Belgen over de grens te hebben gebracht.

Beide vonnissen zijn op 8 en 14 September 1916 door den kogel voltrokken.

Hierbij breng ik deze bekendmaking ter kennis der bevolking van het gansche onder mij staande gebied.

Brussel, den 14e September 1916.

Der General-Gouverneur in Belgien,
Freiherr VON BISSING,
Generaloberst.

---

1. Un Belge qui, moyennant payement, se chargeait, à titre professionnel, de faire passer des lettres et des personnes en contrebande, de faire franchir la frontière à des espions ennemis et de faire parvenir en Hollande des rapports d'espionnage concernant les mouvements des troupes allemandes en Belgique, a été condamné à mort, par le tribunal de campagne du gouvernement de la place forte d'Anvers, pour trahison commise pendant l'état de guerre en pratiquant l'espionnage.

2. Un soldat belge en civil qui, sans s'être déclaré, est resté jusqu'à présent en Belgique et s'y est chargé, moyennant payement et comme mandataire d'un commandant anglais, de faire franchir la frontière hollandaise à des Belges aptes à porter les armes, afin qu'ils entrent dans l'armée ennemie ou au service de l'industrie militaire ennemie, a été, par jugement du tribunal de campagne du gouvernement de Bruxelles, condamné à mort pour trahison commise pendant l'état de guerre en faisant passer des hommes à l'ennemi. Il a avoué avoir fait franchir la frontière à plusieurs centaines de recrues.

Les deux condamnés ont été fusillés les 8 et 14 de ce mois.

Je porte le présent avis à la connaissance de la population de tout le territoire placé sous mon autorité.

Bruxelles, le 14 septembre 1916.

Der General-Gouverneur in Belgien,
Freiherr VON BISSING,
Generaloberst.

The German occupying authorities used thousands of posters to discipline and instruct the Belgian population. Thorp often referred to them. On September 16, 1916, she wrote that all of Brussels was shocked at seeing "another fatal red poster"—the color used to announce executions—to inform the populace that two civilian resisters had been shot. This is the poster Thorp saw. LANDESARCHIV BADEN-WÜRTTEMBERG, J 151 NR 336, "BEKANNTMACHUNG" ZWEIER TODESURTEILE DES FELDGERICHTS WEGEN KRIEGSVERRATS, STAATSDRÜCKEREI NR 574

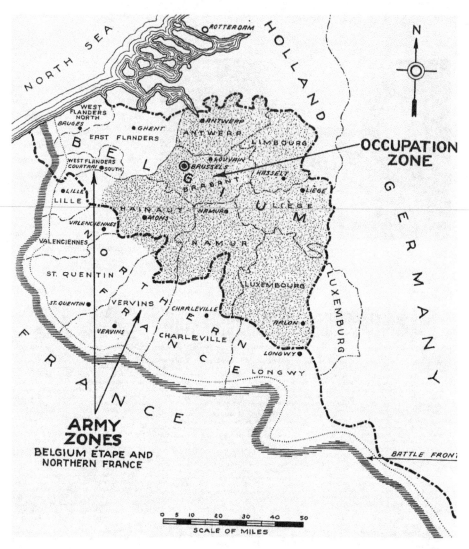

Mary Thorp often refers to the two parts of occupied Belgium: the army zones, or Étape, and the Government-General, where she resided. This food relief map of Belgium shows those boundaries as well as many of the main cities she references. HERBERT HOOVER PRESIDENTIAL LIBRARY AND MUSEUM, WEST BRANCH (IOWA)

bit of revolution we have here. The General of the Staff at Petit Bigard had sentinels all round him on Sunday night, & finally consented to hoist the red flag, when going away. The soldiers simply (make) them submit; nevertheless there is of course, as usual, a counter-current of those who remain faithful to the old army, & they quarrel amongst themselves.

Each night we eagerly look forward to the events of the next day, it is an interesting time to live just now. I wonder if Mlle Bolo remembers how, already in 1914 she & I had decreed that our chastisement for German Imperialism was to make a small republic of Prussia! How chimerical it seemed then, we even laughed at our own audacity, & Yet it seems & has come true!!!

[left margin, vertical] 4 years to-day we buried fr.? Whittock R.I.P. How Stephen his be... was!

Mary Thorp's writing in the diary rarely wavered from the strong, clear strokes demonstrated here. She must have reread entries because she had a habit of inserting additional text in the margins or between lines. IN FLANDERS FIELDS MUSEUM, YPRES, BELGIUM

A nattily dressed Dick Dodson at Ruhleben in 1918, shortly before he was released to the Netherlands as part of a prisoner exchange. Clearly, he sought to reassure his aunt about his health and well-being. IN FLANDERS FIELDS MUSEUM, YPRES, BELGIUM

Mary Thorp's nephew, Dick Dodson, sent snapshots of camp life to his aunt to reassure her about his surroundings and to help explain internment at Ruhleben, outside Berlin. This photo depicts "Bond Street" in Ruhleben, which reminded prisoners of a main shopping street in London. IN FLANDERS FIELDS MUSEUM, YPRES, BELGIUM

Many internees at Ruhleben obtained extra funds by working for other prisoners in camp. Dick Dodson had been a printer before the war, so he set up a temporary shop in camp. This advertisement for his business appeared in the camp periodical, In Ruhleben Camp, *which was produced by prisoners.* IN FLANDERS FIELDS MUSEUM, YPRES, BELGIUM

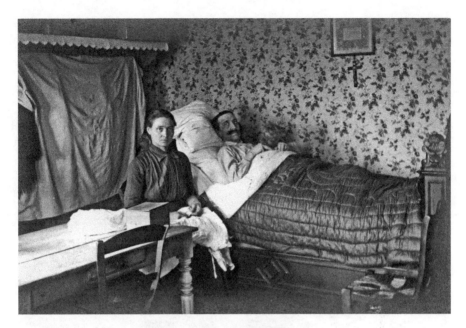

Mary Thorp's charity work brought her face to face with poverty. These undated pictures show domestic interiors in the rue Haute neighborhood, where Mary Thorp often went on house visits. BRUSSELS CITY ARCHIVES, ICONOGRAPHY COLLECTION

Thorp often wrote about the extreme dearth of butter—considered an essential foodstuff at the time. The Brussels press tried to insert humor into the dismal situation. This cartoon, dated July 1917, is captioned "Those Who Queue!" and shows people thronging a food-relief warehouse; the sign on the door reads "Butter for Sale—100 Grams A Person Only." BRUSSELS CITY ARCHIVES, FONDS KEYM

Thorp mourned the fate of forced laborers deported to work in Germany. She also mentioned the mendaciousness of the German posters in the Brussels streets. This Brussels cartoon from about 1917 does both at once. The poster declares that "Many jobless men have done so well in Germany that they have decided to stay there permanently." The bottom image shows a cemetery in Germany, with the caption "Those who stayed permanently." BRUSSELS CITY ARCHIVES, FONDS KEYM

Framing the Diary: A Note from the Editors

Mary Thorp started her wartime diary in September 1916 and ended it in January 1919. The manuscript covers five bound notebooks; it was stored with a few additional materials, including scrapbook pages and some bound prison camp magazines. In order to provide context for the wartime developments Thorp chronicles, we have provided short editorial notes at the start of each notebook. These supplement the diary annotations, which, in the interest of space, we have kept as brief as possible. In the notes, Mary Thorp is referred to as "MT." In the diary, we removed some repetition, indicating those edits with ellipses. On a few occasions, we inserted text between square brackets to clarify the content—for instance, to point out that Thorp meant tanks when she mentioned "cistern Land dreadnoughts." Some entries feature text in italics: these are Thorp's own inserts, which she occasionally added in the margins or between lines for clarification. We have also kept Thorp's strikethroughs. In order to eliminate repetition and trim the size of the diary, we have omitted sections of text and inserted ellipses. Finally, we have translated foreign words and phrases.

A word about Belgian place names: in the First World War era, people like Thorp would have referred to cities in Flanders exclusively by their French name; today, their Flemish name is more often used. Examples from the diary include Tirlemont (today Tienen), Louvain (today Leuven) and Ypres (today Ieper). We indicated both names where necessary.

We have kept the diary structure: Books 1 through 5 correspond to Thorp's notebooks. Inside the entries, to improve readability, we have indented all paragraphs, which Thorp herself did not do consistently. For an example of Thorp's handwriting on a typical diary entry, refer to the photo gallery.

Mary Thorp's Diary

$\mathcal{Book}\ 1$

THE "ELEVENTH HOUR,"

SEPTEMBER 1916–FEBRUARY 1917

*T*horp started her diary on a note of optimism: she expected September 1916 to be the "eleventh hour" of the war. She drew this hope from reports about the fighting in the Somme: the British had introduced tanks; Allied aviators dropped leaflets over Brussels, announcing liberation; the Germans were shortening their front.

Thorp's feelings were widely shared: "The people are really in fear—half fear, half hope—thinking, for some odd reason, that the Germans are about to retreat," wrote Brand Whitlock. "One hears it everywhere. It is interesting as a bit of crowd psychology."[1] He was less sanguine, and he was right. The Somme offensive had by then bogged down into small localized assaults. Other Allied offensives had stalled—at Verdun, on the Eastern Front, on the Isonzo (Soča), in Mesopotamia. Hoping for breakthroughs, armies deployed ever more destructive artillery barrages and huge numbers of infantry, with an appalling toll in lives. Even so, on the Western Front, the inconclusive debacles did not significantly dent the prevailing view that military planners needed to keep pushing. Thorp's diary at first testified to this determination, but like many others, she eventually lost hope.

Shaken by the suffering at the fronts, Thorp paid close attention to the possibility of a negotiated peace. The end of 1916 saw various proposals. On December 12, the Central Powers, now in the ascendant, issued a "Peace Note" that avoided discussing exact terms. A week later, US President Wilson urged both sides to clearly state their war aims. The Allied reply requested the rollback of all Central conquests in this war and of all territories gained in earlier conflicts, which suggested Alsace-Lorraine. It also hinted at the breakup of the Habsburg and Ottoman Empires. The Central

---

[1] Allan Nevins, ed., *The Letters and Journals of Brand Whitlock* (New York: Appleton-Century, 1936), 292.

Powers rejected this. The underlying assumption for both parties was that the war could still be won; the Allies banked on attritional warfare, the Germans on submarines. Though Thorp could not have known all of the details, she followed events avidly. The coming and going of the prospect of peace was hard on her. She refrained from commenting on the Allied rejection of the German peace proposal, and eventually she resigned herself to a military rather than a diplomatic "solution," hoping against hope for a military breakthrough via a "shortcut" not on the Western Front. But she was painfully aware of horrors to come.

Meanwhile, life under German occupation had become, if anything, even harder. The occupation regime had started forced-labor drives and heightened its requisitions of goods. This in a winter of food shortages and exceptional cold—off the Belgian coast, the North Sea froze. For the German military, the deepened exploitation and indeed dismantling of Belgium, while it precluded chances of negotiated peace, served the immediate needs of the expected knockout blow. It also helped to break civilians' resolve. Ludendorff declared in February 1917 that Belgium had to "help carry the war's burden" to such an extreme extent that it would make "the wish for peace break forth ferociously" among the occupied population.[2] Thorp's diary documents this tremendous strain.

LOCAL GOSSIP AND "SIDE-SHOWS" OF THE WAR, DURING THE GERMAN OCCUPATION OF BELGIUM, FROM SEPTEMBER 15, 1916

Several times, in the beginning of the war, I wanted to start a diary, but was dissuaded from doing so, because it was considered dangerous; a Jesuit father was shot during the tragic Louvain days of August 1914, for having written a few impressions. . . .[3]

As we consider now, that events are entering on a very interesting period, I decide to follow my fancy at (let us hope), "the eleventh hour."

FRIDAY, SEPTEMBER 15

Brussels is expiating cheerfully its enthusiasm, manifested when the Allies' airship took a peep at us at 10-15 pm on Sept 6th, *and after relieving itself of a few well aimed bombs, threw down papers announcing our near delivery & let off fireworks, of which I had a good view on our lawn.*[4]

[2] Quoted in Sophie De Schaepdrijver, *La Belgique et la Première Guerre Mondiale* (Frankfurt: P.I.E.-Peter Lang, 2004), 228.

[3] MT refers to the well-known fate of Eugène Dupiéreux [or Dupierreux], a young Jesuit student executed during the invasion at Louvain for keeping a diary of the "atrocities."

[4] On September 6, an Allied biplane flew low over central Brussels, dropping leaflets assuring civilians that "the moment of deliverance is near." Louis Gille, Alphonse Ooms and Paul

No circulation in town from our[5] 8:30 pm to 3 a.m.: all places of amusement & public resort closed, from Sept 12th to 18th. The districts of two railway stations outside the Boulevards being also "cleared," we infer troops are moving. The great rumour to-day is: that on the 21st, 22nd, & 23rd we shall be kept indoors on account of our "gentle invaders" moving eastward somewhat to shorten their front. If only I dared to believe it! Too good to be true I fear!

SATURDAY, SEPTEMBER 16

The excitement in town to-day was another fatal red poster saying two more men had been shot, on the 8th and the 14th, for communicating with the Allies' front & passing men. R.I.P.[6]

Very few bicycles, they are all to be suppressed on the 20th, according to a German decree. The people who give up their bicycle tyres between the 15th & 20th are paid a little more than those who simply declare them, & continue riding till the 20th....

Mme. W has to appear before the German police on the 19th, concerning the affair for which she spent the night in prison, at Liège, on Aug 26th.[7]

SUNDAY, SEPTEMBER 17

Last Sunday for bicycles, fortunately a fine, mild day, very few to be seen in the forest.... The rumour of our having to be "kept in" three days this week is no longer believed by the sanguine.

News from our front in the West good. We wonder how much truth there is in the victory of the enemy announced in Doubroutcha?[8]

Delandsheere, *Cinquante mois d'occupation allemande* (Brussels: Albert Dewit, 1919), 2:288–290; Nevins, *Journals*, 290–291.

[5] In November 1914, the occupation authorities had substituted Central European Time for Greenwich Mean Time. Out of patriotism, many Belgians refused to acknowledge the shift and kept referring to "our" or "Belgian" time. The introduction of daylight saving time did not alter this.

[6] The Germans executed the two men for helping trapped Belgian and Allied soldiers escape the occupied country. This what MT refers to as "'passing' men." One of them was a young, invalided Belgian soldier, Mathieu Bodson, whose last letter to his mother did the rounds in patriotic circles. Gille et al., *Cinquante mois d'occupation allemande*, 2:302–304.

[7] Madame Wittouck, MT's employer, spent a night in prison in Liège for her intent to carry two personal letters from Vielsalm (a small town southeast of Liège) to Brussels.

[8] In Dobrudja (Romania), the Allied forces were in full retreat by September 18. German posters in the streets of Brussels had announced successes on this front since September 8. Charles Gheude, *Nos années terribles* (Brussels: Oscar Lamberty, n.d. [1919]), 2:342.

Had a cheerful letter from Dick in Ruhleben; he has been changed to Barrack 14—more space & light; the "Authorities" are evidently "seeing to it" since the complaints were made. Only four men allowed now in each box, instead of five or six.[9]

MONDAY, SEPTEMBER 18

... To-day ends Brussels' punishment of keeping indoors from 8:30 pm. I heard a neutral diplomatist remark the other day, that if in England anyone shouted for instance "Hurrah for Turkey"! his punishment would merely be to be pointed out as a madman—no official reprisals—and that besides "all that won't win the war."

TUESDAY, SEPTEMBER 19

Just dined with M. & Mme. *Billings* Ruddock. He is the new Secretary of the American Legation.[10] Charming, both of them, & so desirous of helping us. . . .

I heard to-day that the most precious, beautiful stuffs, silks, velvet, linen, damask table clothes etc etc are used in Brussels, by the Germans, for making bags to be filled with earth to barricade their trenches. (This from a German woman who works in the factory). Mme. W. was called up by the "occupiers" to be questioned on letters they found in the perquisitions they made in both our houses on Aug 27th when she was detained at Liège. We think the matter ends there. She answered very cleverly.

WEDNESDAY, SEPTEMBER 20

Heard the cannon very distinctly in the garden this afternoon. Tournai is in the "Étape" (war zone) since Saturday. The civil administration that was centralized at Lille has been moved there.[11]

They say Bissing has gone to have a look at the West Front. How lovely if he could witness the fall of Thiepval, Combles, Péronne, Chaulnes.

I do wonder what will happen when we take that line. Have just been introduced, on paper, to the wonderful cistern Land dreadnoughts [tanks]—a hearty welcome to them! for sparing our brave men.[12]

---

[9] The new barracks described in his letter were a response to a March 1915 inspection of the camp by the American ambassador.

[10] Albert Billings Ruddock, secretary of the US Legation in Brussels, and his wife, Margaret.

[11] Tournai, on the Belgian-French border, had been on the outer edge of the Government-General; from September 1916, it belonged to the Étape.

[12] The armored vehicles referred to by their code name of "tanks" (hence MT's "cisterns") were introduced by the British army on the Somme on September 15.

THURSDAY, SEPTEMBER 21

Nothing to say of the war to-day, unfortunately.

Was rather amused just now to read, in a Dutch paper, that a German has been imprisoned, in Germany, for having said, in a train that the "Deutchsland" [*sic*] type of submarine was invented merely for the escape, to America, of Kaiser & Kronprinz, in a certain time.

Was told that business men, coming from Ghent on urgent affairs, are accompanied by a German soldier. Otherwise no communication with the "étape."

FRIDAY, SEPTEMBER 22

At 8:45 a.m two German emissaries came again, to interview Mme. W concerning answers they considered unsatisfactory at her interrogation last Tuesday, concerning letters found in her desk at the B[d].[13]

I went to see Mme. Groenvelt about her husband's imprisonment. . . . [H]e has been shut up two months, has nine more to go through, for having had in his shop Tipperary (music only) national anthems etc.[14] I found the poor woman almost dying from heart trouble, after an awful night. Went to the American Legation & exposed the case to the secretary, Mr. [Ruddock] who promised to do his best to have poor Groenvelt released.

SATURDAY, SEPTEMBER 23

. . . This evening two Zeppelins passed over the town—I fear on their way to England again; nearly every time they attack during the night of Saturday to Sunday.[15]

Read a bill thrown out of one of our airships at Antwerp, telling us raids will be made between the 22nd & 30th, warning people to take shelter far from railways & promising us a general offensive on every front towards October 10th.

SUNDAY, SEPTEMBER 24

. . . Had a letter to-day from the American Legation: Mr. Ruddock says he has put the Groenvelt case before the Political Department, which advises an application for pardon, by the wife, to the Governor General.

I will see about this to-morrow.

[13] The Wittouck residence on Boulevard de Waterloo.

[14] Printed music in Belgium was now subject to censorship (Avis [Official Poster] no. 559, August 29, 1916).

[15] From Zeppelin bases in Belgium, the Germans attacked Britain and France. These bases in turn were targeted by Allied bombers.

MONDAY, SEPTEMBER 25

I went to tell Mme. G[roenvelt] that she must make a written application to Von Bissing for her husband's pardon. I am to make her a copy.

Lovely weather for our "getting on". Greece seems very revolutionary.[16]

While we were at dinner this evening, about 8-45, a zepp[elin] passed quite near; we went out on the terrace on hearing the motor. I wonder where it is going. We knew this evening by German paper, that there <u>was</u>, as I thought, another raid over England from Saturday to Sunday, & that one of their 2 Zepps was burnt and another fell, the occupants being taken prisoners.[17]

TUESDAY, SEPTEMBER 26

To-day we had the details of the big Zeppelin raid of the 22nd 23rd over England. Wonder if the two we saw here on Saturday evening were those brought down in Essex. I wonder also what became of the one that was near the Fougeraie during dinner that night.

Bissing has ordered back to Germany all the female relations & followers of the German soldiers and officers.

Another gloriously fine day for our advances on the Somme. I went to-day to my monthly German control; all was dull and quiet there. When we return to town I shall have to go every Tuesday as before. I obtained to go only once a month from here.

WEDNESDAY, SEPTEMBER 27

A tragic day for Brussels! Alas for the poor victims. R.I.P. [18]

At 4:45 a.m. all the cannons of the town and suburbs began shooting at two airships that were in sight. *The airships & shots & clouds of smoke were seen from our windows.* All the trams were stopped. Several of the shots fired by the Germans, instead of exploding in the air, fell on different houses, causing great havoc & loss of life in different quarters. Of course, nothing official is ever known, just so far they say there are 6 people killed & 20 to 30 wounded.

A servant cleaning his boots in the cellar kitchen at the B[rnne] d'Hoogvoorsts' was killed. I was anxious for the boys who had just started to school through the forest, but the victims were mostly people in their houses. . . .

---

[16] In ostensibly neutral Greece, pro-Allied former Prime Minister Eleutherios Venizelos opposed the German-leaning King Constantine; the Allies progressively took over control.

[17] Zeppelins raided the English coast, Midlands, and London on September 23. In retaliation, British naval airplanes attacked Zeppelin sheds near Brussels and Antwerp.

[18] On the morning of September 27, after two Allied planes had passed Brussels, there was a detonation. Several houses on the east side of town were badly damaged. Ten people were

THURSDAY, SEPTEMBER 28

Deo Gratias! We have taken Combles! And a brief telegram in the Dutch papers say Thiepval has fallen also! How I have longed for this! En avant [onward] now for Péronne & Chaulnes ... and then what will be the next move???

Indignation very great in Brussels at the deaths & injuries caused yesterday by the German shots exploding when falling on the houses & in the streets. They say the neutral ministers are making investigations to establish responsibilities. We never, since the Gs are here, get anything in the censored daily papers concerning such occurrences.

FRIDAY, SEPTEMBER 29, ST. MICHAEL'S DAY

Great devotion at St. Gudule in honour of St. Michael, patron of Brussels, "l'ange des combats" [the angel of battle], to obtain prompt victory.

Have just been reading particulars of the fall of Combles, from accounts in Dutch papers. Should like to ask each "cultured" Boche[19] I meet—*in the street, for we never speak to them except when compelled officially, on business*—what he thinks now of our "contemptible little army"!!![20]

Please God we may soon admire it here on the spot! The poor are suffering from semi-starvation, food so dear and work so rare, in spite of all the possible help that is given. I was very affected by the change in my little dressmaker, wasting away from want of nourishment. The German communiqués report: 13 Belgians killed, 28 wounded, 15 houses destroyed by bombs from the English airships on Wednesday! Everybody is convinced all is due to German guns.

SATURDAY, SEPTEMBER 30

I have just put my watch back one hour, so to-morrow we get up at the real hour of the sun. ...

Have just read the speech Bethmann Hollweg made on Thursday. We think it feeble, denoting discouragement & greater comprehension than ever of the "will power" of England.[21]

Heard distressing particulars concerning the death of Count Robert de Lesseps, killed mortally wounded on the 4th inst [instante mense, i.e., of this month] ... in

killed, including the janitor at the Baroness d'Hoogvoorst's. Gille et al., *Cinquante mois d'occupation allemande*, 2:314–320.

[19] Insulting term used to describe the Germans during World War I.

[20] In August 1914, German Emperor Wilhelm II referred to the British Expeditionary Force as "General French's contemptible little army."

[21] Theobald von Bethmann-Hollweg, chancellor of Germany from 1909 to 1917.

the battle of the Somme, in a special act of heroism, died next day in a hospital near Péronne. R.I.P.[22]

SUNDAY, OCTOBER I

Another zepp. passed over the house while we were at dinner this evening; please God it may make no victims in England!

We heard the cannon <u>most</u> <u>distantly</u> & <u>loudly</u> all the afternoon—but we never get to know exactly from what point the sound proceeds: North Sea, Somme, Belgian front???

The patriotic barrister M. S.K. who defends *in their trials* all the Belgians & Allies "par patriotisme" [out of patriotism] against the Germans, called on me to ask me to render a [*sic*] him a little service.[23] He has been interested in thousands of such cases. He says that <u>Germans</u> who are convicted of treason are never condemned to death, but to penal servitude, according to their laws, but that a code of laws was made in view of this war, condemning to be <u>shot</u>, all inhabitants of invaded countries who betray German military interests. Just now there are 17 for whom the Pope & different great personages are trying to get a reprieve.[24]

MONDAY, OCTOBER 2

We were awakened this morning by another air fight at a quarter to six. Shooting went on for half an hour.

I hear there were accidents again; a girl, in bed, in Avenue de la Couronne, had a leg cut off. God have pity on all the poor victims of the war! . . .

TUESDAY, OCTOBER 3

Each time a zeppelin passes this way in the evening, I am right—in fearing it is bound for England. The one we heard on Sunday most probably took part in the raid we have just read of in the Dutch papers. *What luck that Zepp the 4th was brought down near London again!*

[22] Robert de Lesseps, son of the Suez Canal engineer Ferdinand de Lesseps, died on the Somme on September 4, 1916. MT knew him: he married a niece of Paul Wittouck, Marthe Allard.

[23] The prominent Brussels lawyer Sadi Kirschen, a naturalized Belgian born in Romania, was one of the Belgian lawyers allowed, under restrictions, to defend civilian resisters before the German military tribunals. He pleaded the Edith Cavell case, among others.

[24] The 1872 German military penal code called for the death penalty for war treason for crimes such as spying for the enemy. In addition, the Imperial Decree of 1899 allowed military commanders to execute foreign civilians for aiding the enemy.

What a boon those Dutch papers are under the present circumstances, & how famished for news must be the poor people who live in the "Etape" (*war zone*), like the 't Kints who never get any papers except the local censored.[25] We hear an aeroplane (perhaps one that was here yesterday morning,) was brought down near Tirlemont, the English airman was able to burn his machine and escaped, (before the arrival on the spot of the Boches), in civilian attire provided by the onlookers, who were all arrested at once for letting the Englishman escape. I wonder how he fared!!![26]

WEDNESDAY, OCTOBER 4

... Shoe-leather gets dearer every day... 9 fr. for soleing & heeling boys' boots. About 7 to 8 for mine, & the leather so inferior in quality. Dress materials hardly to be found. About 2 months ago every stock was examined by the G's & eight ninths had to be stored away.... why??? & only 1/9 sold. I don't know when a second ninth will be freed.[27]

THURSDAY, OCTOBER 5

Heavy showers all day, and strong wind, am afraid it was unfavourable for our front.

The cannonading we heard so plainly on Sunday afternoon was from the Belgian coast, hydroavions (seaplanes) [*sic*] fighting.

I am told that a German paper announces that all the Court jewels (except the historical ones) and all Society's private jewels have been sold to make money for the war.

FRIDAY, OCTOBER 6

... "Potatoes" are the object of the greatest interest just now. All those who have a crop are hiding them, so as not to sell them at the prices fixed by our "temporary masters" who have forbidden them to be carried about. No end of funny things happen through people trying to smuggle, but the tragic side of it is, that thousands are hungry for want of potatoes & ~~food~~ bread.

---

[25] Count Arnold 't Kint de Roodenbeke, a Catholic senator.

[26] The airplane landed in a field near Tienen [Tirlemont]; the pilots, a Frenchman and a Belgian (not, as MT wrote, an Englishman), destroyed it and escaped in civilian clothes, given to them by locals. The German military conducted a large-scale search. Gille et al., *Cinquante mois d'occupation allemande*, 2:324–325.

[27] The Militärisches Textilbeschaffungsamt, created on July 30, 1916, ordered textile dealers to inventory their stocks and keep nine-tenths at the disposal of the German authorities. Gille et al., *Cinquante mois d'occupation allemande*, 2:270–272.

Butter is in the same boat as potatoes, & only the very rich have any now; my own personal friends are deprived of it.

SATURDAY, OCTOBER 7

Saw M. Sadi Kirschen, who will have Mme. Groenvelt's second application for her husband's release, remitted to Von Bissing.

Had a call, at the B^d [Boulevard de Waterloo], from a policeman—the police are having to ascertain if all foreigners are really residing where they have declared. He told me the policemen get imprisoned if they are not careful about saluting the Boche officers.

We are glad to know that 150 Japanese officers are going to help in Dobroudscha. Very squally weather, alas for our airmen & advance!

SUNDAY, OCTOBER 8

Madame Wittouck thought she was not going to be "punished" for having travelled back from Vielsalm with two letters—I didn't agree with her. To-day she is informed she is sentenced to 18 days imprisonment, or a fine of 300 marks. I presume she will pay the fine, & not have the same pluck as Mary d'Alcantara who went to prison for 10 days, just a year ago, because she would not pay the Germans a fine of 80 marks for an opinion she expressed to a cousin, & which was "overheard" by a German.[28]

MONDAY, OCTOBER 9

I was told, but can hardly believe, that Count Amédée Visart, Burgomaster of Bruges, has been sent to Germany, for having refused to provide 500 Belgian men, to make trenches for "the gentle invaders", north of Bruges, on the Dutch frontier.[29]

I paid 7 fr. 50 for soleing & heeling my boots, the price, before war, was 3 fr. 50!

Potatoes & butter (or rather, their absence) are the topics of general conversation.

No more flour is allowed to go to confectioners. Sweetmeats only to be had in the shops that don't close, & few of those, sugar not being very available either.[30] None to be had for private people, except for a few grammes from the "Alimentation." All the

---

[28] Marie 't Kint de Roodenbeke, wife of Count Juan d'Alcantara de Querrieu.

[29] In September 1916, the German Marine Corps Flanders, which ruled Bruges, demanded 400 workmen to work on German fortifications. The city government refused. The Marine Corps deposed Burgomaster Visart (though he was not sent to Germany), fined the town, and seized men in a street raid.

[30] The CRB (Commission for Relief in Belgium) and the CN (Comité National) no longer allowed flour to be used for cakes; in response, the *pâtissiers* of Brussels decided no longer to bake any from October 27. Many *bruxellois* applauded this measure (Gille et al., *Cinquante*

Belgians are starting learning English, quite a craze! & all the English Grammars & exercise books arrive from Leipzig!!!

TUESDAY, OCTOBER 10

Heard nothing special to-day concerning the war.

Read of the arrival at New Port *U.S.* of the German war submarine U53, that went over in 17 days. As it only remained in harbor 2 hours, presume it was most undesirable.[31]

The Roumanians are, alas! being beaten back to their frontiers in Transylvania— God grant the Centrals don't reach Roumania.

Motono, Mme. W's great friend, is leaving Petrograd to become Minister of Foreign Affairs in Japan. He always declared, even immediately after the Russo-Japanese war, that the aim of his life was to create durable friendship between Japan and Russia.[32] . . .

WEDNESDAY, OCTOBER 11

They say Mr Amédée Visart has been deposed as burgomaster of Bruges by the Germans, & on account of his age, about 80, has not been sent to Germany, but in his stead, his son Étienne & grandson François have been deported, that they have had trouble with the Germans through their betrayal by a servant, & that Fräulein Strasser came from Germany to give testimony in their favor. It is said too that Bruges is terribly fined, but so far no one knows the truth, though something im- portant must have occurred there.[33]

Lena Ford was delighted to-day because our concierge said he would procure for her a kilo of butter for nine francs & a half![34]

THURSDAY, OCTOBER 12

Great indignant excitement in the American & Dutch Press concerning the de- struction of neutral & English ships, by German submarines, on the American coast. Have they or have they not a secret base on the American coast!!!

---

mois d'occupation allemande, 2:313); Whitlock thought it excessive (Nevins, *Letters and Journal of Brand Whitlock, Journal*, 297; September 27, 1916).

[31] German submarine *U-53* delivered letters for the German ambassador. After leaving the US shore, *U-53* sank several ships (four British, one Norwegian, and one Dutch). Survivors were picked up by US destroyers. This action led to a search for a "secret" submarine base near the North American coastline (*New York Times*, October 9, 1916).

[32] Viscount Motono Ichirō.

[33] Burgomaster Visart's son and grandson were deported to Germany. His daughter-in-law and granddaughter were briefly imprisoned in Bruges.

[34] Lena and Alec Ford were MT's English friends in Brussels. He traded in sodium nitrate, a fertilizer harvested mainly in Chile.

It makes it very hard on Wilson to act either way just now, at the eve of the presidential elections. . . .

FRIDAY, OCTOBER 13

I went to the Rinquets & read them Dick's last good letter.[35]

Ernest rather optimistic about the war, thinks Belgium will be evacuated for the New Year—I don't alas! He fancies we shall advance more rapidly when Péronne falls. . . .

Ernest told me the German officers occupying houses on the Avenue Louise all left last night, in motors, saying they will not return.

Good riddance!!!

SATURDAY, OCTOBER 14

Heard nothing special connected with the war.

Yesterday Ellen R [Rinquet] told me she had been horrified when a G. officer put out his hand to help her into a tram. She exclaimed with indignation "Ne me touchez pas"; he became very red & didn't attempt to assist any other women. I don't approve Ellen's attitude under the circumstances (I mean a man trying to be commonly polite) but she declares she can't help it, & that she sees their hands stained with blood. She is ferocious enough to get into trouble; Ernest & I told her so; he says he will never let her enter another tram where there are Boches, for fear of an incident.

SUNDAY, OCTOBER 15

The wind has dropped at last, after blowing hard for ever so long. I wonder if the change will bring us any more air fights. . . .

The measures taken by the Germans against anyone carrying potatoes get more rigorous every day. Even private people who grow them, may not dispose of any & may are only entitled to keep a certain quantity for themselves—the result is "smuggling" in every manner. We hear that Germans living in Brussels obtain much greater quantities from their alimentation than the wretched pittances allowed to the Belgians.

MONDAY, OCTOBER 17

All day long, from early morning till dark, we heard the continual roar of cannon, louder than ever before, never ceasing a moment. It was like everlasting, not distant

---

[35] Ernest Antoine Désiré Rinquet and "Ellen" [Charlotte Hélène Dodson Rinquet], Dick Dodson's aunt and uncle.

thunder. What was it? We never get to know really what has happened. I presume it was something on the Belgian coast. Even in town the roar was most distinct.

We hear that many of the "chômeurs" [the unemployed] are being compelled to go to Germany to work there for the G's. How are they going to be fed? It means more starvation than here! Some of the Dutch papers suppressed yesterday & to-day. . . .

TUESDAY, OCTOBER 18

This morning a German aeroplane was seen over Place Ste Croix as I was passing in a tram. When I got out at Rue de la Paix, it was shot at 4 times, to the general astonishment, as everyone had seen it was a Boche airship—so now to crown it all, they are getting blind. . . .

Someone told me she saw a hare in the forest, stop & make her a military salute. . . . [T]he Germans may not know, they would put it in their picture papers, to show the "Vaterland" that even animals, & wild ones too, have become Prussianised in Belgium!!! . . .

WEDNESDAY, OCTOBER 18

Heard nothing special concerning the war, except that in certain localities, Alost, Ninove, the "chômeurs" are resisting the German authority that is sending them off, against their will, to work for them in Germany.[36]

I had a very nice letter last week from Dick at Ruhleben, of Oct 9th; he keeps up his good spirits & earns 15 marks a week giving lessons. He is more satisfied than formerly with his "diggings" in a good corner, with three congenial companions.[37]

THURSDAY, OCTOBER 19

To-day is the 808th day of War. It rained all day long in spite of which we heard very loud cannonading, not distant, all the afternoon, the same as on Monday. The cause of latter has not yet transpired.

They say a man was killed by one of the 4 shots fired by the Boches, on Tuesday, at their own aeroplane. . . . [T]his time they owned to their mistake (privately, to a neutral diplomat) they can't possibly deny it for once.

It seems that the "chômeurs" to be sent off to Germany are rebelling in different localities. . . . [W]e think this sending away is preparatory to emptying Belgium of

[36] In the East Flemish Étape, deportations of the jobless had started. Gille et al., *Cinquante mois d'occupation allemande*, 2:340–342.

[37] Education was an important pastime for the men of Ruhleben camp. The British government allotted all prisoners a stipend of 5, later 4 marks per week.

all able bodied men—for there are prisoners enough in Germany who could work on the land & at peaceful trades.

FRIDAY, OCTOBER 20

Had such a bright cheerful letter from Ruhleben to-day, they <u>do</u> make the best of it. . . .

It is said that the Germans have been interfered with by the American legation, in their sending away the "chômeurs." Someone saw a train full of them, going off, in the middle of which was a flat truck with Howitzers pointing towards the engine & the rear "in case of rebellion." . . .

SATURDAY, OCTOBER 21

The Boches are getting simply ferocious about sending away to Germany the "men out of work" (chômeurs). The neutral diplomats say they <u>can't</u> interfere (if they did so they probably would be invited to go to the Hâvre!)[38] The Belgians fight with the Germans on the trains, but are soon put "hors de combat" [they are soon knocked out] by machine guns.

For the closing of the Boche exhibition at Luna-Park on the 15th, they made the women sand-bag makers dress up & dance with the German soldiers, and had the scene photoed for cinemas & their illustrated papers to make the world believe that the Belgians fraternize with them (like the affair of distributing petroleum to the Louvain women in 1914).[39]

SUNDAY, OCTOBER 22

. . . Had a little conversation with M. Ruddock, thanks to whom S[idonie]'s monthly allowance from British Relief fund has been raised.[40]

In the *Belgique*, there is a great tendency (prompted by the Germans) to have peace spoken of & discussed. Am disappointed that the extraordinary & distinct roar of cannon <u>all</u> <u>the</u> <u>week</u> has not brought us greater advances in the "communiqués."

[38] Le Havre, France, residence of the Belgian government in exile.

[39] From June 15 through October 15, 1916, at the Luna Park amusement site, the occupation authorities ran an exhibition on social security in Germany intended to bolster German rule; Belgians were encouraged to visit. The "women sand-bag makers" worked for the German army in a model workshop with a day-care center.

[40] Sidonie Dodson née Van Strydonck, wife of MT's nephew, Dick. The British Relief Fund provided assistance for British subjects. Sidonie, although born in Belgium, had British nationality through her marriage.

MONDAY, OCTOBER 23

It appears that the Bruges men who were compelled "by force" to go to the Dutch frontier to work for the Boches, absolutely refused to dig trenches, but consented to fell trees. They made them fall on the barbed wire separating the frontiers, & thus climbed over them & escaped into Holland. Well done, Brugeois! The German burgomaster that replaces Count Amédée Visart can't manage the town, & has had to call the "Counseil Communal" [Municipal Council] to his aid—they consented, on their own conditions: "being free to consult Mʳ Visart & that no more men shall be levied."[41] Oxen now draw heavy carts in the Brussels streets, instead of the absent horses. . . .

TUESDAY, OCTOBER 24

I am very sad about the fall of Constanza![42] All the Belgian burgomasters are in a great dilemma, if they don't give the Boches the lists of all the "chômeurs" to send to Germany (& they won't) there are to be terrible penalties. The Germans want to replace their 400.000 men still employed in Germany, by civilians of the invaded countries, so as to send their 400.000 more to battle.

To-day I cut the last rose-buds, already nipped by the three days recent frost—three times the roses have faded since we lost our dear liberty!!! . . .

WEDNESDAY, OCTOBER 25

Lady Phipps had an interview with the Boches about getting some money they have blocked.[43] Asked why she wanted it, she invoked the expenses occurred [*sic*] by her recent change of residence, bathroom to be fitted up. . . . [T]hey answered baths were "luxure" in war-time, that she & the English ought to be in a concentration camp, & that the Belgians are "false serpents"!!! I must add that the very first thing the Boches do, on going to reside anywhere, is to fix up a bathroom if there is none. . . .

At Velaines, as reprisals for the refusal of the Burgomaster to give the list of the men out of work "chômeurs," the Boches took a number of the villagers indiscriminately, little boys & big ones, & shut them up in the church.[44] What will be their next move!

[41] A German officer had briefly taken charge in Bruges; then, local government was reinstated with a substitute burgomaster. MT's tale of the workmen's escape to Holland seems wishful thinking.

[42] The Germans captured the Romanian seaport of Constanza on October 22, 1916.

[43] Alexandra Wassilewna, widow of Sir Constantine Phipps, British envoy to Belgium from 1900 to 1906.

[44] The village of Velaines, northeast of Tournai, became part of the Étape on October 1, 1916; three weeks later, deportations of workmen started.

Several people are trying for passports, to remain away till the end of the war. If only the Romanians could have held their own (or have been helped to do so!) I <u>do</u> deplore the loss of Constanza!

THURSDAY, OCTOBER 16

Several burgomasters we know have been arrested for not giving up the names of the "chômeurs."

The town of Tournai is punished for the same: "till further orders all the inhabitants are forbidden to be out of doors after 4 pm."[45] ...

Now, all skins of any kind have to be declared, even if one only possesses <u>one</u> sheep skin! Soon we shall only be allowed a certain number of teeth in our mouths!

FRIDAY, OCTOBER 27

The splendid success of the French at Verdun (Douaumont & Vaux) comfort us rather for the loss of Constanza. Please God they may continue, & the Russians help Romania to resist invasion.

How I deplore Kitchener is no longer there to guide![46] I shall <u>never</u> forget how I felt, when I heard of his sad end. . . . I was waiting for a tram at the top of Rue du Luxembourg, an English person came across the road & asked if I had heard the awful news. . . . I felt I wanted to sit down on the curb & howl, then I went on to mass 11.30 at St Jacques,[47] & just as I prayed for Kitchener & all of us, the German military music, that [illegible] Place Royale every day to give a serenade to Von Bissing at noon, struck up the tune of "God save the King"; it is one of their national tunes, & has clashed so often upon English feelings since we are their prisoners. I think we ought to change our own anthem! ...

SATURDAY, OCTOBER 28

Had a letter from Valérie, 10 lines <u>only</u> on each page according to a new decree at Ghent; & the answers may be <u>only</u> in the same measure.[48] Post cards also 10 lines

---

[45] Because the Tournai leadership refused to hand over the list of jobless laborers, four of them were taken to German prisons. The city was punished with a fine and a curfew. Roundups of workingmen soon followed.

[46] Horatio Herbert Kitchener, secretary of state for war, died at sea on June 9, 1916 (together with 634 men), after his ship struck a mine.

[47] Saint-Jacques-sur-Coudenberg on Place Royale.

[48] MT's friend Valérie at Ghent remains unidentified.

<u>only</u>. (When will it be each person may have only so many hairs on his head!!!) . . . No one may come to Brussels from the Flanders "Etape"; Baron Max Pycke not allowed to come from Peteghem[49] to see his mother who is dying—(& this is a continual occurrence) the Boches say "humanity" doesn't exist in war time.

SUNDAY, OCTOBER 29

I am <u>very</u> anxious about Romania! What a catastrophe if she is invaded. . . .

MONDAY, OCTOBER 30

Squalls & high wind all day, so dull & sad, impossible to forget the Romanian disaster. I saw a German battalion marching with music & some men singing; they looked like leaving for the front.

The Forest is invaded for some time by people picking up beech nuts, horse chestnuts, acorns, wood—nothing is despised just now. Beech nuts are roasted by some people, to be used instead of coffee. All those nuts are sold to be crushed for oil. German soldiers glean in the Forest also.

The cannon was heard to-day in spite of the roaring wind.

TUESDAY, OCTOBER 31

I wish our English soldiers knew what a warm welcome they will have in Brussels when the day of our deliverance dawns! . . .

What a blessing our taking back Douaumont coincides with our reverses in Dobroutcha (Dobrudja) & Transylvania! There are persistent rumours that the Roumanian "Etat Major" [General Staff] betrayed, sold themselves out to the Germans, but those rumours seem founded on nothing, we've not met with them in the Dutch papers, it is true the latter were suppressed several times recently.

WEDNESDAY, NOVEMBER 1

All Saints Day

Great devotion in our churches. Thousands implore God's mercy in our terrible trial, & pray for the innumerable souls fallen on the battle fields. R.I.P.

The Germans declare they will take 300.000 civilians from Belgium & send them to Germany??? Why? Wherever they meet with resistance, they take indiscriminately old & young; at Hornu they even took a hunchback, 65 years old![50]

---

[49] Baron Max Pycke de Peteghem, burgomaster of Petegem, proprietor of a château there, and of a townhouse in Brussels.

[50] In the Hainaut mining region, many men were deported who were not out of work or who were incapable. In Hornu, 140 men were taken in October 1916.

No wonder there is worry in England about the German ships attacking ours in the Channel … and the new development of their submarine War is alarming.[51] I fear not only Germany, but the whole of Europe is en route for decadence & ruin.

THURSDAY, NOVEMBER 2

All Souls.

Had a chat with the Curé (curate) after mass, he heard that young fellows having finished their course of studies preparatory to the University will be considered as "chômeurs" & compelled either to frequent the "German" Flemish University at Ghent or be "sent to Germany." He also was told that, at the moment, the Belgian government at the Hâvre tolerated the acceptance of professorship by Belgians, at the Ghent University.

It seems the French have retaken the fort of Vaux—may it be true!!![52] General feeling here doleful concerning the long time War may still last. . . .

FRIDAY, NOVEMBER 3

A glorious Autumn day! The Forest a mass of gold & burnished copper, & the cannon sounding in the distance. Thank God it is true Vaux is retaken. The Kronprinz can't feel very "Kolossaal!"

Had a sad letter from poor Ellen so anxious about her boys; there has been fighting for the Belgians these days, a friend of theirs badly wounded.[53] Poor mothers! My heart bleeds for them all. The taking away of the Belgians "by force" to Germany is very cruel—all in this War is cruel in the extreme. And what losses on both sides trying to take or keep Péronne! . . .

SATURDAY, NOVEMBER 4

Mr W. told me that my friends (& everyone) could only get sugar from Tirlemont by obtaining a permit from the German Sugar Central, established at Hotel de Flandre. I went to see how the wind blew in that quarter … not in favor of my wishes! A very polite, clean old German gentleman, who "Chère Madamed" me, told me it was an impossibility, as all the sugar manufactured must pass through the Central for general sale, but that he would give me "hints": with a Dr's certificate that a certain

---

[51] The German Marine Corps' new destroyer flotillas had made a very successful raid in the Channel on October 26, 1916.

[52] Fort Vaux near Verdun.

[53] Ellen Rinquet had sons in the Belgian army.

quantity is needed for invalids, the "communes" are obliged to sell what is ordained, & that if the Burgomaster is obstinate, to apply to the "Commissaire Civil."[54] He held forth also about the horror of the Belgians forestalling foodstuffs & hiding them. I had to bottle up what I could have answered to this about the G's sending to their own.

SUNDAY, NOVEMBER 5

What may be the consequence of the Centrals reforming the Kingdom of Poland? Announcement of which appeared to-day.[55]

An English lady I know has a Boche woman enemy, who is seeking vengeance. A woman went in tears to the lady's house, asking for help to get to, or communicate with the front. The lady has never done anything of this kind, & sent her maid to tell the weeping woman so. She suspects it is her German enemy who is trying to ensnare her in some manner to get her into trouble with the Germans, & sent "to camp."

MONDAY, NOVEMBER 6

I wonder what is written in our papers about the proclamation of the Kingdom of Poland by the Centrals! The article of the "Gazette de l'Allemagne du Nord" [Norddeutsche Zeitung] (officious organ of the Berlin government) betrays great fear of the Russians in the future, says openly they won't always have a Hindenburg[56] to protect them against the Russians & that they prefer a free Poland as neighbor (and battlefield of course). Developments of this affair will be interesting. Perhaps Courland will also get Germany to establish it as an independent country!!! (With a German Medem as sovereign!!!)[57]

Hundreds of Belgian civilians are being daily packed off, by force, to Germany, taken just as they are arrested, without warm clothing or anything—this revolts me, it is real slavery. Why don't the neutral countries shame the Germans!

TUESDAY, NOVEMBER 7

The taking away of the Belgian men, by force, to Germany, is absolutely a return to "slavery." How don't the neutral countries rise up against this unheard of cruel

---

[54] The Zivilkommissar, the local representative of the civilian occupation authorities.

[55] In occupied Poland, the German and Habsburg authorities had created the framework for a Polish vassal state.

[56] Paul von Hindenburg, chief of the German General Staff.

[57] Courland (western Latvia) was under German occupation. In March 1918, the German Empire did create a (short-lived) Duchy of Courland and Semigallia.

injustice! The tragedy gets worse every day. To-morrow <u>all</u> the men of Nivelles are to assemble on the Grand Place, & bring light luggage.[58] They say 83 thousand men are to be taken out of Brussels alone. An artist, who lunched with us to-day, told us of a widower he knows, who has been taken off, leaving 4 children. . . .

Are the Germans going to use our 300.000 civilians they are taking away as an argument against the blocus [the blockade]: "if you famish Germany you famish them?" or are they to line their frontiers in case of our advance? This new affliction is causing <u>heartbreaking</u> distress in thousands of homes!!! . . . We are facing gloomier days than ever. To-morrow we leave the Fougeraie. Please God we may be happier when we next come back!

WEDNESDAY, NOVEMBER 8

My first ride in a motor since the war. Mr. Ruddock very kindly picked me up as I was trotting off from the Fougeraie to the tram, for the last time this season. Interesting letter from Dick, though he says he has had a fit of the blues. Cheerful news from Edith.[59]

. . . Great distress about the taking away of the Belgians! I heard confidentially that even some of the German authorities here are ashamed of what certain others have done in this matter, & one of them has gone off to Berlin to see if things can be righted in some measure.[60] I wonder how the world will stand when the time comes for our next move to the Fougeraie.

THURSDAY, NOVEMBER 9

The sending away of the "chômeurs" & others that are not "chômeurs" at all is the topic of every conversation & causes terrible indignation & grief. Pavlick[61] will be called up soon—please God he may not be sent off.

When the last aeroplanes came here, it was said a young English airman who fell near Tirlemont, escaped into Holland. . . . I dreamt a distinct dream that ~~someone~~ this 20 years old hero, whose machine had been damaged by the German guns in Brussels, lowered it a field near Tirlemont, jumped from it to prevent leaving traces, soon came to a little rivulet, in which he walked with the current till he reached a house, where the peasants hid him 3 weeks, in spite of constant German perquisitions & imminent danger of discovery, & that he got off safely into Holland & reported himself since. Too grand a dream to be true, one would say!

---

[58] A meticulously organized roundup of men from Nivelles (south of Brussels) on November 8.

[59] Edith Dodson, MT's niece.

[60] Von der Lancken had traveled to Berlin in October to seek to halt the deportations. Nevins, *Journals*, 304.

[61] He turned seventeen in late September.

FRIDAY, NOVEMBER 10

Every day the German screw is tightened a little more, & our anguish is greater. There are indescribable scenes of sorrow & despair at the entraining of the "white men slaves" for Germany. The poor mechanic, Philip Morris, that I have helped before, called on me at his wits end. No more work, no means of getting any, physically run down. I gave him something & he will come & tell me the result of his last hope for work, a man he must see to-morrow. If that fails, he says he can't do anything but go & sign at the German labour office, as in any case he is doomed to be sent away. The men who sign acceptance of departure for work in Germany are <u>promised</u> a good salary & are sent off in reasonable conditions. The 2.000 who accepted at Antwerp received 50 fr or marks each & 20 for their wife in awaiting [*sic*] they can send her their earnings.[62]

Those who protest, & are entrained <u>by</u> <u>force</u>, travel in cattle vans, without food, air convenience for sleeping etc etc. These last horrors of the Boches will make them hated more than ever. When the trains in which these poor fellows travel stop at Belgian stations, there are heartrending scenes between them & the onlookers.... As I write now, between 10 & 11 pm I hear the whistles of the night trains full of the poor slaves & wounded soldiers.

God help them & us all!

SATURDAY, NOVEMBER 11

In to-days *Belgique*, a very mollified article "to order" I am sure, by the Boches, about the mistakes committed with regard to the "slaves" that have been exported. Brussels is invited to be "calm & trustful," that chômeurs only will be dispatched. This officious announcement is certainly the result of Van den Lancker's [Von der Lancken's][63] rapid trip to Berlin. I went to Anderlecht to make "une enquête" [an inquiry] concerning an anonymous letter received at the Union Patriotique, & saw a train full of "chômeurs" en route for Bocheland, pass over the bridge at the station. The men were all shouting & waving & the people responding. The strain is loosened in Brussels for all the men who are not "chômeurs"—for as long as it lasts.

SUNDAY, NOVEMBER 12

... There are rumours of Bissing being displaced as Governor General of Belgium & our having a <u>harsher</u> man; the orders from Berlin about the "white men slaves"

---

[62] Conditions were better, though still harsh, for men who went to work in Germany voluntarily.

[63] MT consistently misspells German names and words. Because of the large number of references in the diary to Von der Lancken, we have corrected those in subsequent entries.

seemed too cruel to Von Bissing who sent Von der Lancken to Berlin to try & get them repealed in a certain measure. The comments of the papers on Bethman-Holweg's [Bethmann Hollweg] speech seem to infer that he would prefer peace to a certain victory just now. I am glad the papers in general all look upon the famous proclamation of the "Kingdom of Poland" as I do: more as a vaudeville & merely invented to levy half a million men for the present German army.

MONDAY, NOVEMBER 13

I took a kilo of smuggled butter (12 fs) to Lena [Ford] this afternoon, they hadn't been able to get any for a long time. I lunched next to the Secretary of the Swedish legation, back from Stockholm, through Berlin, ten days ago. On leaving the station at Berlin, he saw women mending the roads, & pulling down sewer pipes. He was 2 days in Berlin, & could not obtain at his (good) hotel, meat, eggs, milk, butter or sugar. He had to live on fish, rice & potatoes. He says everyone in Sweden believes in our victory.

The rumour of our having Rupprecht de Bavière for governor instead of Von Bissing makes us think that it would mean Brussels being in the "Étape!"[64] ...

TUESDAY, NOVEMBER 14

I have now to resume (since my return to town) my weekly expiation of my nationality by going to sign at the Prussians'. They gave us all new cards—I asked why? Eicholt replied: orders from above!!![65] I hadn't seen him there for some time; he was in the best of humours, & satisfied my desire to get poor Philip Morrison's[66] address (I had forgotten number) though he remarked it wasn't habitually done. Alec Ford says Eicholt is not anti-English "au fond" [at heart]. He remarked once himself that his mother was English, & now some people attribute an English wife to him, but I don't know on what grounds. News from our front good, we are to be informed to-morrow of an English success on the Somme. ...

WEDNESDAY, NOVEMBER 15
KING ALBERT'S FEAST

Grand high Mass & Te Deum[67] at Ste Gudule at 11 a.m., at St. Jacques at 11:30. I went to former. ... After the Te Deum, the organ struck up the "Brabançonne"

---

[64] Rupprecht, crown prince of Bavaria, since August 1916 commander of Army Group Rupprecht, which held the northernmost sector of the Western Front.

[65] Unidentified German occupation official.

[66] The British national named above as "Philip Morris."

[67] A short religious service based on the hymn "Te Deum Laudamus" (We Praise Thee, O Lord), held to bless an event or give thanks.

(Belgian national anthem), the people joined in the chorus "le roi, la loi, la liberté," & hearty patriotic shouts of "Vive le Roi," went up all over the Church. It was grand!!! I cheered for all I was worth, & if the town is fined for cheering the King, I think I must contribute 10 fr to pay for my share. It did me good to see & hear the enthusiasm. It is the first time the new [papal] nuncio has assisted at such a demonstration, & I know he will admire it.[68]

We are so glad of what must be a big English victory, from the way the Boches announce it in their communiqués; we haven't yet the English version but it is thought the Germans have lost about 30 thousand, killed, wounded & prisoners.

I heard more people from the provinces say, in church, that the only way they dare celebrate the king's feast there, is by "requiem masses"; they couldn't risk the Te Deum & the Brabançonne which is played in churches here continually, & after all requiem masses for the soldiers killed at war!

THURSDAY, NOVEMBER 16

No Dutch papers at all were allowed in Brussels to-day, so we know very little so far of our English success at Beaumont Hamel, St Pierre-Division & those parts; the English communiqués gave already 4.000 prisoners.[69]

In spite of their fine phrases in the papers & Bissing's interview in Berlin, with an American journalist, saying only "Chômeurs" (unemployed) are being taken away to Germany, they still continue carrying off "all sorts of men"; & some of the non "chômeurs" that had already been to Bocheland are being brought back.[70] Great confusion, incomprehensible, like it generally is in all those unjust measures.

FRIDAY, NOVEMBER 17

... I went to see the Rinquets, Ellen a little less anxious, heard from Holland yesterday the boys were all right.

A memorable day for Brussels: the burgomasters (mayors) of all the "communes" of Grand Brussels having refused giving the Prussians the list of "chômeurs" were shut up in their respective town-halls which were surrounded by Boche troops. I haven't yet heard

---

[68] In July 1916, Achille Locatelli replaced Giovanni Tacci Porcelli, who was considered too critical of the occupation regime.

[69] Part of the larger Battle of the Ancre, the last big British push in the Somme campaign.

[70] Cyril Brown, "Belgians Exiled for Their Good," *New York Times*, November 12, 1916. In this interview, Bissing blamed the British blockade for reducing Belgian workers to poverty and defended German deportation of Belgian unemployed workers as "aid." On November 15, the censored *La Belgique* placed a French translation of this interview, to, as Whitlock noted, "no effect other than to inflame the hatred of the populace" (Nevins, *Letters and Journal of Brand Whitlock, Journal*, 322 [November 15, 1916]).

what is to be their fate. I had a little talk with a Swedish diplomat; <u>he</u> says the burgo-master may not, morally, give away the "chômeurs". *Not even to save the many victims who are not out of work.* The Germans have posted up that because ~~they~~ we will not yield, men of all classes will be carried off to Germany (as they have done all the time). The Swede told me also that he had just sent off a long report on the subject to his government. . . . Every day brings its new painful excitement! Oh! for the sight of our soldiers!!!

SATURDAY, NOVEMBER 18

. . . Was told the Emperor of Germany has been to Bruges, & on that account, all his soldiers had been disarmed.[71] Nine workmen from M. Emmanuel Janssen's es-tate have been <u>forced</u> <u>away</u> to Boche land.[72] There is a rumour that all those who go voluntarily have to sign a contract for <u>four</u> years! Valérie writes me that Cardinal Mercier officiated at the funeral of Mgr Stillemans . . . bishop of Ghent,[73] & that there were "naturally" <u>crowds</u> to see him. He is the most popular Belgian after the King. The papers say the German governor of Ghent & his staff also assisted at the bishop's funeral, uninvited of course by the people.

SUNDAY, NOVEMBER 19

Sidonie [Dodson] writes me she had to appear twice before "our invaders" because she was not at home at 9 o'clock one evening they came to enquire, so I conclude that at Antwerp, like in many other places, but not in Brussels, the English are not allowed out after a certain hour. Her step-father & two uncles have been carried off to Germany, her mother is in despair, & expecting her sons to be taken also.

Mr. E. Janssens [Emmanuel Janssen], who followed to the station the band in which were the 9 men taken from his estate, was quite sick & indignant at the way they were treated: if anyone tried to escape, he was brought back to the ranks by whips. He says <u>he</u> can tell the Americans what he <u>saw</u>. There is a rumour that on account of the interference of the neutral countries, this "slave-driving" will cease or be mitigated; we are told the American papers are appearing with sensational headings: "Slavery in Belgium under the Germans", but we know next to noth-ing these days, the Dutch paper having been so frequently stopped all this week. Rumours also of the evacuation of Monastir & a French victory somewhere. . . .[74]

[71] On October 21, 1916, Emperor Wilhelm II visited Bruges.

[72] Emmanuel Janssen, a Belgian financier and industrialist, headed the relief department of the CN.

[73] Monseigneur Antoon Stillemans died on November 5.

[74] On the Macedonian front, French-Serbian forces took Monastir (today Bitola) on November 19, 1916.

MONDAY, NOVEMBER 20

A very bright red poster announcing that Brussels is punished for having cried: "Vive le roi" at Ste. Gudule & St. Jacques on the 15th. All shops, places of amusement etc to be closed at Boche 8 our 7 o'clock & no one to be in the streets after 7.30—except Boches & neutrals, & this till further orders. As I don't often go out after dinner, I don't feel punished. To those who don't obey, 3 months imprisonment or 10 thousand marks fine! Wouldn't they love to catch a few thousand marks!

I hope all the naughty children will be docile and <u>ever</u> do it again at the next opportunity. . . .

TUESDAY, NOVEMBER 21

This evening began our "punishment"! At 7.30, the streets were dark & empty, only Germans & neutrals being allowed out! They say it is for one week! . . . I read Cardinal Mercier's "Cri d'Alarme," [Alarm Cry] appeal to the neutrals concerning the violation of the assurance given by former German Governors in Belgium, that they <u>never</u> would send our men to Germany! He once more tells them plainly their truths.[75] . . .

Lemonnier f.f. bourgmestre [substitute Burgomaster], when threatened to Germany [sic] for not giving lists of chômeurs said, I will go, but my honour will remain here![76]

WEDNESDAY, NOVEMBER 22

. . . François Joseph, Emperor of ~~Germany~~ Austria, died last evening, at 9 pm at Schoenbrunn.[77] I wonder if Hungary will meekly submit to his successor. I went this afternoon to see Melle Van den Plas;[78] she seemed rather downcast about the work for the women, who may now only get work for 3 fr every 3 weeks—stuffs are so

[75] On November 7, 1916, Cardinal Mercier launched an open "Cri d'Alarme des Évêques belges à l'Opinion publique [Cry of Alarm of the Belgian Bishops to Public Opinion]" to protest the deportations.

[76] Alderman Maurice Lemonnier had taken over the mayor's seat after Burgomaster Adolphe Max was sent to prison in Germany in late September 1914. (The term "f.f.," "faisant fonction," means "substitute.") Lemonnier was briefly arrested on November 17 for refusing to hand over the lists of the out-of-work (Gille et al., *Cinquante mois d'occupation allemande*, 2:404–407).

[77] In the margin of this entry, she wrote: "Fee d'Alcantara's great-grandfather. Note of April 1941." This refers to Princess Stéphanie (nicknamed Fee) zu Windisch-Graetz, great-granddaughter of Francis Joseph. In 1933, she married the Belgian count Pierre d'Alcantara de Querrieu. As MT was writing this note in 1941, Count d'Alcantara was engaging in resistance against the Nazi occupation regime. He was arrested by the Gestapo in August 1942 and died in Sachsenhausen concentration camp in October 1944.

[78] Louise Van den Plas, one of the founders of the Union Patriotique des Femmes Belges.

rare. Bills are being slipped into letter boxes by the Belgians, telling all the men of Brussels not to present themselves when they are called up. . . .

THURSDAY, NOVEMBER 23

. . . We have heard some instances of pity shown to poor women in despair, by the German officers in command of entraining the chômeurs; one woman was at the train with her 9 children & said to the officer: "As you send my bread-winner away, I will leave you my 9 children to look after" & the man was allowed to remain. Some of the German soldiers themselves are affected by the pitiful sights of despair they witness— & others are brutal in the extreme.

FRIDAY, NOVEMBER 24

. . . The terrible explosion in the port of Archangel seems to be a national catastrophe for Russia & for the Allies.[79] People's state of mind here just now is rather "blue": the "chômeurs" question, the being kept in after 7.30 pm (not knowing for how long) the general monotony of things make it more dismal than for those who are behind the front of the Allies. Shall we ever be! & how will it come to pass!

SATURDAY, NOVEMBER 25

Now that the year has expired during which Belgium had to pay Germany 40 million francs a month (for them to make war against us!) the tax has been raised to 50 million a month, & this by "special great bounty," said the two officers who received the deputation of bankers, as Berlin wanted 80 million a month, or at the very least 60; so the 50 are only to be allowed during 6 months; after that, the tax must be raised. Please God all that is Boche will be erased from Belgium ere that & our money flowing home again! It seemed to me, from the Prussian communiqués that they are preparing the opinion for our taking Bapaume. The Dutch papers continue to be stopped most frequently.

SUNDAY, NOVEMBER 26

This morning Cardinal Mercier preached at S^te. Gudule; specially for the "chômeurs" question. Though the sermon was only announced on Saturday, on the quiet, there were crowds listening. We read all his correspondence with Bissing concerning this

---

[79] On November 9, 1916, a munitions explosion in the Russian port of Archangelsk killed several thousand people.

affair—he doesn't fear to tell the Boches all their truths.[80] This afternoon, tea & the du Chastaing's, father & son, at Mme. F. [Frantz] Wittouck's obliged to have these "séances" before dinner during our "punishment." The sight of all the Sunday people clearing out of the Cafés & Cinemas & rushing for trams, or on foot to be home by 7.30 was quite a comedy! . . .

MONDAY, NOVEMBER 27

I went to see Mme. Cousin, & saw also her husband, to whom I didn't dare mention Zeebrugge, his great work, that has, alas, too admirably served Prussian interests! He told me that if ~~all the~~ only one of the "Counseils provinciaux" [Provincial Councils] ~~refuses~~ objects to the 50 million monthly war tax, our "gentle invaders" will help themselves, no matter where & how, to 80 per month! There was a funeral service for the emperor of Austria at S^te. Gudule this morning, in grand style, only Austrians and Germans present of course, music, organ, etc, all done by themselves. After sugar has been made from this year's beet root crop, all the brass & copper of the machinery will be taken to Germany, & no more sugar will be able to be made here.[81]

TUESDAY, NOVEMBER 28

. . . Mgr Locatelli, who was to have lunched here on Sunday, can't come, but he had tea with Mr. W. to-day & saw Micha & Serge. He disapproves both England & Germany for not ceasing the war; is absorbed by the different causes of distress in Belgium & sends voluminous reports to the Holy See. He communicates over the heads of the Boches <u>here</u>, direct with Berlin & Rome, so is not "persona grata" with them & there is no love lost either between him & Villalobar. . . .

WEDNESDAY, NOVEMBER 29

Count 't Kint in town for a few days, I had a chat with him at his breakfast Rue Ducale. He thinks the war will end soon by a "discussed peace" not "imposed peace" on either side. Mme. Wittouck went to see Von Bredo about getting a Petit Bigard horse . . . back, didn't succeed.[82] Von B [Von Bredow] told her Bucharest will fall in a fortnight; that Germany will then make war against Holland & ~~Germany~~ Denmark, that the war will last 2 years more, & that he is quite broken-hearted & neurasthenic

---

[80] On October 19, Mercier sharply protested the deportations in a letter to von Bissing, which did the rounds clandestinely.

[81] As it turned out, sugar production was never halted.

[82] Horses kept at the château of Petit Bigard (Klein-Bijgaarden) near Brussels, property of the late Félix Wittouck, Paul Wittouck's older brother.

at having to witness the despair of the poor people whose horses he is forced to commandeer. His office was full of flowers offered him by different people, *mostly businesswomen* whose horses he had been able to leave to them.[83]

THURSDAY, NOVEMBER 30

What will be the result of the rapid advance of the Centrals in Roumania! How I deplore Kitchener's death, I think <u>he</u> would have advised Roumania before it was too late.

I bought 3 pairs of boots for the boys, 50 fr a pair, price before the war 34 fr 50. The shops look <u>so</u> piteous in their efforts to make something of a show for St. Nicolas. . . .[84] [N]o cakes or pastry; the confectioners that remain open show a <u>small</u> quantity of marsepain [marzipan], 4 times the ordinary price, & little sticks of chocolate ditto. The *Belgique* yesterday & to-day points out that theatre going people & Liberals don't cheer for their king in Churches, & that only those who do ought to be punished for instance in being shut up in church for 24 hours!!! Horrid article yesterday.[85]

FRIDAY, DECEMBER 1

I was told that a Prussian officer had said if we had been under military "regime" in Brussels, Cardinal Mercier would have been shot long since.

The Bishop of Liege [Liège] & the Senators of Brussels, have sent strong protestations to von Bissing concerning the "white men's slavery." Rumor says that our "punishment" may be increased to having to be indoors at 5 instead of 7:30 pm. . . .

The Germans in Germany are being prepared to being "compelled" to work for the state, in case anyone doesn't yield with good grace. The word "contrainte" [coercion] is repeated constantly in Helferich's [Helfferich's] speech. They always lay stress on the "punishment" before making full statements.[86]

---

[83] In the summer of 1916, the occupying army sped up its requisitioning of draft horses in greater Brussels. At war's end, Belgium had lost an estimated 50,000 mares and 5,000 stallions. Gille et al., *Cinquante mois d'occupation allemande*, 2:276–277, 351. "Von Bredo" is Major von Bredow, the director of the horse depot of the Government-General in Brussels. This may have been Count Gerhard von Bredow, a Prussian estate-owner who, immediately after the war, would express critical views of the deposed emperor (as reported in the Liberal Brussels *La Gazette*, December 13, 1918).

[84] At the feast of Saint Nicolas on December 6, children received gifts and sweets.

[85] The editorial "Bon sens," *La Belgique*, November 1916, 2.

[86] The Auxiliary Service Law of December 5, 1916, required mandatory service for all ablebodied Germans during the war. Karl Theodor Helfferich, secretary of the treasury, had to see this unpopular measure through the Reichstag.

SATURDAY DECEMBER 2

We are more & more depressed about the Germans nearing Bucharest.... How much more cohesion there seems to have been all the time between the centrals than between our allies. It is said that the "Brussels" men will be taken up next week, & if the Burgomaster won't give the list of chômeurs, the town will be super punished, people to be in at 5 pm. I wonder what is thought, in England, of Bethman-Holweg's [Bethmann Hollweg] continual talking of peace whenever he has an opportunity....

Sidonie writes me her step-father has been forced away to Germany just 3 weeks, & they haven't had any news whatever of him yet.

SUNDAY, DECEMBER 3

... Everyone is very glum & there is great nervous tension concerning the rapid advance of the Boches to Bucharest! Would it be possible they find there their "Moscow"!!! for no one knows what Russia is doing in that direction. A lady I know took a long walk last night, pretending she was Austrian when challenged by the police, she had an Austrian woman's identity card & got home quite safely, without being fined the 10 thousand marks promised as penalty to Belgians & belligerents.

MONDAY, DECEMBER 4

This morning at 6:30, I was awakened by Prussian fifes & drums playing their victory tune ... concluded it was to celebrate the fall of Bucharest, but it appears they were anticipating, all the church bells of Prussia & Alsace-Lorraine being ordered to ring in honour of a victory in Roumania.

I went to see the poor old misses Allan—recollections of my childhood at Ostend—it meant a lesson of patience & endurance for me. How such old people suffer from the war—their wants are small, but all is so expensive, eggs 50 c each....

TUESDAY, DECEMBER 5

This morning we paid our last weekly visit to the Boches, in future it is to be the 1st Tuesday of the month only, as it was formerly. I met Alec & Lena Ford going there; he is as optimistic as ever concerning our victory, says the Roumanian catastrophe will only!!! add 6 months to the war, & that Lena & I ought to feed on nothing but starch for a fortnight, to strengthen our backbone... [O]f course I know we must win in the long run, but how long must the run be! Really the prospect of years of our present conditions here is despair.

...

WEDNESDAY, DECEMBER 6

The cannon was very loud again this afternoon, heard in the house, with windows closed. Alec & Lena Ford told me an American friend of theirs has a married daughter at Berlin. She wrote to her mother that she wanted to buy a new dress, but that when in Berlin, one gets a government permit for such a purpose, one has to give up to the authorities, the old dress that is to be replaced. So this lady concluded she would not buy a new dress, but stick to the old one. . . .

THURSDAY, DECEMBER 7

. . . The Prussians announced this morning, by a little blue poster, their entrance in Bucharest. Music all the afternoon in the barracks at the back of our house to celebrate the event, & this evening a torch light military procession with music & grand tra-la-la. . . .

. . . Great satisfaction amongst the Allies at Trepow [Trepov] proclaiming Russia is to share (when?) Constantinople & the Dardanelles.

Mme. W's opinion of Trepow [Trepov], whom she knows personally is: that he is far too autocratic to be the right hand man in Russian politics just now (& small minded). He was very coolly received by the Duma. Qui vivra verra! [Time will tell.][87]

FRIDAY, DECEMBER 8

I keep wondering all the time how & when England will be able to give Constantinople to Russia, according to Trepow's [Trepov] proclamation. I feel so humiliated about the Boches being at Bucharest, & I won't believe they were presented with flowers by the inhabitants as they say in their lying communiqués to-day.

All is very dismal, & we hear nothing *of the outcome* of the cannonading that goes on continually—our communiqués give no news of the Somme, except that the Germans are bombarding violently. What next??? . . .

SATURDAY, DECEMBER 9

. . . The British charitable fund is a real Providence to the poor English in Belgium; I went to see Mrs Churchill, a poor consumptive woman, who receives 12 fr 50 a week Dr. & medicine gratis.[88] It is a trouble to all Englishwomen that tea is so

[87] Prime Minister Alexander Fyodorovitch Trepov revealed to the Duma on December 2, 1916, that Britain and France had promised Constantinople and the Dardanelles to Russia after the war. He did this to prove that Russia stood to gain from the war.

[88] Lily Churchill, who suffered from tuberculosis, was helped by MT with her claims to the British Relief Fund.

dear, about 20 fr the kilo, & difficult to get. I have some, for the house, from Perry's every week, at 3 fr 50 the ¼ kilo, but they won't sell to new people tho' I begged a ¼ kilo (3 fr 50) the other day, for some poor Englishwomen. The impossibility of getting sugar is also a terrible trial, the alimentation sells only a tiny supply, not nearly enough.

SUNDAY, DECEMBER 10

I was up in the Cinquantenaire this afternoon[89] & heard the cannon all the time....

I passed by the main entrance of the military school, on either side of which there is a huge symbolical statue of war. The Boches had placed a big bunch of newly cut laurel branches in the arms of these statues—their laurels of Bucharest of course! alas!

They have given notice, by registered letter, to all of the people whose houses or buildings have been damaged by the war, that they have to pull them down entirely & without delay, but I think those interested take no notice of the order.

MONDAY, DECEMBER 11

Mr Beaudoin[90] told us to-day, that 1120 men were taken from Tirlemont & the environs; only 11 signed an engagement for Germany. He made a written report to the Americans on the heart-rending scenes of departure he witnessed: the lines of soldiers broken through by women & children, men clinging to lamp-posts etc. not to be driven on to the station etc etc, & the crowd of women & children returning from the station after the entraining of the men, singing the Brabançonne & hooting all the Germans they met & in front of the Commandature [Kommandantur][91] ... and the German print in all their papers that the Belgians are delighted to be taken to Germany & horrible lies of that sort!!! It makes me simply ferocious!

TUESDAY, DECEMBER 12

Sensational news in the German papers this evening!!! Kaiser has made proposals of peace to the Allies—so that must have been the pith of the famous assembly of the

[89] The 1880 Parc du Cinquantenaire in Brussels, a grand ensemble of park and buildings.

[90] Lucien Beaudoin was director of the sugar refinery at Tienen (Tirlemont). The Beaudoin family had been long associated with the Wittoucks and their enterprises.

[91] The local headquarters of the German military police.

Reichstag to-day; we were all anxiously awaiting to-morrow's papers to see what it meant.[92]

I think the Allies won't hear of peace. . . . [W]e'll wait & see! Such a vain-glorious description of the Boche's entrance in Bucharest, in their official communiqués: they were covered with flowers, warmly & respectfully welcomed etc, such nonsensical humbug for an official report. Brussels streets are like a tomb ever since Nov 21st, from 7:30 pm. A tram passes every ½ hour for convenience of the G's, who then have to pay their fare.[93] Our penance still continues it is said till the 23rd.

WEDNESDAY, DECEMBER 13

Chancellor Bethman-Holweg's [Bethmann Hollweg] speech in the Reichstag yesterday & the Emperor's proclamation of his proposal of peace to the allies the subject of every conversation to-day. . . . I am determined to think right whatever our leaders decide. God grant they may consider the aim of the war sufficiently attained, though I fear not. The Germans are such hypocrites, even now they tell the neutrals they only send to Germany men out of work, & we all know of quantities torn away from their work & earnings, who were independent of all public & private relief. As I write the cannon is heard, & has been all day, in fact it hasn't ceased now for many a day & still nothing comes of it on our front, alas! except continual loss of young lives.

THURSDAY, DECEMBER 14

. . . We are burning with anxiety to know what the Allies think of Wilhem's [sic] proposal of peace. Here some wish for peace almost at any price, but not I, nor many I know, it must not be a humiliating one for us!!!

Our coachman Joseph was arrested yesterday by the Boches, & shut up in St Gilles' prison to-day, "au secret," [in solitary confinement] likewise his son, who, it appears was caught (or betrayed) as he was trying to get away to Holland. No one can tell how long in prison it may mean to both. . . . The being kept isolated "au secret" such a long time is (victims tell me) the most awful & enervating, maddening part of the trouble.

FRIDAY, DECEMBER 15

I went to see Joseph's wife, made enquiries for her. Nothing can be done for him as he is kept "au secret", except send him clean linen, food, tobacco every Wednesday, & await events.

[92] Germany held an emergency session of the Reichstag and then issued through neutral channels a call for peace discussions. The overture was predicated on the notion that Germany was "winning" the war and may have been timed to take advantage of the shakeup in the British cabinet.

[93] Germans did not have to pay public transport fare when in front of Belgians, emphasizing their status in the conquered city.

Went to see Ellen [Rinquet]—poor thing, she is so grieved, no news of her boys since October 28th. . . .

I hear there have been "squabbles" amongst the diplomats here in Brussels & the consequence is none of them will any longer accept anything for their respective friends in their diplomatic valise, which henceforth must be controlled by the Germans, so goodbye to the plan of sending my photos to my friends in England! Alec & Lena Ford came to discuss the "situation." He is always most optimistic, but we (all English) agree that we don't want German offered peace.

SATURDAY, DECEMBER 16

The commentaries of the different papers on the proposal of peace all point the same way: that we can't accept it. I am curious to know what the allies' answer will be.

The cannon is heard all the time, & yet our "communiqués" don't mention anything special. This evening there was a rumour of a victory for us at Verdun. When will the terrible strain on our hearts & nerves be somewhat relaxed! Though I see so much misery visiting the poor sick for our work of the Assistance Discrète, & nearly all of it is caused or increased through the terrible war.

SUNDAY, DECEMBER 17

I went with Serge this morning to see a rabbit exhibition. Since the war, rabbit rearing, by all classes of people, has developed immensely, owing to the high price of meat & the great use made of the fur of special species of rabbits. . . .

MONDAY, DECEMBER 18

Our 4 weeks of being kept in from 7:30 pm to 3 am have just expired; we are free to come & go, but shops are to be closed at 6 pm. . . . We had an assembly this morning for our section of the Oeuvre Discrète [Discreet Assistance], several interesting reports concerning the American supplies etc etc. . . .

TUESDAY, DECEMBER 19

I went to-day to see a poor English family in distress, mother & 5 children. The father had a good situation [position] until the war, when he went away. The family gets 25 fr a week from the British relief, & is helped by our Assistance Discrète, but all that just keeps them alive.

At Malines the Boches have taken 20 boys aged 17, who were still studying at the College in the same case as Pavlick here. I trust he will be spared! . . .

WEDNESDAY, DECEMBER 20

Zeppelins passed over Brussels last evening. I wonder if they were bound for mischief in England—it would be just like the German diplomacy to bombard London the night Lloyd George was to announce their wish for peace in the House of Commons!

THURSDAY, DECEMBER 21

I went to the Maison Communale [City Hall] at Ixelles, about getting the monthly kilo of sugar for the sick & people over 70. There must be an examination of the invalid by the "communal" doctor, & the "pièce d'identité" [identity document] must be exhibited to prove age.

We read Lloyd George's speech, very little of it was given in the *Belgique*; a little more in our Dutch communiqués, but all the Dutch papers were stopped this morning.[94] . . . Many German soldiers carrying Xmas trees to their quarters. . . . [T]hey have Xmas trees even for men all alone.

FRIDAY, DECEMBER 22

. . . The wife of the Swiss consul, Mme Borel, is at Ouchy.[95] Her little girl wrote her a card, the governess added a word, but the card was not allowed to go by the diplomatic valise—the Germans have become simply ferocious on that matter. We all think Lloyd George's speech splendid—the commentaries of the press judge that he hasn't closed the door on "Peace." . . .

SATURDAY, DECEMBER 23

Had a letter from Dick and the Ruhleben Xmas card, which made me weep; it came just as I was making the "crib", & represents two poor captives behind their wire enclosure, gazing sadly & wonderingly at the rising sun *of 1917*. . . . [W]ill the new year mean deliverance? Dick writes the Xmas attraction at Ruhleben is a series of representations of the "Mikado."[96]

The event of the day, Wilson's message of mediation to the belligerents. And what will be the Allies' reply to the German proposal of "conversation"! All the world is breathlessly awaiting the important historical document it will mean.[97]

---

[94] Lloyd George rejected the German peace overture.

[95] Ouchy near Lausanne, Switzerland. Jules Borel was Swiss consul general in Brussels.

[96] *The Mikado*, a comic opera by Gilbert and Sullivan, was performed at Ruhleben at Christmas 1916.

[97] Wilson's December 1916 note asked for a "sounding out" of belligerents' war aims.

SUNDAY, DECEMBER 24, & MONDAY, DECEMBER 25, XMAS DAY

... Nothing special to write about, nor to-day either, except that our regretted Kitchener said it was to be a 3 Xmas war.... [W]ell, let us now hope for a brighter period. The English papers don't seem to think a "conversation" with the enemy possible, but we must await our answer to the Germans & see what they think of it. My thoughts have been all day with our soldiers, dead & living & all those who mourn for or tremble for them.

Peace on earth to men of good will!!!

Gloria in excelsis deo!!!

TUESDAY, DECEMBER 26

No news whatever to write.

No papers of any kind to-day, the Germans keeping their Xmas. Will to-morrow bring us the Allies' answer to the German proposition??? ...

WEDNESDAY, DECEMBER 27

... No newspapers yet. Sidonie writes me that since her mother has heard from her step-father (after 4 weeks since he had been forced to Germany as a chômeur, though he worked 4 days a week) she is more miserable than ever, for he complains bitterly of being starved, implores her to send food, but it is not allowed to go.... Another "chômeur" found means of writing from Bocheland that if we correspondent heard & saw all he does, we should know the end of the War is near—so great is the misery there.

THURSDAY, DECEMBER 28

We went to a fête, this afternoon, for the benefit of the "oeuvre" "Aide aux villageois" [Aid to the Villagers], a very good institution, as the poor in the country get much less help now than those in towns, where so much is done for them.[98] I am surprised to see that there is always money forthcoming for good works, "tant mieux!" (so much the better!).

The Hall was crammed with children taken as a treat to see the "danses plastiques"[99] & share in the lottery of toys.

---

[98] A relief organization founded in December 1914 by a group of Brussels women that provided impoverished village children and their families with clothing, toys, bedding, and other goods.

[99] Eurythmic dances.

FRIDAY, DECEMBER 29

This morning another great requisition of poor old light cart-horses, belonging to poor people: bakers, laundrymen, vegetable sellers etc. I watched the sad faces of the men taking them in to the Boches, & the relieved smiling ones who came out with their "bread-winners", too miserable to satisfy our tyrants. Most distressing scenes *of despair* generally take place at these requisitions. . . .

1917

MONDAY, JANUARY 1

I see I forgot my diary on Saturday Dec 30th. Last night I wrote nothing, because Isie[100] was here to see "the New year in" with me. At 11 pm, the Boches' midnight, they played *(we heard them)* their national anthem *& the Austrian* in the Barracks & illuminated the tower of the Palais de Justice [the Palace of Justice]. How we hope next New Year all may be different!!! This morning I was awakened at 7:30 by a Grand German band on the Boulevard!

I ought to have written yesterday, that Joseph was let out of prison late on Saturday evening, on Mr. W's bail of 1000 marks. To-day I had a long talk with him about his impressions & life during his detention. A very dismal New Year's day, mild & dark & rainy.[101] We got a slight notion this evening, from Dutch extracts, of the Allies answer to the German proposal.

The recently named papal nuncio, Mgr Locatelli, who was considered very pro-Belgian, (probably too much so by the Boches) has suddenly been called away, it is said for good. Such a pity, he was quite "for us".[102] It is thought that Villalobar has a perverse finger in the pie; Mgr L. was not under his thumb, & there was no love lost between them. . . .

TUESDAY, JANUARY 2

A dramatic occurrence at the Meldeamt [registration office] to-day, a young fellow who went to sign was offended with a Boche soldier; he drew out a dagger & stabbed the soldier right through the neck. An officer present, took out his revolver

[100] MT's Brussels friend remains unidentified.

[101] The weather was particularly bad that New Year's Day, and the heavy rain caused flooding in lower Brussels. In one district alone, 2,000 houses were damaged. Gille et al., *Cinquante mois d'occupation allemande*, 3:3–4.

[102] On Locatelli's insistence, the Vatican condemned the deportation of laborers on December 5, 1916. He was not removed, but was named apostolic internuncio in the Netherlands in March and continued his role in Belgium.

& shot the young man on the spot. Glad it didn't happen while I was there; we had to pay our monthly visit this morning. Cannon very loud.

Have seen the reply of the Allies to the German proposal of peace-making. Am curious to see commentaries of the same in different papers. . . .

WEDNESDAY, JANUARY 3, & THURSDAY, JANUARY 4

I didn't write yesterday, was in bed with a threat of "flue". Hope it has vanished. . . .

In the pays [area nearby] d'Audenarde, barbed wire is being placed on many points to prevent people & "foodstuffs" getting from one village to another. . . . We have <u>our</u> answer to the so-called German call for peace. . . . [N]ow we anxiously await <u>our</u> reply to Wilson's message. . . .

VENDREDI [FRIDAY], 5 JANVIER [JANUARY 5]

Not one single Dutch paper allowed in Belgium to-day! <u>What</u> does it mean? Rumour says a Russian victory??? A mere breath of another vague rumour is . . . the death of Hindenburg??? I often wondered how it would fare with the Boches if <u>he</u> disappeared.

Had a visit from Jeanne Neuhausen who was in town for the day. She told me of the <u>heart-rending</u> scenes she witnessed the day the "white slaves" of their village were taken. She & Henri de M. saved about 20.[103] She ~~spoke~~ *deigned to speak* German for the <u>first</u> time since the war, and that to the "Kriegschef," [*Kreischef*[104]] <u>imploring</u> pity for the poor men. We both & Isie who was here, cried at her description of the *moral* agony they all suffered. She felt that day added 10 years to her age, & she looks a wreck!

SATURDAY, JANUARY 6

No Dutch papers allowed in Belgium again to-day. . . . [W]e wonder why! is it because they are pitiful & indignant concerning the "chômeurs"???

Unfortunately the Russians & Roumanians are retreating all the time. . . . [H]ow will that end? . . .

SUNDAY, JANUARY 7

No end of cases of "itch" (gale) amongst the poor classes, owing to the lack of soap which is the most practical of disinfectants.[105] Whatever must be the consequences of the greater lack of things essential in Germany than here!

---

[103] Jeanne Neuhausen remains unidentified, as is "Henri de M."

[104] The military district commander.

[105] Scabies (French: *la gale*), a mite infestation of the skin, spreads through contact with unwashed clothes.

MONDAY, JANUARY 8

Not much about the war to-day, the Dutch extracts speak mostly of hunger in Germany. Van Vollenhoven said, the other day, a friend of his who had lived at Hamburg 24 years, had been compelled, through lack of all things, to return with his family to Holland.

Brussels gossip just now is chiefly about the intrigues of—a certain Spanish Marquis [Villalobar] who has certainly, since the beginning of the war, wanted all the feathers in <u>his</u> hat & none in those of any other "dips" who have helped us. . . .

TUESDAY, JANUARY 9

Very dull day, not a scrap of news, supposed or real. A story goes that the Benedictines at Maredsous were betrayed by some German amongst or near them, for having hidden 500 guns in their church steeple. One of the monks claimed the entire responsibility, said the guns were there since the fight between the French & the Boches in August 1914, & that if the Benedictines had wanted to make use of them, they had had the choicest of opportunities, for . . . Kaiser paid them a visit not very long since. I recollect it was told then, that having been forewarned of this "honour," all the pupils "were out walking," & the Father who accompanied Kaiser to the door of the Abbey was sharp enough to detect a photographer posted there by *Boche* order, to immortalize Guillaume on "good terms" with the monks, but the host was nimble enough in his movements to disappoint the cinemas & illustrated papers that were to have communicated that touching friendship to the world.[106] I wonder what will be the result of the discovery of the 500 guns!

WEDNESDAY, JANUARY 10

A German officer, after spending a holiday at Hambourg [Hamburg] told someone I know, that famine & distress are so great there, that all the children are dying off. . . . Am impatient to read the speech Lloyd George is to make to-morrow in London.[107]

THURSDAY, JANUARY 11

. . . No possibility to get from village to village, except for "born smugglers" who bribe the sentinels & get their farm produce into towns where they get <u>enormous prices</u> for all. All the farmers are "coining money," *(more or less honestly—rather less than more!!!)* many paying their rent years in advance.

---

[106] The Benedictine Abbey at Maredsous near Namur.

[107] On January 11, 1917, Lloyd George launched the new British War Loan and predicted Allied victory in the next months.

FRIDAY, JANUARY 12

A German servant *in Brussels* allowed to go home for a month, came back after 10 days. When giving in her passport at the Commandanture, she was asked why she returned before it expired. She said: because she was starved there, there being no food. Asked if she had told this to her employers here, she said yes, of course, to justify her prompt return. The girl was sent to prison by the Boches for 20 days!!!

Villalobar is back from Paris & Berlin. He talks more than ever with admiration of the Boches . . . says there is plenty to eat there!!! But that one only gets "messes", mixed up food one can't recognize. Well! Perhaps they thought they couldn't quite starve the Marquis, still if all is plentiful, why couldn't they give him good nameable eatables!!!!!!

SATURDAY, JANUARY 13

Had a good letter from Dick. . . . The English government sends them all "sugar & margarine" every week, & has sent from Denmark, 2 to 3 kilos of white bread weekly, for each prisoner. Isn't that splendid! Dick gets regularly 3 other parcels a month from England, besides mine & others from here! I hope those soldiers, prisoners in Germany, receive the same from the old country! Hurrah for England! She's a grand country! . . .

SUNDAY, JANUARY 14

The Allies' reply to Wilson & Kaiser's de-preciation of it have appeared & been commented. . . . How will the war end! . . . It seems to me it will take a long time to bring the Centrals to all the Allies desire. . . . Let us hope latter will find a "short cut" to bring them round, not like "the short cut through little Belgium is the longest way we know" (to Paris) but a real short cut to Constantinople & the rest. . . . Just now there is nothing gladdening anywhere, alas!

MONDAY, JANUARY 15

So glad! This morning, Dick's delayed letter of Dec 27th & Xmas Ruhleben camp number arrived. They bear the *Ruhleben* Spandau post-mark of January 4th. Dick writes he had to get special leave of the Censors to send it me, as it was forbidden to send it any place in Germany or the occupied territories. Their parody of the Mikado "Makeado" very amusing. The American Embassy & Colony of Berlin[108] assisted at a matinee. The Ruddocks were in Berlin, I must ask if they went. . . .

---

[108] The embassy staff and other Americans living in Berlin went to see *The Mikado* at Ruhleben in January 1917.

TUESDAY, JANUARY 16

. . . Went to Wygaerts' to-day to buy tinned vegetables to send to Dick. There was a German officer buying for nearly 300 fr of vegetables & other eatables to send to Germany. . . .

We long now for the end of the bad weather, so that "something" may happen on the Somme. A meter of ordinary common cotton, for mending old shirt collars, I paid to-day 3 fr 45!

WEDNESDAY, JANUARY 17

Cannon loud again all day. I've just read that the "Morning Post" says, there are in England 7,500 *German* "forty-fivers"[109] as they call them at Ruhleben, but that the half of them refuse to be sent back to Germany, & ask to be kept in England!!! What an excellent argument for us! I don't think even one English forty-fiver, will want to remain in Germany! Their Xmas camp magazine shows their intense longing to quit. Skits on "birth certificates wanted, not after 1871" & other jokes on the subject are very significant.

THURSDAY, JANUARY 18

. . . Men *so called "chômeurs"* who have returned from Germany because they refused to work say that to try to force them to sign, 25 of a band were picked out as victims, stripped to the waist and severely beaten, but all the time they cried out to the others: don't sign. The men of Anderlecht, St. Gilles & different suburbs are to present themselves to-morrow at the Gare du Midi. It will soon be Pavlick's turn. . . .

FRIDAY, JANUARY 19

Till now the Brabançonne was played now & again after certain services in our churches—it has just been forbidden. Two Boche soldiers, policemen, have been found murdered at Stockel;[110] a thousand marks offered to discover the culprits and in future no one allowed to be out after 10 pm. All cafés & places of amusement continue having to close at our 9 pm.

Mr. & Mrs. Ruddock did go to the matinee of the "Mikado" at Ruhleben, said it was very well done, but that the men seemed less lively than last year—no wonder. An extra year's captivity counts. There is any amount of mud at Ruhleben camp. They regretted not having thought of making a point to see Dick.

[109] Civilian internees forty-five or older were eligible for repatriation.

[110] An outlying western district of greater Brussels, still densely wooded at the time, where two German guards had been attacked (though not killed) by firewood smugglers. Gille et al., *Cinquante mois d'occupation allemande*, 3:31–32.

Franchomme's big store[111] has been closed by the Boches, & the owner is in prison or fined enormously because . . . a German shopwoman they had for 35 years (a confidential employée) is said to have betrayed to the Germans that her employers had hidden, & not declared, a portion of their stock.

The "Grand Bazar" is closed also, because . . . in the toy soldiers that were for sale, some of the Germans were lying down, or holding up their hands, or supposed to be in a conquered position!!! Isn't it "grand culture" to stop such childish nonsense!!!

SATURDAY, JANUARY 22 [*sic*: SHOULD BE 20]

To-day the men of certain parts of Brussels (Anderlecht, Cureghem) had to assemble at the Gare du Midi, guarded militarily, to be picked out (without any sort of discrimination) & entrained at once to Germany. One man straight from his service on a tram, in uniform, & numbers of other "workers" were sent off. Oh! the grief & anguish in many homes near us to-night! Some men that were sent back from Germany, because they would <u>not</u> sign or work, were travelling 4 days & nights in a cattle van, without being able to sit down. On arriving at Antwerp, they were kept at the station 24 hours, with the result that 2 men died, and how many must have been near death after such treatment. Oh! the hypocrites & brutes those Boches are!

SUNDAY, JANUARY 21

This is Pavlick's second day in bed with chicken-pox, & I haven't been out for two days, except to rush to Mass in tram. Isie came in to tea, notwithstanding chicken-pox, looking very cold & ill, is suffering from sciatica, & general cold & discomfort. . . . [T]hey say that on [*sic*] 1,800 men convoked [summoned] yesterday by the Boches, from Cureghem Anderlecht, only 700 presented themselves, half of whom were packed off at once in the train waiting in the Gare du Midi.[112] Those who came back from Germany, are all wrecks, some die. We "glean" that only infants in Germany are allowed milk, all that remains is used for making glycerine for ammunition. <u>When</u> will the end of cruel ordeal arrive!

MONDAY, JANUARY 22

. . . Many of the Belgians forced to go to Germany die there or on their return here after being so ill-treated. We all wonder what benefit (except to satisfy their brutality) the Boches have in taking the men away, starving & ill-treating them

---

[111] A large textile store in Brussels. In March 1917, most of its stock was confiscated and sent to Germany. Gille et al., *Cinquante mois d'occupation allemande*, 3:129.

[112] For the first four days (January 20 and 22–24), the occupation authorities had summoned 8,000 men (and even some women) in total from greater Brussels; 409 were deported, 251 of

for a certain time & sending them back quite broken down. It seems 13 men from Éghezée have died of their deportation.[113]

It is freezing hard to-night. Will that hasten on our advance in any manner! German papers seem to hanker after Belgium being at least partly annexed to Germany! God forbid![114]

TUESDAY, JANUARY 23

My dressmaker was out on Sunday, with her grand-child, 7 years old, who was laughing and chatting; she said to her grand-mother: "Je vais mettre mes mains dans votre poche." ["I will put my hands in your pocket."] A Boche *soldier* was passing [and] understood "boche" for poche, apostrophized the woman & child, threatened to carry them off to the "commandanture" for mocking him etc. etc. Fortunately the grand-mother succeeded in making him understand his stupid mistake.

Oh! Poor fellows in the trenches! 10 degrees under zero last night, 5 all day long & it will freeze hard again to-night. Tant mieux [so much the better] for the very numerous cases of cutaneous [skin] diseases about, but alas! for those who are underfed (they are legion) & have no fire.

WEDNESDAY, JANUARY 24

More heart-rending accounts from the "deported men" who are sent back from Germany, about the treatment inflicted to try & make them work. . . .

Many more were forced away to-day; American delegates[115] were with them at the last moment, to give them each 10 marks & a supply of white bread. Bravo!

I know that at Ruhleben industrious English civilian prisoners are offered good positions in Berlin & to have their wives & families, in Belgium, join them there. . . . I hope none will be so blind to circumstances as to think it possible to accept.

THURSDAY, JANUARY 25

. . . Oh God! how long will these horrors last! I think constantly of the poor fellows frozen to death in the trenches & while on duty. God help them! . . . 200

them from the largely Flemish-speaking, working-class municipality of Anderlecht. Gille et al., *Cinquante mois d'occupation allemande*, 3:37; see also 28.

[113] This is correct. At the triage camp at Güben (southeast of Berlin), where pneumonia was rampant, thirteen men from the district of Éghezée (Namur province) had died by January 11.

[114] In Germany, annexationist lobbies were now openly demanding (parts of) Belgium.

[115] CRB delegates.

horses passed here, requisitioned by the Boches; they will not leave one horse in the country. It breaks my heart to see these last resources of hard working people being wrenched from them! Yesterday at 1:30 pm, what everyone took for a Boche aeroplane passed over our house & the Porte de Namur, quite low down. It flew over the St Michel college, & threw down into the play ground, where the boys were at recreation, a Belgian coloured bag, containing a ball of clay, in which was a paper, bearing greetings to the rector of the College, signed by an old pupil, who was in the aeroplane. This same man sent a message down to his father, near their own house at Etterbeek.[116] . . .

FRIDAY, JANUARY 26

Kaiser's birthday is to-day or to-morrow, for there has been boche music about to-day, & this evening a torch-light procession in a freezing cold East wind. The manager of the "Grand Bazar" condemned to pay 80 thousand marks fine, undermanager prison & fine (the former is ill in bed, so can't go to prison) some employees fined also because . . . some of the toy soldiers here were Boches, holding up their hands (to show they were articulated) & other nonsense of that kind.[117] Reminds one of the Saverne incidents![118] Oh Prussian militarism, when wilt thou cease making tragedies out of humbug and . . . Bosh!

SATURDAY, JANUARY 27, 1917

Young de Bousies & several other young fellows who had got safely through to Holland, were going to England to join the front, on the "Prins Hendrik" Dutch mail-boat, that was taken to Zeebrugge by the Prussians. I suppose their presence on board was signaled. <u>Why</u> can't <u>we</u> prevent the Boches seizing those mail boats! No more young men will be able to get to their army, if the Dutch boats are captured! All funds belonging to belligerents, in banks in Belgium, are seized & will be sent to Germany to help their war-loans. My little stock at C^sse des R.[119] is in the number;

---

[116] On January 24, Belgian aviator Edmond Thieffry flew over his old school, the Collège Saint-Michel, dropping a Belgian tricolor flag with the words "Bravo Jesuits! From your alumnus Edmond Thieffry." He then dropped a flag nearby with greetings to his fiancée. Gille et al., *Cinquante mois d'occupation allemande*, 3:38–40.

[117] Military Governor Friedrich von Hurt closed down the Grand Bazar department store and condemned the managers to three months' imprisonment and fines. The Brussels police superintendent had (clandestinely) broken the story. Gille et al., *Cinquante mois d'occupation allemande*, 3:25–26.

[118] A 1913 incident in Saverne, Alsace, where a German officer publicly insulted locals before arresting them.

[119] The Caisse Générale de Reports et de Dépôts, a Brussels bank specializing in modest stock portfolios.

if only I had known what to do & had taken it away from the beginning but no-body could advise me! Please God, I don't have to lose it, the savings of so many years' work!

SUNDAY, JANUARY 28

Frost continues, skating everywhere. Nothing of the war to-day except that papers seem to think we shall soon have a terrible offensive on the Somme. When & how will it happen! I am very disturbed about the German sub-marine war! I met Mr. Cousin to-day; each time I see him I think what a thorn it must be to him to see his famous Zee-Brugge, his greatest work, used by the Boches against us, without it ever having served the great ambitious aims Belgium had in creating it. . . . [I]t has really never served but the Germans, as if it were made to await the fatal use they make of it! Who could have foreseen such events![120]

MONDAY, JANUARY 29

Nothing to write about to-day, except that it is almost an impossibility to obtain any glycerine[121] from the chemists; they have hardly any left, & when they do consent to sell a little, it is only 30 grammes at a time. How nice it will be, after the war??? To be able to get things as we were accustomed to. . . .

  This terribly frosty weather grieves me for the men wounded in battle who can't be attended to immediately—how many cases of gangrene there must be, alas! God help them! and us all!

TUESDAY, JANUARY 30

. . . I heard that 80 thousand German soldiers had arrived in Bruges, it is thought the Germans will take the offensive on the Flemish front.[122] On dit [they say] that after February 7th no passenger trains will be seen, all being reserved for the German army. So many people are already or nearly without coal, none arrives, no means of conveyance. Men that have been sent back from Germany because they would not work for the Boches are in an awful state of *ill* health, tuberculosis, etc. They say that German soldiers (meaning well) advised them to lie flat on their stomach to quell the terrible hunger they endured there.

---

[120] Jean Cousin, an engineer, had developed the port of Zeebrugge.

[121] A skin moisturizer.

[122] Marine Corps reinforcements linked to the resumption of unrestricted submarine warfare.

WEDNESDAY, JANUARY 31

... Had a card from dear Valérie, she is not well, suffers from cold & can't get her usual supply for milk. Poor Dear! & to think we are losing three years of the happiness of friendship! it means so much at our, & especially her age.

THURSDAY, FEBRUARY 1

We were all surprised & couldn't understand why the <u>town</u> authorities (Belgians) did not allow skating on the ponds in the big public places: Bois, Parc Léopold, etc, & ordered the ice to be broken up on the edges & thrown on to the middle. It appears it is to avoid having the Belgians meet the Boches & be photoed for cinemas (as they love to do, as soon as they get a chance) to make the world believe we are on good terms with them in every day life.

Had a visit from dear good Carola,[123] as hopeful & cheerful as ever; she doesn't believe in the awful offensive we are awaiting, thinks the belligerents will come to terms of peace diplomatically. . . . I don't.

To-day began the famous Boche sub-marine blockade of England! How many of it is bluff, I wonder.

FRIDAY, FEBRUARY 2

What <u>will</u> be the result of the German sub-marine blockade of the Allies' countries! Will it be as bad as the Boche papers & their speeches proclaim? or no worse than before, & is it only bluff? I fancy they have always done their "level best" against us & can't do much worse. . . .

Dieu nous aide!!! [God help us]

SATURDAY, FEBRUARY 3

... Lots of money was taken from the German Bank to Cologne the other day; I wonder if my little packet was in it from Caisse des Reports.

SUNDAY, FEBRUARY 4

Pavlick is returning to college to-morrow after his chicken-pox, & to-day Micha went to bed with the same complaint, so no leisure yet for me!

What will America do about the sub-marine blockade! We must wait & see, but I wonder. It is <u>so</u> <u>cold</u>, & no coals to be had; the poor are being frozen to death in their attics, alas! alas!

---

[123] MT's friend Caroline "Carola" de Crombrugghe de Picquendaele.

We had an excellent charity sermon at the Carmes this morning,[124] & afterwards the "Brabançonne" & Lion de Flandre very beautifully on the organ.[125] I thought it was no longer tolerated by the Boches—perhaps they didn't think of forbidding it in chapels.

MONDAY, FEBRUARY 5

To-day we heard by the German papers of the cessation of diplomatic relations between the States & Germany.... What will Holland & the other neutrals do! I have been wondering (& I hear others have had the same thoughts) if all the bluff about the Blockade is not simply meant to make all the world rise up against our enemies, who then, would have a plausible reason, before their people, for accepting our conditions of peace....

The man who brought the ice here this morning, said a child 3 years old, living next door to him, was frozen to death last night in its cradle.

The coal crisis is a terrible one. I am praying the wind may change & start the thaw, on the day of the full moon, the 7th.

If all nations make war on Germany, her blockade will mean her own suicide.

As usual, we must wait & see!

Our chef's sister-in-law, whose son had been taken to Germany as a *chômeur* (he had work here) took steps to have him back, but was informed, by the Germans, that he was dying & could not travel. On hearing this, the poor woman fell down dead ... two more victims of the war! they are <u>legion</u>, directly & indirectly.

TUESDAY, FEBRUARY 6

So far, the American Legation have received no "walking papers." Pavlick saw Mr. Ruddock, who said they had received no instructions up to this.[126]

The men from 17 to 55, of villages west of Brussels, have to present themselves "to be sent to Germany" to-morrow.

It was said this slave driving would cease during this excessive severe weather, but the "Boches" <u>don't</u> care. They have deprived us of means of getting coal, people here are freezing to death & many of those sent to Germany die there, or return here with health shattered for good.

WEDNESDAY, FEBRUARY 7, THURSDAY; FRIDAY 9, SATURDAY 10

In bed with grippe [flu] ...

[124] The little Carmelite church on Avenue de la Toison d'Or, opposite the Wittouck residence.

[125] "De Leeuw van Vlaanderen," (Lion of Flanders), Flemish patriotic hymn.

[126] The diplomats (Whitlock and Ruddock) and the CRB officials remained until April.

SUNDAY, FEBRUARY 22

How many lives lost, alas, ~~by~~ *through* the German submarines, since I wrote last! I feel I must read all I can get, yet I know all those disasters prey on my mind & prevent me getting well.... Oh! the poor people innocent & inoffensive, cut down without warning by those pirates—God help them!

I am so glad to think the English blockade never caused any willful loss of life! How long will the neutrals tolerate the killing of their nationals! The American Legation are remaining here, so far, & the Relief Committee also. I am sure a "certain Marquis" [Villalobar] is jubilating at the idea that the United States are now quite "out of it" concerning the glory of the conclusion of peace, <u>when</u> it comes, & that his country will probably gather all the laurels alone—& he a few more decorations & the highest post of ambassador....

MONDAY, FEBRUARY 12

It is probably [*sic*] the Americans will leave here for the Hague (of their own accord). Holland will then attend to the interests of the English. I hope, for all those it concerns, the English Relief Fund will continue to work well.

The Papal Nuncio, Mᵍʳ Locatelli <u>has</u> returned, in spite of the Marquis' intrigues. We had a little coal brought here to-day, from a depot where they had a small quantity left— we had to send two of the coachmen to guard it (from being robbed) on its way.[127] ...

TUESDAY, FEBRUARY 13

The American Legation haven't yet left Brussels, though the "Relief" is going over to the Spanish & Dutch diplomats. How will latter agree with the Marquis [Villalobar] in this! ...

WEDNESDAY, FEBRUARY 14

Had a good letter from Dick.... He has received a splendid parcel of clothes & different useful things, from Edith in America. He also received clothes from the English Red Cross.... Mr. W gave to-day 25 thousand francs *to his sister Mme de Beeckman*[128] for the "Assistance Discrète," ~~his sister who told~~ so our poor people won't want yet. An article in the *Belgique* says English *aeroplane* bombs killed people at Bruges—perhaps the German guns, like here in October.

---

[127] In desperation, people had started pilfering the coal brought in for those families who could still afford it. Gille et al., *Cinquante mois d'occupation allemande*, 3:62–63.

[128] Paul Wittouck's sister, Emilie, wife of Baron Fernand de Beeckman, had inherited a 500-hectare estate in Limburg province and used her considerable resources for charitable work. She was one of the patrons of the Discreet Assistance.

THURSDAY, FEBRUARY 15

Five months exactly since I began this diary. I didn't think then, we should, at this date, be practically no nearer the end of the tragedy than then. . . . How long is it still to be! These days we know & hear <u>absolutely</u> <u>nothing</u> about events, except hard local fighting here & there on the Somme.

A letter from dear Valérie to-day written on the 9th. ~~All the~~ No gas-light in the streets at Ghent in the evening, not even between 5 & 7, so she will have to give up her reading at Mme V's. Thank God she writes she suffers less from pain, but cold intense. The thaw is too slow, it freezes 3 to 5 degrees at night; 4 above zero in the shade in the day.

FRIDAY, FEBRUARY 16, & SATURDAY, FEBRUARY 17

Excitement to-day through German posters announcing that all schools have to be closed; they ~~Boches~~ say on account of the coal question—but that is absurd, & everyone thinks they will be lodging troops everywhere very soon.[129] All shops, except those which sell food-stuffs only, are to be closed at our 5 pm.

I saw V^{ctesse} F. De Beughem to-day & went up to her to congratulate her (an American) on belonging to a country that won't be dictated to by Germany.[130] She said she thinks there will be war, & it seems to read so from extracts of Dutch papers to-day. Alec F[ord]. is very exercised about how his money will arrive now that the Americans have no more diplomatic valise.[131]

SUNDAY, FEBRUARY 18

Nothing whatever of the war to-day; we are more & more "au fond de l'entonnoir" [at the bottom of the funnel] & don't know anything, & scraps of news in the horrid Boche paper *La Belgique* are daily more demoralizing. . . .

MONDAY, FEBRUARY 19

[A friend] got a post-card from a German lady friend of his, in Berlin, begging him to send her some eatables! . . .

[129] The school closings, decreed on February 17, 1917, were a catastrophe for many *bruxellois* because at school their children were warm and received free meals. The measure served to channel coal away from the schools. Gille et al., *Cinquante mois d'occupation allemande*, 3:62–63, III, 122–123, and 134–135.

[130] The Vicomtesse de Beughem de Houthem, née Irene Hare from New York. During the war, she was one of the organizers of the CRB's Lace Committee, dedicated to preserving the livelihood of Belgium's lacemakers.

[131] As a trader in Chile-harvested sodium nitrate, Ford's business interests were largely in South America, hence the concerns about funds that had been funneled through neutral US channels.

There is no more sugar to be had in Germany—it goes for making chemicals for ammunition, in some of the best hotels, one gets a little saccharine. . . .

TUESDAY, FEBRUARY 20

The boys returned to College, in spite of the German poster, & were told that, by order of the Archbishop, Cardinal Mercier, his episcopal schools are to remain open, until the Boches go & close them by force. We suppose that will happen shortly—wait & see. I heard the cannon as I was walking in Rue de la Régence. When will the famous offensive begin!!!

WEDNESDAY, FEBRUARY 21

No news. Very foggy & dirty thaw. Germans went to some schools & forced them to close. Every day they are expected at St. Boniface.[132] . . . It is said a Zepp. came down in Ghent.

THURSDAY, FEBRUARY 22

The boys were sent back from school to-day—the authorities were forced to submit to the Boches. We suppose that there will be no more school till the end of the war—in many schools of the suburbs, beds are being placed—is it for ambulances or passing troops! The German posters give a list of 12 people killed at Bruges & several wounded "by the English aeroplanes;" that means by the German guns trying to bring them down, as it was the case here in Brussels last October, especially on the B^d de la Grande Ceinture.

Everything is done *here*, in papers & posters, by the Boches, to injure the English in the minds of the Belgians & neutrals. Am glad to see the new *war* loan in England is such a success & that nearly 5.000 boats have entered British ports from 1st to 15th of Feb, the losses through submarines being only 1 percent!

FRIDAY, FEBRUARY 23

. . . I wonder what Germany thinks of the nearly 6 thousand boats that have entered British ports the 1st fortnight of their famous blockade! And what of the enormous success of our new loan! When they are forced to call for all the jewelry in the land to have it sold to make money for their loan!!!

---

[132] The Institut Saint-Boniface, a Catholic school in Ixelles, one kilometer from the Wittouck residence.

SATURDAY, FEBRUARY 24

... When <u>will</u> the fine weather & fine offensive come!!! Have been worried by the "soap" problem to-day; a cake that used to cost 25 or 30 centimes is now 2 fr 50 or 3 fr & only muck at that. <u>When</u> shall I get my good Pears soap again! ...

SUNDAY, FEBRUARY 25

Have just read that 6 Dutch boats were torpedoed & sunk as they were leaving England on the 22nd, date that was given out by the Germans as a day of security! They say a German officer committed suicide in the "aubette" of the Porte de Namur,[133] just opposite, ~~at de~~ between 4 & 5 this morning.

The Germans seem to be making all kinds of mischief in the U.S.... and now it is averred that their sub-marines were supplied with food & ammunition off the Spanish coast. Which country will possibly be able to remain friendly with Germany???

~~TUESDAY~~ MONDAY, FEBRUARY 26

It's a terrible thing to have all the schools closed by the Germans, all is at sixes & sevens. The professors try to take a few pupils at different hours, clandestinely, in their own rooms at the schools, but there is great confusion & the children's lives are upset.

Another calamity: a new *Arrêté* [Order] forcing all factories to be closed.... [W]here will this lead! & the thousands of poor workmen who will suffer!

It is said the Kaiser & Hindenburg are in Brussels—we feel we are on the verge of something immense—on which side will the offensive start? The torpedoing ~~the~~ of the Dutch steamers leaving Falmouth has done the Boches <u>no good</u>—the Dutch don't seem to like it <u>this</u> time, but I doubt it will make them declare war—they don't dare!!! The Dutch flag is now floating on the English legation here. Brand Whitlock won't use his motor any longer, because he has had to take off his "Stars & Stripes" & he won't ride without them; the Ruddocks, who never sported a flag, still continue to use theirs but tyres are getting scarce even for the few remaining legation motors. What will March & the fine weather bring! We feel we are destined to witness & suffer extraordinary things before our deliverance dawns! God help us all!

TUESDAY, FEBRUARY 27

On March 1st, the Boches <u>compel</u> us to deliver all the brass & copper one possesses: kitchen utensils, stair-carpet rods etc etc, in fact no one knows exactly if

---

[133] A kiosk on Porte de Namur, opposite the Wittouck residence. The Brussels chronicles do not mention this event.

photo-frames & such trifles are condemned too. And to think all that is to make ammunition to kill <u>our</u> men! Every day is more painful.

It is said there was a terrible air-battle from Calais to Bruges, after a Zepp, which fell at Bruges, rose again & finally fell at Gent. Many people killed at Bruges! alas! alas![134] Coal from Belgium is being drafted off to Holland by the Boches, & we can't get any—some of the miners have refused to work on that account. I am trying to take this awful period just "day by day" & trust in God for the rest.

WEDNESDAY, FEBRUARY 28

… The town of Ghent & its burgomaster are both heavily fined. The Germans had placarded a list of people killed at Bruges during the last air-battle as having succumbed to the Allies' bombs. The burgomaster was plucky enough to stick up a counter-placard, saying the deaths & damages were due to the Boches' firing at our airships—hence the punishment.

I must take some steps to try to get back from Germany Sidonie's stepfather who is dying of starvation & reproaching his wife & family for not sending him food. They have sent numerous parcels, <u>none</u> have reached the poor man, I suppose he doesn't quite realize that food passing through Germany is sore temptation just now for honesty. . . .

When I began this book 4 and a half months ago, I thought & hoped we should have "got on" towards the end more than we have done. <u>How</u> will the world stand at the end of the red book that I begin to-morrow!

---

[134] In Bruges, the air raid and flak counter-fire violence became intense after February.

Book 2

"QUI VIVRA VERRA,"

MARCH–SEPTEMBER 1917

T *he year 1917 was momentous for Thorp and the Wittouck household, as they were per-*
sonally affected by global events. The US entry into war meant the departure of the
American diplomats who had been fixtures in the Wittoucks' social life. Thorp saw more of
the Dutch, Spanish, and Swedish diplomats afterward. The Russian revolutions touched
the Wittoucks even more, since Madame Wittouck was Russian by birth and many mem-
bers of her family were caught up in the turmoil, most devastatingly her brother-in-law,
who was murdered.

Thorp's diary mixed global war news with events close to home, and she recounted
any rumors she heard. The diary shows striking instances of Thorp's access to information:
when, on the Macedonian front, French-Serbian forces took Monastir (today Bitola) on
November 19, 1916, she heard about it on the same day. The sound of cannon, a constant
backdrop in their lives, is mentioned more than a hundred times. While it might portend
an Allied breakthrough, she feared the destruction this might bring; it was widely known
that the German army's retreat on the Somme had left a wasteland. The artillery she heard
was coming from the fierce battles that began in the spring of 1917 near Ypres (Belgium)
and in the French theaters of Lens, Arras, and the Aisne River. By late 1917, the cannons
were in Cambrai and Messines and in the muds at Passchendaele. These offensives and
strategic retreats led to massive displacement of civilians from front zones. Thorp person-
ally felt its tragedy through her friendships with Mademoiselle Cazé (displaced from La
Fère) and with the Boulez family (in Waregem). It made her ever more aware of the war's
toll on civilian lives.

And it was a year not only of abysmal material misery but of growing fis-
sures inside occupied society. For all the outcry over forced labor, for instance, many

commentators, Thorp included, reserved their greatest indignation for the deportation of men with jobs, which suggested that the unemployed, while deserving of sympathy, were more expendable than others. Another type of fissure was linguistic: even though the "activists" who chose to work with the Germans were a despised minority, they remained a segment of Belgian opinion, and some of them were members of the bourgeoisie. All in all, the year 1917 heralded a harsh period with no clear end in sight.

CONTINUATION OF "LOCAL GOSSIP" ETC.

It is quite by want of choice I had to buy this startling red covered book to continue my diary, but it suggests too vividly <u>how much</u> blood must be shed before I come to the end—if I am spared to do so. God grant the calamity be over, or very nearly so, when this book is filled, four or five months hence. When I began my diary on September 15th 1916, I thought & hoped it was at the "eleventh hour," but alas! alas! . . .

THURSDAY, MARCH 1

Better news to-day—we have retaken Kout-el-Amara[1] & the English have advanced ₅ 11 or 4 miles on the Ancre![2] When will Bapaume fall! . . .

So two American women have perished from cold in the boat lowered from the Lucania [*RMS Laconia*].[3] What will Wilson do now! . . .

FRIDAY, MARCH 2

I've just had the "treat" of looking at the Xmas number of "Vogue." Now & then, at very long intervals, we are lent an English illustration, brought in by a diplomatist or some "noble stranger", & it goes on a big round as a curiosity.

To-day German civilians invaded the St. Michel College, while the boys were there, striving for "Belgian culture" on the sly; they were questioned, dismissed, & the college is once more in for a bad fine or something worse for continuing a little teaching!!!

Everyone has been preparing the brass & metal to be sent in to the Boches to-morrow, alas! alas! We all hope that by giving something we are accomplishing "de deux maux le moindre" [the lesser of two evils].

[1] Kut al Amara (modern Iraq) had been the site of a humiliating defeat for Britain in April 1916.

[2] In the Ancre (Somme), British forces pushed German lines back more than five miles.

[3] A German U-boat sank the RMS *Laconia* on February 25, 1917, and two American citizens (a mother and daughter from Chicago) died.

SATURDAY, MARCH 3

To-day began the heart-rending procession of people condemned to take their metal to the "Barbarians" to make ammunition for killing our own brave men! This is one of the many "worst" things of the war. Please God our metal will arrive too late to harm our heroes, that the war may be over before it can be used.

Every day brings its share of sorrows to add to the former ones. This morning a nice woman, wife of an engine-driver (machiniste de l'État) [engine-driver working for the Belgian state railways] came to ask my help to get her sick husband back from Germany, where he was sent without any warning, & in spite of his Dr's certificate that he is seriously ill, having been ratified by a German Dr. I will do all I can in this case, Mme. Frantz Wittouck had offered the St. Michel College a room in her house to hold the class Jean is in, 2nd latine.⁴ About 27 boys were to have assembled there this morning. The "Marquis" [Villalobar] has told her the Boches won't allow it—no teaching may be given anywhere . . . & no one can understand the reason.

Poor Maria Scholler had organized a concert at the Salle de l'Union Coloniale for the 15th inst. [of this month]; bills & 2 thousand programmes printed, tickets sold etc, programme censored— now, a new decree: "No public concert without modern German music, & the Belgian Artists won't submit. Maria had the old German masters in her programme, all the concerts had, as usual, but Prussia must command . . . so now my poor friend has to give a private concert in a small hall & lose the money she so much deserves.⁵

SUNDAY, MARCH 4

Heart-breaking accounts of the state the poor "deported" men are in when sent back to Belgium, exhausted & dying of hunger, cold & neglect. The way they were treated in Germany because they would not work is real martyrdom. . . .

The Americans, even Bryan⁶ & the pacifists, are desirous of arming their merchant ships since they know of the plot that was sent against them by the Germans wanting to debauch Mexico & Japan.⁷ Their "gaffes" once more serve for their confusion.

---

⁴ The second year of the six-year Latin secondary school curriculum.

⁵ Maria Scholler remains unidentified.

⁶ William Jennings Bryan, Woodrow Wilson's secretary of state until 1915, promoted strict US neutrality.

⁷ In January 1917, British Naval Intelligence intercepted a telegram between German Minister of Foreign Affairs Arthur Zimmermann and Mexican authorities. This telegram suggested that Mexico form an alliance with Germany and invade the United States. This affair, once revealed to the Americans, helped lead to the US entry into war.

MONDAY, MARCH 5

A big fall of snow, alas for our soldiers. New "arrêté": all the men from 17 to 40 (it was 30 before) & all retired officers (Belgian) have now to go to sign at the "controle." What <u>do</u> the Boches finally mean to do with those men!!![8] . . .

We are wrathful & indignant at the behaviour of a few mad & treacherous "Flamingants" who have been to Berlin, to discuss "with gratitude!!!" the Flemish question with the Chancellor "Scrap of Paper".

His answer most perfidious; the game is merely to divide the Flemish & Walloons in Belgium just as they make every effort to put Belgium against England. Their pretext is that Flemish & German are so near in language etc etc, but the Dutch are the nearest to Flemish, so why don't those mad idiots of Flamingants go over to the Dutch!!!

Fortunately they don't represent all the Flemish people, & I hope no one will be misled, which is the Germans' object. . . .

TUESDAY, MARCH 6

. . . If I were in England, how glad I should be to volunteer for the civil service, in such great need just now; still I feel I did my duty in remaining at my post & trying to make good men of the three boys—they are still in great need of guidance, moral & other.

String & paper are getting so scarce. Yesterday I bought 48 cakes of Lanoline soap, at 2 frs a *small* cake, what might have cost formerly 20 to 25 centimes in a good quality, whereas now it is "savon de guerre." [wartime soap]

WEDNESDAY, MARCH 7

. . . Mme. Joseph Bulon, the engine-driver's wife, came to see me again about her husband's release. I sent her to Mr. Sadi Kirschen, the avocat who has done <u>so much</u> for thousands of Belgians in trouble with the Germans, & he won't receive a penny from anyone, even the rich, he does all for patriotism. I hope, after the war, that his practical & truly patriotic zeal will be handsomely recognized by the country.

THURSDAY, MARCH 8

. . . People are freezing to death. It is pitiful, heart-rending to see how the poor suffer; even those I visit I can't help, because the difficulty is to <u>find</u> coal for sale and those who do succeed have to pay unheard of prices. . . .

---

[8] At the Meldeamt (registration office), young men ages sixteen to twenty-nine had to present themselves at regular intervals to demonstrate that they had not left the country to join the Belgian army. In March 1917, this was extended to men up to age forty. Louis Gille, Alphonse Ooms and Paul Delandsheere, *Cinquante mois d'occupation allemande* (Brussels: Albert Dewit, 1919), 3:167.

FRIDAY, MARCH 9

... I went to the Annex of the Dutch Legation to see Mr. Kattendyk [Van Kattendijke] about getting Sidonie's step-father back from Germany—he gave me indications & said the Boches don't like them to bother them much about "so called chômeurs" because they (the Germans) say that all those who haven't signed to work are being sent back; but how slowly! ... The coal crisis continues. Two barges of coal were bought at the mine & were en route to Petit-Bigard, but were seized by the Germans—so poor Mme. Félix Wittouck is almost coal-less with her big establishment.[9]

Severe winter weather & snow this afternoon again. One hears so much German spoken in the streets by civilians, men & women. I suppose many have come here for to avoid famine, for we are not yet in the straits they are in Germany. The German soldiers we see in our churches pray most devoutly, three were doing the Way of the Cross at the Carmes[10] this evening; I asked God to spare them for worshipping Him so humbly.

SATURDAY, MARCH 10

... Mme. Josse Allard has exported, this year (2 months & 9 days) for 800.000 frs of lace, made in Belgium by the women whose interests she has in hand.[11] ...

Mr. W. gave everyone in the house 5 kilos of delicious sugar, & I have made 20 ½ lb packets to give to the needy. ...

SUNDAY, MARCH 11

... Had a card from Dick yesterday; he had received, at least, a letter from Edith dated Dec. 28th 1916. All the men at Ruhleben are to be vaccinated; I read there were cases of small-pox at Berlin. God preserve our camp![12]

One of the 7 Flamingants, who went & degraded themselves at Berlin, received & complimented by Bethmann-Holweg was Dr. Dumon of Bruges![13] They surely can't remain Belgian after that! ...

[9] Widow of Félix Wittouck who owned the château of Petit Bigard [Klein-Bijgaarden].

[10] The Église des Carmes on Avenue de la Toison d'Or, opposite the Wittouck residence.

[11] The CRB Lace Committee. This refers to Marie-Antoinette Calley Saint Paul de Sinçay, wife of the Brussels banker and businessman Josse Allard, stepson of Paul Wittouck's sister.

[12] Ruhleben had fairly good sanitary conditions for a prisoner of war camp. Matthew Stibbe, *British Civilian Internees in Germany: The Ruhleben Camp, 1914–18* (Manchester: Manchester University Press, 2008), 151.

[13] The Bruges physician Emiel Dumon. Sophie De Schaepdrijver, *Bastion: Occupied Bruges in the First World War* (Bruges: Hannibal Publishing, 2014), 42, 142–144.

MONDAY, MARCH 12

We are told that the German Brussels paper *Belgischer Kurier* announces this morning the taking of Baghdad by the English. May it be the beginning of the end of our struggle with the Turks, at least in Asia Minor.

I wanted to order fancy coloured striped shirts for Micha, at Darchambaud's [a shop in Brussels] to-day. They have the proper stuff "before the war", at 9 f 50 the shirt, but they are forbidden to use it. It has been put aside by the Boches, to be exported *by them* to Germany (or elsewhere) in exchange for <u>money</u> & Darchambaud had to buy material where he could, & charges now 25 frs per shirt. . . . The G's <u>are</u> slack of money, part of the brass they commandeered was paid for in "Bons" [Receipts] to be refunded after the war.

TUESDAY, MARCH 13

This afternoon we had a German soldier & an officer in the house to "see what they could still discover" in the way of copper & other metal. They were inoffensive, didn't come into the rooms, except at no. 20, in the apartments of the married servants (concierges, Jean, chauffeur) & into the kitchen. They took some notes, so will probably send for certain things. I hear 485 frs were paid for the metal sent them by Mr W, but they "make a perquisition" nevertheless. It seems they photographed the people carrying their metal to the Luxembourg station; it will probably appear in their illustrated papers as: "The Belgians are so poor, they run to sell us their copper ware"!

WEDNESDAY, MARCH 14

This morning two more Boches came to the house, to inspect the new Minerva open motor-car Mr. W bought just before the war.[14] Of course it is going to be taken—for a small sum, not nearly cost price, like all the rest. We feel the Germans will take <u>all</u> they can out of the country. The ~~sub~~ officer who went to see the motor told one of our men: "this war was terrible, away from home nearly 3 years, they don't eat potatoes every day, & have to fight for other fat fellows who want for nothing." St Quentin has been evacuated, thousands of people drafted off, standing up in railway trucks, to Charleroi, Namur, Tournai etc. We expect "réfugiés" in Brussels as districts are gradually evacuated.[15]

THURSDAY, MARCH 15

. . . What can be true about the riots in Petrograd?[16] To-day I took all the papers, signed in due form, concerning Sidonie's step-father's return from Germany, to the

[14] A Belgian luxury car manufactured from 1902.

[15] Since late February, people from northern France, evacuated by the Germans in the context of their "defence in depth" strategy, had been arriving in Belgium.

[16] The February Revolution.

Annex of Dutch Legation to send to von Bissing, with my request to him to free the man. Let us hope for success. They told me the Boches don't like their being so methodical & careful, because the Dutch keep a document to show the Belgian Government on its return, what they have done for us.

FRIDAY, MARCH 16

My dear friend Mlle Cazé, who was at La Fère since the beginning of the war, arrived at Rochefort last Monday.[17] . . . The inhabitants of La Fère were allowed 4 hours to pack a trunk each, & say good bye to their homes & furniture. . . . They travelled to Rochefort in cattle cars, & were standing up in them, 30 hours en route. Mlle C had taken a chair for her old mother, 86, who had to leave a sick bed for the cattle-car. It is supposed that all the houses at La Fère (like *they were* at St Quentin) have been blown up. The Boches, in their retreat, leave nothing whatever standing, & no inhabitants to help the Allies on the road. . . .

Mme W. joined me at Maria S's concert [Maria Scholler], & announced the crisis at Petrograde, departure & abdication? of the Czar, according to the German papers, but we must see. . . . Will the Russian democrats want to make a separate peace? Revolutions are epidemic—I shouldn't mind one at Berlin just now. How shall we fare here? Shall we be evacuated & have all burnt before the Allies can arrive! God help us all, and bring the war to an end soon!

SATURDAY, MARCH 17

No accurate information yet concerning the revolution in Russia, but the Brussels boche papers are amusing in the way they lay all the blame (as usual) on the English!!! What a lot of reading we shall have for the rest of our lives! Napoleon & his wars have quite "fini de chanter," [they are done singing] after having been harped upon for a hundred years! Comparatively, this war, to be as thoroughly sifted by history, will need quite a thousand years.

How will the German retreat from the Somme end? This morning, the two German soldiers who came after the copper last Tuesday, came again, but really only for forms' sake, were on my storey [floor], went into one bedroom, didn't open my door, had a look round the garret & into the kitchen ovens!

SUNDAY, MARCH 18

The German Brussels paper announces this evening, that the English have entered Bapaume, Péronne, Noyon. . . . Thank God! What can be the plan of the Boches now over there? At ~~Virelles, near~~ Chimay they have expelled nuns & professors from their

---

convents & schools, disinfected all the premises during 4 days, & brought in quantities of beds. There are about 150 German doctors in the district. Does it mean a battle in that direction? or simply a make belief again? The events in Russia are very absorbing, as far as we can get any information, but we cannot realise why the Czar could not remain & make all the reforms that he asks his brother Michel (a man inferior to himself) to make.

MONDAY, MARCH 19, 1917

Hardly any particulars yet concerning our great advance on the Somme. I wonder if our soldiers found any inhabitants left there to welcome & cheer them! How weary they must be of seeing desolation everywhere! News from Russia still very confused, & Mme W. terribly grieved & upset because the *Belgischer Kurier* says the Governor of the Province of Tver (her brother-in-law Nicolas (Nix) Bunting) has been murdered.[18] She rushed to Villalobar to try to send a telegram to Petrograde, but no means of wiring out of Belgium. The impression is now, that the revolution is against the *Russian* pro-Germans & that the Russian people are very Germanophobe & furious because there were so many Germanophiles at court & in the aristocracy.

TUESDAY, MARCH 20

Nothing very definite yet about the turn of affairs in Russia. They seem to accuse the Czarina of being pro-German. A few particulars about our advance on the Somme, but I fear all the Germans abandoned was reduced to ruins. Shall we have the same fate here? . . . A post card from Dick at Ruhleben, written only yesterday—very rapid between Berlin & Brussels, but 10 to 12 days from there to Antwerp, in Flemish. Dear Val's [Valérie] last lines to me were of Feb 25th. I wrote her in haste this evening, after reading that shortly we may correspond no longer with the "villes d'Étape" except for business purposes, & even that with great restrictions. Poor Valérie will be <u>so</u> grieved, & so am I for us both.

WEDNESDAY, MARCH 21

A cold, snowy day for the opening of spring. It is freezing again to-night. . . .

As we were coming out from lunch, three German "sous-officiers" entered the hall to come & seize 2 *copper* boilers of the kitchen stove, & one in the garage. They had their "plunder" cart at the door, but as the boilers are fixtures, they couldn't take them

---

[18] Anonymous [Albert Stopford], *The Russian Diary of an Englishman: Petrograd, 1915–1917* (London: W. Heinemann, 1919), 123. On March 2 (15), 1917, the day of the tsar's abdication, the governor of Tver oblast (north of Moscow), Nicolas Bunting, Catherine Wittouck's sister's husband, was killed allegedly for refusing to hand over his sword to rebellious soldiers. William H. Chamberlin, *The Russian Revolution* (Princeton: Princeton University Press, 2014), 1:85, observes

at once. They were polite, regretted having to do it etc. To a neighbor who remarked to them they must be hard up to have come to this, they replied: Yes, we are hard-up. Alec Ford told me this evening, he had had a message from his brother Abbot *Hugh Ford*[19] in Rome, through the Nuncio, asking if he was in want of anything. Was able to write a line or two on a scrap of paper. Some of the American ~~Committee~~ Relief Committee told him 60 Americans of the Relief are leaving for Baden-Baden this week, under German escort, which is to guard & watch them a fortnight there; *so as to let news from here get stale* then they go to Basle [Basel] & on to Paris, Barcelona & to Key West Florida & on to N. York. This particular man thinks he will remain in Paris, ready to go to the front as soon as Wilson declares war; he says Germany is done for & no mistake.

THURSDAY, MARCH 22

... What do the Boches mean to do, & where will they stop their retreat????? Alas for all the plunder & destruction they accomplish. When will our brave men enter a town where they can be properly welcomed & treated! If only we could rush them on & drive them out, but the state of the land they leave makes it impossible. The soap crisis is to end by only a few people being allowed *by the G's* to make it, & it must be sold wrapped in certain stamped paper, & no other than this official soap may be sold after April 15th.

FRIDAY, MARCH 23

... Lady Phipps told me the traitor Sir Roger Casement was the cause of her husband, Sir Constantine, having to give up the diplomatic career, that Casement had untruthfully made out that Phipps, who he had seen in Brussels, was ~~working~~ holding with Belgium in the then very "tendue" [tense] question of the Congo.[20] ...

SATURDAY, MARCH 24

Had a letter from Dear Val [Valérie], written on the 4th! ... the last I presume alas! till the end of the war, correspondence now being forbidden in the Étape—such a blow to us both.

that such incidents were rare in the spring revolution. Nicolas (or Nicolai) von Bunting's German ancestry had earlier played a role: on December 2, 1916, in a speech in the Duma, the xenophobe deputy Vladimir Purishkevitch had accused him of repressing pro-Allied discourse. Frank Alfred Golder, ed., *Documents of Russian History 1914–1917* (New York-London: Century Co., 1927), 172.

[19] Edmund Hugh Ford, a Benedictine abbot of Glastonbury.

[20] Sir Roger Casement investigated human rights abuses in the Congo before the war. When war broke out, he pushed for Irish independence; he was arrested and executed for his alleged role in the 1916 Easter Rising.

I made several "enquêtes" pour l'Union des Femmes Belges. I am always edified by the good qualities of thrift & love of work in the class of Belgian workwomen— so many eager to ~~get~~ earn the 3 to 4 frs fortnightly at the Union F.B. [Femmes Belges]. I have started collecting the tea that remains in tea-pots, & straining it off into bottles for different poor English women who miss their tea so much—it is now 30 frs & more the kilo 15 to 17 frs the lb. so no question of buying any. I have a little provision for the schoolroom. Cannon loud again today.

SUNDAY, MARCH 25

Cannon very audible again to-day. I am told the Germans are inquiring, in private houses, how many French refugees each one can take in—it is thought it is in view of evacuating Lille??? It would be <u>awful</u> if they destroy such a big town, the desolation they leave behind them, in their retreat, is heart-breaking.

A half tipsy Boche "sous-officier" informed people in a tram the other day: "Nous sommes foutus"! [We are done for] & kept on repeating it. Two officers got up on the platform, & the "sous" put his hand to his mouth to hide his words & repeated them, adding: "et ceux là le savent bien." [And those there know it] The latter handed the tippler out of the tram at the first stop.

MONDAY, MARCH 26

... Good letter from Dick—it was 2 years on the 23rd he is a prisoner. ... [H]e thinks he'll be home in November. God grant it may even be before! ...

TUESDAY, MARCH 27

... I begin to wonder if the Boches mean to retreat slowly right back to Germany, being famished & exhausted, & if the idea they want us to adopt, of a decisive battle "somewhere" in open country, is not simply a snare. ... How much longer must we wait & see! Van Vollenhoven returned from the Hague to-day. The Russian Legation there has no news whatever from Petrograd, & he wasn't able to send a telegram, so Mme W is still in suspense about her brother-in-law having been killed in the revolution, not having been able to get confirmation of the fact we read in different papers about the governor of Tver.

WEDNESDAY, MARCH 28

Saw a poor English woman to-day who <u>can't</u> do without her tea—she pays it <u>3 frs 75</u> the 100 grammes, so 37 frs 50 the kilo, but only a hundred grammes at a time. Another English family who <u>can't</u>!! go to the Alimentation pays the same for a franc's worth of tea at a time & 9 frs the kilo for sugar, when they <u>can</u> get any (smuggled) from shops! My bottles of tea strained off when we have taken ours, have great success; it means better quality & great saving to those poor women. All the people of the American legation are leaving, in a few days, for Le Hâvre via Switzerland. Weather still so cold & no coal to be had anywhere.

THURSDAY, MARCH 29

I have just heard, from Sidonie, that her step-father, for whom I applied to the Dutch Legation & wrote to von Bissing came home last Tuesday, 27th. Deo Gratias! [God be thanked!]

Mrs. Ruddock lunched here to-day, her husband unfortunately, had business elsewhere. They & all the ~~Ger~~ American Legation, C.R.B committee & members all leave for Switzerland, on Saturday or Sunday. We expect the declaration of war with Germany on Monday. Mrs. Ruddock kindly offered to do messages for me.... I gave her one for [a list of friends ...]. I hope they will arrive safely....

FRIDAY, MARCH 30

To-day Brussels is full of rumours concerning something having happened to Hindenbourg, he has committed suicide in despair of what is happening on the Somme—or, he has been seriously wounded by a German who tried to murder him.... I think it is merely a "poisson d'Avril" [April fish]. Mr. Baudoin sees all the "deported" men who return to Tirlemont—some & most of them are in pitiable condition of exhaustion & ill-health, & bear traces of ill-usage. They tell how they were made to stand in rows & be examined by men who wanted them for their different industries, & were picked out "au choix" [chosen] exactly like in a slave-market. The <u>people</u> in Belgium won't forget!

SATURDAY, MARCH 31

I've just read the letter (handed round on the quiet) written by our beloved & admired Archbishop Cardinal Mercier to von Bissing, about his priests *at Malines* being condemned to 100 marks fine, because they would not accept any favours nor have their "cartes d'identité" stamped to escape being sent to Germany with the poor deported men.[x] The Cardinal speaks <u>plain</u> <u>truths</u> to Bissing & makes me think of St. Paul in his epistles.

There was a big adieu lunch somewhere to-day, for all the American gentlemen of Legation & C.R.B. Mr. Ruddock says Brand Whitlock [the American minister] was so eloquent & pathetic that he made them all weep.

[x]The clergy wished to accompany the men in their exile, to help them morally.

SUNDAY, APRIL 1

What will this month mean towards the end of the terrible calamity! . . . It seems that last Thursday, while we were at dinner, all the lights of the town, trams etc were put out suddenly by order of the Boches, for an experiment. I suppose they think we might be having airships this way again. There was a ~~small~~ short panic in consequence, no warning having been given. We all seem to feel something important will happen this week. God grant it may hasten the end of War!

MONDAY, APRIL 2

Our American protectors left for Switzerland this evening . . . weakening somewhat my feeling of being protected against the Boches.[21] At last, we got some decent coal to-day, & have felt warmer than for some time, 15 degrees in my room instead of 12 or 13. Everywhere *that* coal is being carted (by oxen) or shoveled down into cellars, numerous urchins are to be seen, with pails or bags or any kind of recipient, ready to pilfer all they can—it is quite a "spectacle de la rue" [street scene].

. . . Seven years ago to-day I saw Mr. & Mme Wittouck for the first time. . . . I came from Bruges—a warmer spring than this.

TUESDAY, APRIL 3

. . . Read this evening that *in Germany* people's clothes (even for babies 1 to 2 years old) are regulated by government: so many dresses, handkerchiefs, undergarments & so on, & house & bed linen likewise. Really the Germans seem blind to ridicule when they descend to <u>such</u> <u>trivial</u> details. I wonder what a person, who has a cold in the head can do with 6 handkerchiefs!

WEDNESDAY, APRIL 4

Last week *here in Brussels* 60 Boche officers, who had paid "not to be sent to the front" were ordered off nevertheless. They rebelled; some tried to run away; there were shots exchanged, & maxim guns brought out against them. The 60 are now imprisoned at St. Gilles, we wonder what will be their fate. Maria S. [Maria Scholler] lunched to-day with a lady from Bonn. (B^mne de Loë, née d'Hoogvorst)[22] She told

---

[21] Whitlock and the US Legation left on April 2 along with twenty-four US CRB (Commission for Relief in Belgium) delegates. Huge crowds came to the Gare du Nord rail station to see them off. Seven CRB officials remained behind to transfer the food relief program. The men chosen to remain were those the Germans thought had been too near the front in recent weeks and who might have useful intelligence.

[22] Marguerite van der Linden d'Hoogvorst, wife of the Dutch aristocrat Levinus de Loë Imstenraedt.

Marie that there a ham costs 250 marks, that she & her family haven't eaten butter or meat for an age. . . .

She also told Maria that the women who make ammunition earn fabulous wages, & it is they who buy the good expensive smuggled food. They also indulge in furs & jewelry. A big ammunition factory, not far from Bonn is situated by the side of the prison where all the Belgian women are sent—so they preserve the factory from our *air* attacks.[23]

THURSDAY, APRIL 5

Germany is exceedingly vexed that the U.S. have declared war. A German paper says to-day, that new proposals of peace are coming from Vienna. This has been expected this last week.

~~One of the pr~~ It seems that three of the officers that refused to go to the front were shot while trying to escape, in the Park. . . .

GOOD FRIDAY, APRIL 6

Mme W thought she would have news of her brother-in-law, said to have been killed in the Russian revolution but . . . it was a government letter, of February, to her Dutch friend Van Vollenhoven announcing some order of honour was conferred on him. Quite uncommon, this message from a government that no longer exists—nor probably the order either. . . .

SATURDAY, APRIL 7

The Boche authorities here & in the Étape don't seem to agree at all. People there may write here, we get their letters, but we may not write there. Marthe Kervyn came from St. André, by Bruges, yesterday, with her little Henri.[24] She had been asking for this permission for a year. They walked to Bruges station, 3/4 of an hour at 3 am, in pouring rain, & seeing bombs falling at some distance. That happens all the time in the Bruges district, when there is moonlight—constant air-fights. At Bruges station, a German sailor was told off to accompany Marthe wherever she went & to bring her back on Sunday. He lodges in her grandmother's house also. He followed her to shops, friends' houses, where he awaited her in the street. In the afternoon she went with him to report herself at the Commandanture, where the

[23] Siegburg Prison, near Köln, was an internment center for female political prisoners from Belgium and France.

[24] Baroness Marthe du Roy de Blicquy, spouse at that time of Baron Eugène Kervyn de Lettenhove, mother of Henri and Roger. With thanks to Benoît Kervyn de Volkaersbeke for clarifying.

officers were indignant at a lady having been given into such custody, *they* asked her from what <u>barbarous part</u> of <u>the world</u> she had come! . . . & to try to make amends they phoned to Bruges to obtain a prolongation of her passport—it was refused. They then obtained, from Thielt,[25] that she might remain till Monday & be rid of her naval escort while in Brussels—thereupon, after a hearty tea, he went to bed at 8 pm & slept till 10 this morning. He has to accompany her back to Bruges on Monday. They talk <u>English</u> to each other, he not knowing French, & Marthe no German!!!

EASTER SUNDAY (THE 3RD OF THE WAR), APRIL 8

What can the Czar & Czarina have done to be treated as they are, shut up in the fortress of St. Pierre & St. Paul??[26] We know nothing yet here of any documents that may have been found. <u>What</u> a lot there will be to read after the war & when history gets settled. No more Napoleon stories that have filled a century. The Russian communiqués are worded as they never were before in their worst defeats. They own to regiments having been almost wiped out by the Germans. What can it mean? *La Belgique* to-day gives a horrid article, trying to make believe England prevents American food coming here, but omits to mention the many C.R.B. ships that have been destroyed by the Boches.

EASTER MONDAY, APRIL 9

. . . A big tea party here this afternoon in honour of the (very) young Dutchmen who have come to replace the Americans on the Commission for Relief in Belgium. C.R.B. I poured out tea & helped to entertain them. They are young fellows of the highest Dutch society, the cream of Holland they are called. (I say there will be no cream left there to make cheese) . . .

TUESDAY & WEDNESDAY, APRIL 10 AND 11

Serge & I joined the others *here* at La Fougeraie yesterday Tuesday, in storms of snow & icy cold, it was like midwinter. . . . We don't hear any war gossip here, but have read of our English success between Lens & Arras, & 5 thousand prisoners already & "beaucoup de butin." [a great many spoils][27]

---

[25] Tielt was the headquarters of the German Fourth Army, which oversaw that part of the Étape.

[26] The Peter and Paul Fortress in Saint Petersburg.

[27] The British attacked at Arras at first successfully, but the German counterattack from April 14 led to a new stalemate. The Arras offensive was designed to be coordinated with the Chemin des Dames (French) offensive, which failed.

Please God we may speedily have final success, that victorious peace may be restored. May "God's Kingdom come"! Que Votre règne arrive! [May Your reign come] over every nation on earth!

THURSDAY, APRIL 12

A fearfully wild, windy night last night; no sleep, I thought so much of those on sea. . . . Snow again this afternoon, <u>when</u> will it cease! Little news of war; only *from* what the Germans publish, our victory near Arras has been brilliant. The Dutch papers were not allowed in to-day, so we presume we had a great success.

Mme. Josse Al. [Josse Allard] coming from Holland & Villalobar ditto, brought news that the English say the war will be finished for September. Marthe Kervyn's "sailor" said it would be over in July, & that there are 850.000 men round Bruges where a great battle is expected. Please God save dear old Bruges!

FRIDAY, APRIL 13

Mme W. has had news, through Bréda,[28] of the murder of her brother-in-law, Mr. Nix [Nicholas] Bunting, governor of the Province of Tver. He was killed in the Government House, which was plundered. His wife & five daughters have taken refuge with her sister, Mme. D at Petrograde.[29] God help them! No snow yesterday, the first time for many days.

We heard the cannon.

From the little we can make out from the papers, we are anxious about the Socialists in Russia—they seem to want to force the moderate Government to make peace??? . . .

SATURDAY, APRIL 14

Mme. Frantz W. [Wittouck] came to tea & brought us the persistent rumour that war will be over in a month or two. Mr. Cavalcanti, the Brazil Chargé d'affaires, who is leaving Belgium for the Havre, owing to the rupture of Brazil with Germany, feels confident he will be back here in two months![30] . . .

Had a letter from Dick, of the 11th, he was struggling with a fit of the blues. My February parcel hasn't reached him. . . . I <u>don't</u> like the idea that I spend my money to

---

[28] The Dutch border town of Breda.

[29] At least two of these daughters came to live in Brussels eventually: Marie de Bunting (b. 1898) married Micha Wittouck in 1925 but died young; Sophie (b. 1912) applied for Belgian nationality in 1955, after having lived in Brussels for decades.

[30] Brazil broke off diplomatic relations early in 1917 and then declared war on the Central Powers in October 1917.

feed the famished Boches. Had a card from poor Melle Cazé, still at Rochefort with the La Fère réfugiés, doesn't yet know if she will be allowed to come, Mme. Frantz W. [Wittouck] has been to von Moltke[31] about her.

SUNDAY, APRIL 15

... How will the battle of Arras end! shall we take back St. Quentin? What will be decided in Russia? separate peace exacted by the people, as the horrible paper (boche) *La Belgique* wants to make us believe, or will she remain true to our alliance? I wonder if the Czarina did betray us as they say, & cause the catastrophe that deprived us of Kitchener.

MONDAY, APRIL 16

A stormy, windy night again, so bad for our brave fighters, God help them all the world over, on land & on sea.

No news whatever, but I like the idea of the *Daily Chronicle*: make peace with the German people, but not with the Hohenzollerns.

The Public School children returned to school to-day, after the Easter vacation, but were sent home for a week: too cold to hold classes & no coal for fires. The "astronomers" at the Uccle Observatory say they can't explain the present extraordinary cold & disturbances of atmosphere: the south wind is icy & ... so on. . . .

TUESDAY, APRIL 17

A cold damp, snow wintry day again, alas! . . . The cannon very audible all the time.

An article in the *Belgique* (boche) from Berlin, saying the Dutch complain of their sinking so many C.R.B. boats. . . . [T]hey try to justify & explain, very lamely, as usual.

There is so much about "peace" now in the few things one finds to read, that I begin to think this book will perhaps see the end of the war. Please God <u>many</u> blank pages may remain, & that the last I write may be about "honourable" peace & not a makeshift.

WEDNESDAY, APRIL 18

Great excitement to-day at the news of the great success of the French between Reims & Soissons. The German papers say it is the greatest battle that ever was in

---

[31] Hans-Adolf von Moltke of the German Foreign Office was appointed to the Political Department in Brussels in February 1915.

this war & out of it. More than 40 thousand prisoners between us all on the West Front this week. Please God the success may soon be definite & end the war.[32] ...

Real winter weather again all the morning, snow all the time, everything soaked, I wonder how the poor soldiers can fight through it all.

God help & make them victorious!

THURSDAY, APRIL 19

This morning came the news of the death of Baron von Bissing, General Governor of Belgium, with whom I had an interview in July 1915, about Dick's nationality.[33] We consider this death rather a disadvantage for us, for, in spite of the systematic attacks of the "*Libre Belgique*",[34] we fear we might have a worse man than von Bissing. . . . I think his mission in Belgium was far from pleasant. Villalobar & van Vollenhoven both went off to the Hague yesterday, quite unexpectedly, concerning the C.R.B. question. . . . Holland objects to the C.R.B. boats being destroyed as they continually are by the Boches.[35]

FRIDAY, APRIL 20

To-day, von Bissing's coffin, after having been taken off to the Conservatoire (I suppose for some religious service) was taken processionally to the Gare du Nord, to be sent to Germany. Restaurants & places of amusement had to be closed.

After my visit to him in July 1915, I told "Eicholt" [*sic*] he had received me like an English gentleman. . . . Eicholt said sneeringly "An <u>English</u> gentleman! There is your English conceit!" I replied: until quite recently it was taken as a compliment to be called *compared to* an English gentleman, all over the world, & I daresay you have been compared to one (he has lived years in England) without ever resenting it! ... He made no reply to that![36]

SATURDAY, APRIL 21

Nothing very special to-day; we seem to be getting on very well by degrees, oh! if it could be a little quicker! After all we went through about being compelled to give

---

[32] In the event, the French Chemin des Dames offensive was a disaster.

[33] Von Bissing died in Brussels at age seventy-three.

[34] The longest-running underground newspaper of occupied Belgium, the *Libre Belgique*, had published repeated attacks on Von Bissing.

[35] The CRB held vessels in English ports in the spring of 1917 after several food relief ships were sunk by German submarines. The Spanish and Dutch had to work to reestablish assurances for the cargoes before relief resumed.

[36] Eicholt remains unidentified.

up brass & copper to the Boches, & their repeated visits to houses to enforce the quantity, the following is very characteristic of their usual lies.... [MT inserted an excerpt from the March 29 German *Königsberger Allgemeine Zeitung*. The article blamed Belgium's misery on the Belgian Government's decision to take the deposits of the National Bank when it left in August 1914. The article went on to claim that the ensuing misery had now reached a point where Belgians had to sell their copper and brass to get by. MT added the punctuation to the final sentence, which read "For humanitarian! reasons, the military authorities buy them at very advantageous prices to the sellers!!!"]

SUNDAY, APRIL 22

A bright, clear day, north wind, and cannon <u>so</u> <u>loud</u>, <u>all</u> <u>the</u> <u>time</u>. While I write, at 10 pm, the stars are shining beautifully, and roar of cannon <u>without</u> <u>any</u> <u>interval</u>, like continuous distant thunder—preparing a new attack, I suppose.

Too amusing—in this evening's *Belgischer Kurier*, the Kaiser congratulates his son & their men in Champagne, on the Aisne & everywhere for on their decisive victories, but adds "the battles still continue"!!! ...

MONDAY, APRIL 23, ST. GEORGE'S DAY

I wonder if our brave Englishmen have been able to achieve something special for England's Patron Saint. The cannon was so loud all last night, & especially at dawn, it made our doors & windows rattle. I still hear it in the distance. German airships have been flying about us all day, practicing I presume, in the bright sun & northerly wind. The gardener told me it was the first day he has been able to work in his shirt-sleeves, it being too cold up to this.

TUESDAY, APRIL 24

It was a beautiful bright morning at 6 a.m (really 5, as we have the "summer time" [daylight saving time] since April 15th). I walked over to St. Job to 7:30 mass.[37] When I came out of church there were 6 German aeroplanes in the blue sky, coming from Uccle, their noise accompanied me all the way home. I suppose they were merely exercising. No special news. Heard the cannon again this afternoon, I think something is preparing again on the English front.

To-morrow we return to Bd de W. [Boulevard de Waterloo], the holidays having come to an end, boys resume studies to-morrow morning. What will be the fate of the Allies when we come back to the Fougeraie?

---

[37] A semi-rural church close to La Fougeraie.

WEDNESDAY, APRIL 25

From the Dutch papers I see the English offensive did begin again at dawn, on Monday, 23rd when I heard the cannon so loud & my windows rattling.

To-day the Boche papers have sensational headings, pretending they are victorious—their communiqués so ambiguous, flattering their people . . .

The new governor named for Belgium is von Falkenhausen, I wonder what he will achieve here: von der Goltz & von Bissing didn't survive their post.[38] We returned here from the Fougeraie this morning.

Heard that P.L. has started off . . . on "an interesting journey", without having said a word to anyone. Good luck to the enterprising traveler![39]

THURSDAY, APRIL 26

I made investigations at Central Post office to see if there were any means of writing *or wiring* to dear Val, in the Étape—none, except it serves the furtherance of German affairs. Nevertheless, I tried a 10c post-card pretending something about German lessons— & will see if it comes back to me as it did before. . . .

They say there is now to be a "Centrale" for eggs (after all the rest, & it means their being sent in masses to Bocheland), each person will perhaps be able to buy one, weekly; B^mne de Beeckman has made a provision of a thousand & many are doing likewise.[40]

FRIDAY, APRIL 27

The battle on the Aisne is continuing furiously—many killed I fear, on each side, but we seem to be keeping our ground & pushing on still. Mr. Morel had to see the German who directs the coal department (permission to receive coal) a very nice intelligent man. He told Mr. M. that he has many girl typists in his service, & that they suffer from hunger.[41] He asked Mr. M. if he could let him have jam & vegetables *for them* from the Soleil.[42] Mr. M. answered that for the moment hardly any were left, but that he would send him a price list & that some would be available next August. Oh! August, exclaimed the German, with an eloquent, negative shake of the head,

---

[38] Ludwig Von Falkenhausen served as governor-general from 1917 until the end of the war.

[39] Probably a young man attempting to join the Belgian army.

[40] Paul Wittouck's sister, Emilie. By making "a provision," the baronne was planning for future shortages.

[41] More than 17,000 female auxiliaries (*Etappenhelferinnen*) worked in occupied and front-line jobs in order to free up men for combat in the German army.

[42] Mr. Morel was director of Le Soleil canning factory in Mechelen.

clearly expressing: they will no longer be needed then! (meaning the Boches will be gone by then) let us hope!

SATURDAY, APRIL 28

This is the "Thousandth" day of war *(or is it to-morrow?)*...

I had hoped this terrible war would not have lasted longer than that! My dear Friend, Melle Cazé, who had to evacuate La Fère, was allowed only last evening to arrive in Brussels, *from Rochefort Belgique* with her old mother (86). She came to see me to-day & told me <u>many</u> interesting things about her life at La Fère since the war.

We are told that 3.000 *German* women, who were clamouring for food in Berlin, were shot by "boy scouts" working the "Mitrailleuses" [machine guns], the soldiers having refused to shoot; that cavalry from here have been sent over there to maintain order, & that "admissible"??? proposals of peace are to be made next week ... by the Boches.[43]

SUNDAY, APRIL 29

A long leading article on the 1000th day of war, in the *Belgique* [the censored newspaper], trying to justify its always "making the worst of the war" for <u>us</u>, no matter what the news is.

It speaks of all the square kilometers the Boches have taken in Europe, but ne'er a word of the thousands <u>they</u> have lost in their much beloved colonies.

At Berlin, they seem to be anxious concerning the 1st of May[44]—demonstrations forbidden, work exacted from the Socialists. I am curious to see how the 1st will pass, & what will be proposed for peace the next day.

MONDAY, APRIL 30

I forgot to write. Nothing particular

TUESDAY, MAY 1

A lovely spring day. The night is perfect too, the moon in its first quarter shining brightly & peacefully & yet ... what terrible scenes on the battle-fields not far off! Have just had a letter from Sidonie, Robert has been <u>very</u> bad with measles, his doctor

---

[43] Incorrect rumors, but there were massive protests in April 1917 over severe shortages of food and fuel.

[44] International Workers' Day.

has had 41 mortal cases with children, in his patients only. The illness <u>very</u> bad at Antwerp.

Melle Cazé paid me another visit. Nearly all her belongings were stolen from Linterpoort while the Boches were in the house 3 weeks in 1914.[45] One of her French Grammars they left; at the place [in the book] where *as* an example of a [grammar] rule was given: "Nous n'irons pas à Berlin," [We won't go to Berlin] they had written underneath: "Nous irons à Paris!!!" [We will go to Paris!!!] But the shortcut, through little Belgium, is the longest way we know.

Melle Cazé told me of a German governess, who had been years in France & remained loyal to her country of adoption, having to receive the Germans in the absence of the owners of the Château. When the Boches asked if she could speak German she said she had forgotten it all, except one word: "Schweinen." [*Schweine* means pigs] Jeanne Neuhausen, when in the same predicament, told them: She <u>had</u> been German till the day they treated Belgium as they did, but that since then she had hardly survived the shame of it. . . .

WEDNESDAY, MAY 2

Several men holding posts in the Ministries, that the Germans wanted to send to Namur as the center of the "Wallonie", refused to go, on the ground that all Belgians belong to one country only; they have been dispatched to prison in Germany.[46] . . .

This morning at 5, I was awakened by ~~soldiers~~ military music & regiments going off to the front I presume. We seldom hear musical demonstrations now that they have "d'autres chats à fouetter." [More pressing concerns]

The Refugees' house next door but one to this is full of "chômeurs" [unemployed workers] just out from a long stay in the Brussels' hospitals, where they had to go to get over the pitiful state in which they returned from several months ill-treatment in Germany.

I talked *Flemish* to one of them to-day, a young fellow from Eecloo. He had been 5 months at 20 kilometers from Verdun—forced to work for the Boches. All those men (nearly 100) are waiting now to get passports to return to their respective homes. Last Saturday's battle, the 3rd battle of Arras,[47] seems to have given us but small gain for the <u>many</u> who fell—. . . Dieu nous aide!!!

[45] Castle Linterpoort in Zemst (north of Brussels), a village that had seen heavy fighting and massacres of civilians in August 1914, belonged to the d'Ursel family, who probably employed Miss Cazé at some time.

[46] The occupation authorities had divided Belgium along linguistic lines. Namur became the capital of French-speaking Wallonia. In protest, government officials quit.

[47] The fighting at Arras continued through several waves of attacks in the spring of 1917 with terrible casualties.

THURSDAY, MAY 3

Memorable day. I was presented to His Eminence Cardinal Mercier, Archbishop of Malines, kissed his episcopal ring & asked & received his blessing *on us all* here in the drawing-room.

Mr. W. had responded very generously to some aid needed for one of the War works specifically interesting His Eminence. The Abbé Reyn, who saw Mr. W sev-eral times concerning this, was asked to obtain the Cardinal's autograph on ~~an album~~ the cover of a blotter on which Mme. W. is collecting interesting signatures of "per-sonalities" during the war.[48]

The Cardinal's reply was, that he would pay a visit to Mme. W. & sign the blot-ter in her own home. He did this, most graciously; the boys & I were called down to be presented & exchanged a few words. Our mutual impression was very "sym-pathique", I knew already how charming & simple this eminent Eminence is, & was so glad that Mr. & Mme. W. should know & appreciate him otherwise than by his remarkable writings that defend us against the Germans & comfort & encourage us. He presented Mme. W. with a new work of his, (limited to a few copies) on the manner in which Christian charity demands us to think of & treat our enemies the Germans. (I will comment it when read.)

To-day arrived the new Governor of Belgium: von Falkenhausen—on paper he looks like a hard, rapacious bird of prey.

The cardinal's opinion of the departed governor, von Bissing was is that he was humane, inclined to justice, but weak, easily led, & not very intelligent, he told us he prayed for his soul.

FRIDAY, MAY 4

Met Miss Aherne. She hopes to get away to Holland & Ireland, the Dutch Legation is working for her & two other English women to get passports, but she says the English government forbids (for the moment) any English people to cross the sea. . . .

SATURDAY, MAY 5

Florrie D. who lives near the d'Assche's mansion, where the new governor of Belgium, B^m von Falkenhausen lives, tells me he is very frightened of being blown up, & that is why he prefers living in town, to Trois Fontaines, the country place of Mr. Orban, where von Bissing had elected domicile.[49] The present

---

[48] MT refers to a new vocational school in Schaarbeek (Brussels). In late 1915, in spite of the war, Mercier had decided to go ahead with the building project and enlisted Reverend Théophile Reyn to solicit funds among Belgium's elite. By 1917, the first pupils enrolled in what is today the Institut Cardinal Mercier.

[49] Von Bissing lived in the château of Trois-Fontaines in Vilvoorde outside of Brussels. Ludwig von Falkenhausen resided in the Vandernoot-d'Assche mansion in central Brussels,

man is going to have the Square in front of his house closed to the public, & everything that enters the Beauffort's house next door, has to be examined!!! It is more pitiful every day, to see the extenuated, feeble, pinched faces of all those I meet—even people who can afford to pay, can't buy sufficient food, it is not to be found. . . .

SUNDAY, MAY 6

. . . What is the result of the 4th battle of Arras??? Please God the cavalry, tanks & all the Germans <u>say</u> they <u>spy</u> behind our ranks, may enter into action <u>very</u> soon & make them hurry off. How weary we are of them!!!!! *Belgischer Kurier* announces this evening that Millioukof has had to resign.[50] What can be expected in Russia???

MONDAY, MAY 7

The make-believe "German business" post card I sent to Val on the 26th of April reached her; to-day I got a reply, in the same style, written on May 3rd, so I will try to continue this to tell her I am alive.

The French have got to the top of the famous "Chemin des Dames" & made more than 5 thousand prisoners. On the whole I have a feeling that on our front these titanic battles must be the last, such huge, unheard of massacres cannot be continued for very long, the Germans are losing too many of their best reserve men. I read Cardinal Mercier's "Les vertus pastorales des temps actuels" [today's priestly virtues] that he gave Mme. W. on Thursday, very interesting.

TUESDAY, MAY 8

A balmy soft rainy day, D.G. [Deo Gratias] it was so necessary for the land. I met Alec & Lena Ford. He was as optimistic as ever about the war, I hope he speaks the reality: that the Boche sub-marines won't be able to famish England. The terrific struggle of nations is getting daily harder & harder, how can it end?!!!

I sent a 10c post card to Val, "<u>Affaires</u>" of course in the corner!!! Spoke of her buying a Boche illustrated paper. . . . Darchambeau told me 10.000 meters of his materials have to go to the Germans—he is paid for them, his cost price with 30 to 40% more, but he has to struggle for it.

the private residence of King Albert before he acceded to the throne in 1909. The Beauffort mansion was located around the corner.

[50] Pavel Milyukov, foreign minister under Russia's first Provisional Government. He resigned in May 1917 after street protests against the continuing war.

WEDNESDAY, MAY 9

... The Étienne Visarts have suffered terribly from the Boches, Mr. Ét. V. & his son are in a camp in Germany, Mme. V has been turned out of her house, Suzanne been tracked by them & is finally at Steenhault, but Mme. V. not allowed to come here. Masses of trees are being cut down on all the estates in Flanders, more than 300 at Oydonck & the legendary walnut trees in front of the castle.[51] The Spoelberch's avenue at Deurle is doomed also.[52] What next???

THURSDAY, MAY 10

I have an idea that things are going badly for "Kaiserism" in Germany. . . . We hear that someone attempted to kill him & that a socialist sang the "Marseillaise" in the Reichstag! I think Democracy & Socialism will be the cause of the end of the war; I fancy it can't continue so much longer with so much talk of Peace, Peace on all sides.

The town of Mons is condemned to pay 500.000 marks, because an aviator threw 3 or 4 bombs of on Rupprecht de Bavière's motorcar (brother-in-law of Queen Elisabeth of Belgium, Melle Chalaud knew him at Court), without killing him.[53] Food getting so scarce for cattle, even the craze for keeping rabbits is dying out, no more food to be had.

FRIDAY, MAY 11

Something must be very much changed in Germany for the Censorship to have allowed Maximilien Harden to write such an article in the Zukunft, I think it was.[54] He tries to make the Germans realise the important significance of having America against them & wants peace before the States can be quite ready. This article not having been suppressed means a great change in the German mind—I think the Government ordered it perhaps, to prepare the people to want peace at any price. The Boche malady just now, here, is to insist upon everybody being either Flemish or Walloon—& the unanimous answer is "We are Belgians." Ctesse de Smet[55] told me the "functionaries" of the ministries she knew when her husband was Prime Minister

[51] Ooidonk Castle, west of Ghent.

[52] Deurle Castle, west of Ghent; "avenue" refers to a tree-lined lane.

[53] Rupprecht, crown prince of Bavaria, commander in the northernmost sector of the Western Front. His late first wife was sister to the Belgian Queen Elisabeth.

[54] Maximilian Harden, a German journalist and editor of the Berlin weekly *Die Zukunft*. The issue that MT referred to was devoted to the US entry into war, which Harden considered a devastating blow to Germany's chances, and which he blamed on Germany's foreign policy.

[55] Marie Morel de Westgaver, widow of the former prime minister, Count Paul de Smet de Naeyer.

are having a bad time, between remaining faithful to their King & the Boches try-ing to get them to acknowledge the dividing of Belgian into two parts—their last insanity.

To-day great reception for all the Boche personalities at the new Governor's von Falkenhausen. The Burgomasters of Brussels & several adjoining communes are arrested for not consenting to order enclosure wire to be cut down & given up. Engineers of Namur were called upon to construct bridges over the Meuse??? They have found reasons to refuse to do so. A great many men are being requisitioned again just now, to make roads in Belgium, especially an enormously wide new one, from Virton to the German frontier. Oh! if it could be for their speedy return thither!

The Bavarian minister von Hertling, just back from Vienna, has <u>astounded</u> eve-ryone by preaching peace without any annexations & with concessions—amazing![56] after the King of Bavaria's ferocity for conquests.

I had 4 more of the poor convalescent *Flemish* chômeurs here to-day & heard their tale of woe! These had been very kindly treated by the German nurses in the hospitals they were in in France (sick with bad treatment & famine) before coming here, . . . poor fellows! I expect one from Bruges to-morrow.

SATURDAY, MAY 12

I went to see Mme. Cazé, the old lady (86) who spent 30 hours in the German cattle van, coming from La Fère to Rochefort when the former was evacuated. She is as-tonishing to be as alert after all she went through, & the loss of her home & belong-ings. She doesn't know where her son & his family have been sent. One of our men servants has a cousin, a school teacher in the province of Namur. She had to lodge Germans. One of the officers told her they are in a very bad way; that their official reports about success are all fake; that they had a big ammunition depot blown up in Champagne, 100 men killed, & out of 1.000 men travelling in a train recently, 16 only escaped our aviators' bombs.

SUNDAY, MAY 13

24 years to-day I sailed for N.Y. We are having <u>very</u> <u>hot</u>, sultry weather. Went to La Fougeraie in the little cart, garden & all vegetation simply perfect, what a dif-ference with 3 weeks ago when we were still there, & snow had only ceased three days before. I heard the <u>cannon</u> quite plainly all the time, a continual rumble, & it had been so all night. God grant there may soon be something decisive! . . . Pity for our brave men on land & on sea, near & far, for the latter are terribly out of the "lime-light."

---

[56] Georg Von Hertling, prime minister of Bavaria, became German chancellor on November 1, 1917.

MONDAY, MAY 14

A good storm shower this evening cleared the air & did no end of good to the country. I saw a man fall down insensible in the street, & helped him, he was taken to the hospital. I fear similar cases will be frequent *in the heat*, everyone is so exhausted from want & misery. Mr. Lemonnier, the f.f. [*faisant fonction*, i.e., substitute] burgomaster of Brussels is sent to Germany, because he wouldn't give up the barbed wire in Brussels—he says it shall not be given for war purposes, the Boches answer they consider it as "arms" in which case they may want our knives, forks, railings etc.[57] . . .

TUESDAY, MAY 15

. . . To-morrow Mr. Lemonnier f.f. de bourgmestre, is to be sent to Germany. The "Conseil Communal" [Municipal Council] had a very brief sitting to-day, & decided to hold out about the barbed wire, & <u>not</u> give it up to the Boches.

The *Belgique* says that a Socialist paper of Amsterdam announces that all the employees of banks, prisons etc are to take their holiday before August, because it is supposed Peace will be made then, & that there will be much work for everybody & no question of holidays.

WEDNESDAY, MAY 16

All the people interested in the "Union Patriotique des Femmes Belges" were invited to-day to visit the new premises & see the people at work. It is so nicely installed, Rue des Chartreux; all the services are there: needlework, cutting out, lace department, & the 2 departments of "Jouets Belges," [toys] the wooden ones that men make & the rag ones made by women. I congratulated Melle van den Plas most heartily on her great achievement; the ladies on the Committee have made a splendid success of the whole thing. I spoke to Carola there, & to V^{ctsse} Louis de Spoelberch,[58] who is in the toy department, B^{mne} de Broqueville talked to me for quite a few seconds before I *quite* realized it was she, so very changed & thin she has grown.[59] Told me about Maud's ambulance, how she is the only woman in it, with an excellent Dr. & staff of men.[60] The very worst cases are brought there *St. Pierre-Brouque in*

[57] For his continued lack of cooperation with German orders, Lemonnier was arrested in May 1917 and sent to prison in Germany, together with another burgomaster of Greater Brussels. Gille et al., *Cinquante mois d'occupation allemande*, 3:210–212, 225, 236.

[58] Françoise "Fanchette" de Woelmont, the wife of Viscount Louis de Spoelberch.

[59] Berthe d'Huart, the wife of Prime Minster and Minister of War Charles de Broqueville. He was with the government in French exile. She spent 1914–1917 in Belgium with her daughter, Myriam.

[60] Maud Bainbridge was an English nurse working at a Belgian-run dressing station close to the front (near Hoogstade) and may have worked at more advanced stations as well. She

motors, after immediate operation & while still under chloroform, thanks to which many have been saved. Maud has a room "underground" with a candle to light her, but gets spells of rest which she spends at Broqueville's villa.[61] Mme. De B. said this ambulance will be the first to follow the Allies into Brussels—God grant it may be soon! & that we shall hear more of dear old Maud's glory. . . .

THURSDAY, MAY 17, ASCENSION DAY

This morning at 7, pilgrimage mass, at Ste. Gudule, in honour of Notre Dame de la Délivrance. The boys & I went. Great devotion. Good sermon by a French Barnabite . . . Père Prévost. Plenty of Boche Military present, I wonder what they think of such ceremonies! . . .

Mr. W. has received notice from the Uccle authorities that he is to give up all the wire of the Fougeraie enclosures. Letter from Dick: for 6 weeks he gets an extra parcel weekly from a lady at the Hague; the last contained 1 lb butter, 6 eggs, tin milk, & soap. D.G. [Deo Gratias]

FRIDAY, MAY 18

. . . Mme. De Beeckman told us at lunch that all the peasants bringing in big baskets of eggs by the Place Dailly tram had to unpack them all at a country station, to prove to the Germans they were not smuggling anything forbidden (Our breakfast eggs cost now 75 centimes). The trunks she had in the luggage van were not opened, though they did contain a little butter "tout au fond." [all the way on the bottom] She has often had confiscated butter that was being brought to her from her estate.

SATURDAY, MAY 19

Little of the war. The Italians seem to be progressing on the Isonzo, & the Boches own to having at last "abandoned Bullecourt" to us. The Papal Nuncio, Mgr Locatelli, called on Mme. W. He had just returned from Luxembourg, & had been hearing what the (some) Germans think: that now, they don't want peace!!! but to fight to the end, confident in their 600,000 new yearly recruits; that they mean to keep at least the Flemish part of Belgium etc, but that doesn't impress me & I don't think much of Mgr L. as a diplomatist. The contractor who placed the wire enclosures of the Fougeraie, went to speak with the Boches on the subject, but they would only speak

was decorated by King Albert on June 7, 1920, for her work with the Belgian army's medical services (*London Gazette*, June 7, 1920).

[61] The village of Saint-Pierre-Brouck, southwest of Dunkirk. Zeneghem Yard, a British munitions depot, was installed nearby.

Flemish with him, so as he doesn't know Flemish, they didn't converse. Humbugs! with their Flemish!

SUNDAY, MAY 20

I've just finished reading one of Jules Huret's books on "l'Allemagne: Rhin et Westphalie" [Germany: Rhine and Westphalia].[62] Very interesting & pleasant to read; one can picture every detail that is related. It was written in 1906 & Huret assures us that "Guillaume II est un grand pacifiste." [Wilhelm II is a great pacifist] All he was told concerning the probabilities of a war was quite the reverse by August 1914, alas! . . .

MONDAY, MAY 21

A part of Brussels is punished by the Boches, have to be home at 6 pm till 4 am: someone stole something from a Boche cart, the crowd helped the thief to escape or took his part, hooted the Boche & their police, & I believe came to blows.

Passing by the Palais des Académies, I saw & heard a German band playing for the convalescent soldiers there *in the garden* (I wonder if there are any of <u>ours</u> in the number). Each time I witness that scene, my heart aches because they are not our convalescents & our music. <u>When</u> will it be! The barbed wire of the Fougeraie (part of it) is being taken down to go to the enemy—it makes my blood boil, but not to give any (the same as for the brass) means they take the whole & our money besides, as a fine.

TUESDAY, MAY 22

Went to see the sick—they all suffer so much from the terribly high prices of everything—eggs still 52c each & will probably get dearer still. At the "Alimentation" one is allowed to buy so little; there must be <u>many</u> poor people who die of sheer misery, exhaustion from slow starvation.

The Boches made perquisitions in all the houses round Petit Bigard, to see if the inhabitants were concealing any flour. 10 kilos were found at the Curé's [Curate's] (of Zuen) so he will get into trouble, yet what is a provision of 10 kilos of flour in a decent house![63] No news of the fighting to-day. How are we faring???

---

[62] Huret, a journalist, wrote several books on Germany before the war.
[63] Zuun, a parish of Klein Bijgaarden (Sint-Pieters-Leeuw), southwest of Brussels.

WEDNESDAY, MAY 23

Mr. Gahan, the English clergyman who assisted Miss Cavell just before she was shot called on me yesterday while I was out & I went to see him to-day.[64] I should have liked to ask him about Miss Cavell—perhaps later on.

Things seem to be settling in Russia—what will the Allies in the West say to their proposal of Peace "sans annexions et sans indemnité"!!! [Without annexations and compensations] There is a rumour that our last success near Arras is greater than what the Boches own to in the news they let pass.

Articles in the *Bruxellois* & the *Belgique* [two censored newspapers] say that America is forcing Holland to join us in the war, or else supplies will be stopped—but I don't believe the it.

THURSDAY, MAY 24

Melle Bolo told me a cousin of hers, a pretty girl of 23, was marched off to St. Gilles prison, last Monday, by 3 civilian Boches, who made a perquisition in her father's house (he is a barrister) & found 3 *Libre Belgique* in her room. They suppose it is not on account of the *L.B.*, but for an unknown (to her) reason they came. Events will show. . . . We hear the Boches are making a big retreat from our front, & that the Kronprinz is at the Château de Waulsort. If latter is true, it would mean a big move back of the B's. [the Boche] . . .

FRIDAY, MAY 25

Mr. Kattendyk (the charming Dutchman of the Legation who is told off to attend to the interests of the English & is much liked by them all) lunched here to-day. (He & his wife, half English, are friends of the W's & habitués of the house)

He had a private conversation with me about what is best to be done for several English girls here which proved to me once more how good & earnest he is & just the man to help us. . . . He also thinks Austria will soon make a separate peace with Italy. We are very anxious about a new arrêté [decree] ordering everyone to declare the trees of certain sorts they possess in their grounds. If those of the Fougeraie have to be sacrificed, it <u>will</u> spoil the beauty of the place.

Kaiser, Hindenbourg & Bethman-Holweg [Bethmann Hollweg] were all together behind a hill the other day in Champagne—admiring the French fighting I presume. Mme. W. has heard, that her brother-in-law, the Governor of Tver was killed in the street, by a single shot, during the Revolution. She was relieved to know it, having feared his end might have been more painful. . . .

---

[64] The Reverend Horace Stirling Townsend Gahan, the British vicar of Christ Church in Brussels from 1914 to 1922, had spent time with Edith Cavell on the eve of her execution. His reports on her last hours were widely known.

SATURDAY, MAY 26

The latest sensational rumour, supposed to have come from "Le Temps" is, that the Vatican is surrounded by Italian troops, because someone there is accused of having "wireless" with the enemy. Of course we thought at once of some German or Austrian belonging to the Vatican—but it strongly needs confirmation.

Last night, the new German Governor of Belgium, gave his first dinner, to the "Dips" [diplomats] here; it is said the "menu" was: soup, scrambled eggs with tomatoes & roast pork! How edifying is this Spartan simplicity, trotted out specially, no doubt, for the benefit of the neutrals!!!

Mme. W's brother-in-law Bunting was killed by a single shot, by one of the soldiers who were taking him from a revolutionary committee to be incarcerated somewhere. the Death was instantaneous, but the corpse received several "coups de baïonette" [bayonet thrusts], was stripped, dragged through the streets & into his room in the Government House. His wife, who was away with her daughters at a friend's house, for security, went & laid out her husband's corpse. What a tragic end for the fascinating man I am told he used to be! R.I.P. . . .

WHIT[65] SUNDAY, MAY 27

It appears there were no eggs on the Governor's menu, on Friday, simply: soup, tomato salad, roast pork & wine jelly for dessert. The dinner was at 8 pm. At 9 the Gov. told von der Lancken to dismiss the guests, as he was not well. The Papal Nuncio & Villalobar said they had ordered their motors for 10, so they were allowed to converse in a little drawing-room! The King of Spain interceded for the fine avenue of trees, at Beloeuil, Prince de Ligne's fine place, to be spared, but the Boches took no account of that, & the trees have been felled, in spite of the artistic beauty of the place, the garden was created by Le Nôtre, XVIIth century.

MONDAY, MAY 28

Met Mme. De Broqueville again at an art exhibition in favour of "l'Union patriotique des femmes Belges". She told me a few more interesting things & how the Boches are giving pleasant lectures in <u>Flemish</u> country places, in order to get in sympathy with the Flemish. . . .

TUESDAY, MAY 29

The English communiqués announce 76 people killed & 174 wounded by German aeroplanes in a town on the southeastern coast???[66] R.I.P.

[65] Whitsuntide (Pentecost), an official holiday in the United Kingdom until 1970.

[66] The first large-scale aerial bombing raid using airplanes (Gothas) rather than zeppelins.

I wonder all the time, how my dear friends in England are faring—if dead or living! When shall I see them again!

The papers say that the "soldiers & workmen in Russia have demanded, in an immense majority to know the terms of the famous secret treaties between the Allies & the Czar, of which there has been so much talk lately." What will result from that, & what can the treaties contain???

WEDNESDAY, MAY 30

... We leave for the Fougeraie to-morrow, for our usual summer's stay, many people feel it won't be the usual season; they think the Étape may draw nearer or that we may come back in a hurry to greet the Allies! God grant we may. This is the 3rd summer removal since the war. I've just had Philip Gibb's [Gibbs'] book, "The soul of war" lent me; it has been round to a good many here in Brussels.[67] ...

THURSDAY, MAY 31

Came to the Fougeraie; very tired. Heard nothing whatever of the war, & only read *La Belgique*, which seemed more perverse & perfidious than ever to-day. It never gives but the most discouraging bits of news out of all sorts of papers—a horrid paper to read, but one must, to know how the Boches give the communiqués.

I read last evening, that the Germans in the States are starting the idea of an ~~American~~ German Republic to put an end to Kaiserism. . . . [W]ould it were true!

FRIDAY, JUNE 1

I am astounded to read that <u>after all</u> the French & English Socialists <u>are</u> going to join the Russian & German at the Stockholm conference of June 15th. I think there must be "anguille sous roche" [there's something fishy going on] to account for this abrupt change of intentions. . . . What if it were to overthrow Kaiserism & end the war!!![68]

Mme. De Borman-de Selliers, the champion tennis player, whom I knew as a jolly girl, nicknamed "Mimi Kermesse" ["Funfair Mimi"] for her jovial temper, has been electrocuted as she was passing the electric barbed wire to get into Holland, likewise a Mr d'Andrimont, who was being passed in a barrel that deviated, & the [*sic*] touched the wire as he put out his hand to balance it. Alas! alas! R.I.P.[69]

---

[67] Gibbs was a journalist who published this account in 1915.

[68] The Petrograd soviet called for a conference of antiwar socialists in Stockholm. While the German and Habsburg governments agreed to hand out passports to allow delegates to attend, the US, French, and British governments refused to do so. There was a Stockholm conference in September 1917, but it did not assemble a transnational coalition.

[69] This rumor was only partially correct. Anne de Borman, née de Selliers de Moranville, a champion tennis player, died in 1962. But the businessman Léon Marie d'Andrimont was indeed killed.

SUNDAY, JUNE 3

I didn't write last night, nothing to note down.

They say it is not true about Mimi Kermesse having been killed passing into Holland, let us hope it is not....

We are led to believe there will soon be a general offensive, on all our fronts....

... Our use of electricity & gas is limited—only 30 cubic meters *plus the half of last year's consommation* per month of latter to each gas-meter. We feel the war in every detail of life, I wonder how it is in England!

MONDAY, JUNE 4

... Mr. Ribot's speech at the Chambre des Députés was a grand success of eloquence, but he won't give the Socialists their passports for the Stockholm conference.... What will the English government do? ...

TUESDAY, JUNE 5

"Contrôle" day at the Meldeamt. I wonder how many more months we shall have to go! An ideal day, so bright & warm, real Italian weather.

The cannon is roaring all the time, without any intervals, I suppose it is in Flanders we hear it. God grant we may at last have the success needed, to bring these cruel times to an end.

I see that Philip Gibbs, the journalist, though travelling about as near as possible to the fighting in August 1914, really knew no more than we did, shut up in Brussels.

How unready France & England were for war, & how ready & waiting for the signal were the well equipped & trained Boches—that is why I think we are marvellously strong to check them as we do.

WEDNESDAY, JUNE 6

The bread ration is not to be lessened yet, Vollenhoven having obtained a loan of wheat from Holland. Deo Gratias! I wrote a petition to the new Governor General, B^m von Falkenhausen, to be remitted by Vollenhoven, asking that the boys may make use of their bicycles for going to school. Heard the cannon again. I wonder what will result from the continual artillery duel at Wystchaete [Wytschaete]! Would it might make the Boches flit from the Lille district! I am told Comines & Menin are to be evacuated. I read that Ghent was made lively last Friday night by bombs & fire at the gas factory, (poor dear Valérie) & the Bruges Canal & Docks on Sunday night (poor little Kervyn boys!)

THURSDAY, JUNE 7

Fêté du St. Sacrement

... The latest Boche placard has caused great sorrowful disarray: all the mattresses & woollen pillows <u>have</u> to be declared; the communes have to see to the execution of the order & the delivery of the quantity of wool requisitioned. What next??? How lucky are those who <u>don't</u> live under German invasion!!! ...

FRIDAY, JUNE 8

A lady I know sees Bⁿ Albert Ruzette, from Bruges, once a month, when he comes to Brussels for the "Comité d'Alimentation." He told her people at Bruges can no longer sleep between midnight & 5 pm, on account of the Allies bombarding the Docks & military places; that 43 houses were destroyed at St. Gilles, fortunately no lives lost. A German officer told him the taking away of the wool of our mattresses is going to be a serious matter, only a certain scanty weight will be left per person. The Boches want it to weave, for making clothes.

There is a great English offensive in the Ypres sector. This evening's *Kurier* owns <u>we</u> have already taken Wytschaete ... & Messines.[70] The big battle seems going to extend northwards, on the Belgian front to the sea.... God grant we may succeed in driving the Boches out of Flanders this time! & may the sons of those I know be preserved till the end! ...

I talked to-day with ~~the~~ a tram "contrôleur". He told me the reason of the penury of trams, (there are never seats enough or even sufficient standing place) is due to the fact that it is utterly impossible to keep any of the vehicles in repair, no materials therefore being obtainable.

Yesterday Joseph the coachman was told his son was being set free on coming out of prison, that he was not going to be sent to Germany. I was agreeably astonished. To-day when the poor man went to await the boy's release, he was told his son <u>was</u> going to Germany, to-morrow. Joseph hurried home to prepare a parcel for the boy to take away, & on his return to the prison was told he had left last evening.... Poor Joseph is in despair & that is the way we sufferers of "Invasion" are morally tortured by the Boches when they can't do worse. I have nearly finished Gibb's [Gibbs'] "Soul of the War" & feel I have seen all he relates, that was in 1915, & things have got even much worse since then and <u>oh!</u> the blood-shed & tortures moral & physical endured all the time!!!

---

[70] The British launched a series of successful attacks and detonated a record number of mines (nineteen) in tunnels under the German lines in order to take control of Messines Ridge and some of the towns nearby.

SATURDAY, JUNE 9

Just heard the news of the death (killed at war,) of young Freddy d'Huart, R.I.P.[71] no details yet; will see his mother on Monday. I called on her a short time ago, & all was then so peaceful & serene in that family. *It's* the 2nd nephew of Broqueville's killed....

The English have already taken Wytschaete & Messines, & other places, 5 thousand prisoners, & booty. God grant we may have complete victory there!!!

It is incredible to see how thin so many people are getting.... I have lost 10 kilos ½ in weight since the end of 1915, tant mieux for me, but it is bad for so many who lose flesh from starvation....

SUNDAY, JUNE 10

I haven't seen to-day's communiqués this evening—it is very trying not to know how the battle continues in Flanders. We don't know anything more than yesterday. God grant we may at last push through farther than the first lines....

MONDAY, JUNE 11

We have had some descriptions, from the Dutch papers, of the battle of Messines & the manner in which it & other villages have been completely wiped out. I wonder how proprietor-ship of land can ever be re-established, all land marks must have disappeared.

I have just finished Philip Gibbs' "Soul of the War"—he was already utterly disgusted with it all in 1915—what <u>must</u> he feel now, two years later! We had <u>his</u> description of the battle of Messines in yesterday's communiqués. Storm & rain again to-day, I do hope it is not bad for our front. What loss of young lives again!!! God grant <u>all</u> the souls are safe with Him!

TUESDAY, JUNE 12

Have heard nothing of the war; but of Peace, I read in "La Bonne Semence"[72] that there has been a grand religious ceremony, in the Vienna Cathedral, & that before Cardinal Piffl, the Emperor & Empress made a vow, repeated by the Cardinal & all present: That Vienna would build a church to "Our Lady of Peace" if God grants a speedy Peace to end the war. How we all long for it! but not if the Boches continue to say: "We are victorious."

---

[71] Baron Alfred d'Huart died on June 2, 1917, in Calais. His mother was Marie-Henriette de Spoelberch.

[72] A Catholic periodical.

WEDNESDAY, JUNE 13

Storms & rain & sunshine again to-day, & so hot. Three years [ago] poor Mr. Frantz W. died suddenly, we went to a memoriam mass for him.

It is rumoured that the King of Greece (poor weakling!) has abdicated in favour of his second son.[73] Also that von Bissing left a document in which he urges Prussia to stick to Belgium, & to make Germans especially of the Flemish. . . . A nice incentive to the realization of the Peace the Boches are clamouring for!

THURSDAY, JUNE 14

It seems that von Bissing's "Political Will" is scandalous with regard to Belgium & astonished all those who thought him a just, peaceful man. . . . Even the Boches don't print it in their papers here *Belgique* & *Bruxellois*.

The abdication of the "weakling" Constantine in favour of his second son, brings Venizelos back to power, & Greece, let us hope, to common sense. . . .

FRIDAY, JUNE 15
FEAST OF THE SACRED HEART

A piping hot day, but no storm or rain. Cannon all last night & this morning till after noon. We wonder if Ostend was being bombarded. We read to-day of the cruel Boche raid over the East End of London—so many poor people killed—& the children in a school[74] . . . When will these infernal atrocities cease! & what must the fighting-line be like in this terrible heat! Oh! the poor men who are struck down & remain unaided with the sun darding on [piercing] them! God help them & us all! The Boches seem furious about the change of King in Greece. What will Alexander be like!

SATURDAY, JUNE 16

The hottest, sunniest day we've had, 30 centigrade in the shade.

No news from outside, I haven't been to town since Wednesday, but the Boches admit we have been getting on east of Warneton. Those who talk to the Belgians when they are sent to houses (for brass etc etc) always speak of the war as going to finish in August??? When & how will it end! This great heat grieves me for the soldiers in helmets, masks & the rest. . . .

[73] King Constantine, under foreign pressure, abdicated the Greek throne on June 12, 1917, in favor of his second son, Alexander.

[74] This daylight air raid on June 13, 1917, killed more than 160 civilians, including 16 schoolchildren in London's East End.

SUNDAY, JUNE 17

... Nothing of the war, except that Russia doesn't seem to mean to do anything to help us. A superior German officer told someone we know that the Boches will hold out 6 months longer??? No means of getting any tennis balls from Holland or anywhere—it seems the Dutch got 12 thousand dozen for their clubs & matches, but won't let them go. The children played this afternoon with 5 or 6 only & lost some; they finally remain with 2. I don't know what they'll do.

MONDAY, JUNE 18

There was a heavy storm last night, the lightning struck the entrepôt [warehouse] of the Tour & Taxis station, where the Boches have their sack factory (sand sacks for the trenches) & the whole place was burnt....

There are wild rumours of the boches evacuating Ostend but I can't believe it. A man who was allowed to go to Bruges & St. André [Sint-Andries, a suburb of Brugge] says all *there* is dearer even than here. We can't get the quantity of ice we need for the kitchen & the Boches don't allow sufficient coal to produce it, & we are only allowed a certain quantity of electricity & gas monthly.

Quantities of fresh troops pass through Brussels in trains, bound for our front. What a pity that Russia is not now doing what we expected. I fear she will be the cause of prolonged agony.

The Boches only allow a small patch of ground per person for raising potatoes, & the *Belgian* police have to go round & take declarations concerning this, I had one *of them* to see me about it at the B^d [Boulevard de Waterloo] to-day but couldn't satisfy him.

Everybody one met was so pleased about the fire at the Entrepôt [the warehouse at Tour-et-Taxis freight-station], though it means but an atom in the mighty scheme of our tribulations.

TUESDAY, JUNE 19

Had 2 terrible storms to-day. The Cardinal's secretary, who came with him to see us on May 3rd, has been deported to Germany for something he said in the pulpit, I believe.[75] ...

WEDNESDAY, JUNE 20

I went to the service of poor Freddy d'Huart, at Ste Gudule. Many people. The sarcophagus, placed very high & covered with the Belgian flag, the Brabançonne played

[75] Dominican priest Ceslas Rutten, briefly arrested in the middle of Mass. He was interrogated following the arrest of his brother, a high-ranking civil servant caught preparing

by the organ after the "absoutes" [final absolution]—very stirring—but the sight of Boche officers there out of curiosity goes against the grain. When shall we be delivered ofrom them! . . .

THURSDAY, JUNE 21

. . . The doctors say that cases of tuberculosis & mental disease are innumerable— quite comprehensible when everyone (except the favoured few) is underfed & overworried. I feel how essential it is to be properly fed just now in order to keep one's mental equilibrium. What are we going to do for clothes next winter! . . . I begin to fear there will be a 4th winter campaign.

FRIDAY, JUNE 22

Wednesday the 20th inst. [of this month] was the day on which, or before, people had, by order of the Boche government, to declare the number of their mattresses. No one, so to say, took any notice of the order. It is now rumoured that the town is to be punished therefore??? . . .

How delighted dear Mary Burman must be at the immense majority for women's votes in Parliament![76] How war changes all things & so many opinions!

SATURDAY, JUNE 23

The Boches have *this week* taken away all our telephones at the B[oulevar]ᵈ. We have been deprived of the use of them ever since their invasion (nearly 3 years!) I suppose they want to prevent us from reestablishing them as soon as the Allies arrive. . . . When will that be! I wonder if those on the right side realise what our life is, deprived of liberty & subject to so many worries & vexations, all apart from the misery & want of the poor. The Boches buy up all the country produces (before others have a chance) & send it off to Germany. Their theory is that if people are famished in Bocheland, the Belgians have to share the same fate! How long, how long still!!!

SUNDAY, JUNE 24

We hear the cannon again to-night—we hadn't heard it for some time. . . . What will happen in our next move! Will Russia help or betray us.

to escape to the Netherlands to protest the German-led administrative separation of Belgium into Flemish and Wallon halves. Gille et al., *Cinquante mois d'occupation allemande*, 3:281–283.

[76] The British House of Commons voted 385 to 55 in favor of Woman Suffrage on Tuesday, June 19, 1917.

Mlle Cazé was here this afternoon, & told us many interesting things of La Fère before she was evacuated with the 2 thousand remaining inhabitants. The little town was punished for several days because of a witty small boy, hearing the Boches speak of some little victory, said to them: "mais il y a encore deux autres victoires: la prise des matelas et l'enlèvement des cloches"! ["But there are two other victories: the confiscation of mattresses and the taking of the church bells"] Thereupon he was marched off to the Commandanture, & *his parents* being too poor to pay a fine, the town had to expiate his wit. Quite Boche!

MONDAY, JUNE 25

Didn't write.

TUESDAY, JUNE 26

I have a feeling we are getting no nearer the end of the war. All's so unsatisfactory in Russia & we know the truth about nothing. The German soldiers made a perquisition yesterday at Petit Bigard. One of them saw the Socialist German paper, the Voorwaerts [*Vorwärts*], in the manager's pocket, said he was a Socialist, that the soldiers here were forbidden to read the Voorwaerts, that it is a shame their officers amuse themselves & have a good time while the men are sent to the shambles. The manager answered: "Why don't you rebel"—He replied "We can't during war." I suppose there would be a revolution in Prussia if we had a military victory. How long will it take to achieve it!!!

WEDNESDAY, JUNE 27

Last night, towards midnight, the Germans were having maneuvers in the Forest [de Soignes], shooting & marching to & fro, near here, and singing hymns in parts. Their outdoor singing is generally very good. I got up expecting an aerial attack when I heard the shots.

At Tournai, in the étape, life is very hard. Certain people are forced to deliver 5 eggs & a quantity of butter daily to the Boches—in fault of which they are heavily fined, 1 mark per egg wanting & so on. They are forbidden to deliver any private letters; recently a letter was discovered written to a gentleman by his veterinary surgeon, concerning horses & dogs—the two of them were punished, & also the bearer of the letter. When will poor Belgium be free again! May we escape being in the étape!!!

THURSDAY, JUNE 28

We had a big party here this afternoon, for a "conference" given by Mr. Thiebaut on "l'âme Belge" [The Belgian Soul] very eloquent & literary.[77]

He recited, with the greatest perfection Verhaeren's "Tours des Flandres" Tours de Lisseweghe et de Furnes[78] . . . rather comforting in the proofs he gave us of the moral strength & energy of the Belgians of old, telling in those of to-day [sic].

Charles du R. told me the latest of the Carola's boys. God help her & them through the ordeal.[79] We are hearing the cannon again these days. . . . C[tesse] Paulo de Borchgrave was told to-day that the Deutsches Bank [Deutsche Bank] refuses to pay Austrian coupons! If that is so?[80] . . .

FRIDAY, JUNE 29

To-day, 20 well known Belgian gentlemen, amongst them C[te] John d'Oultremont, *Hip. d'Ursel etc.*, were sent off to Germany, as hostages (it is said *as a reprisal* for something done by the Belgians to Germans in the Congo.)[81] At Mons, the Boches are taking all the men, indiscriminately up to the age of 50 for their military works: trenches etc.

The answer came to-day to the boys' application for permission to ride their bicycles to school—a peremptory no. . . .

[77] Composer Henri Thiébaut, the 1895 founder of the Brussels Music and Declamation School.

[78] The Belgian poet Emile Verhaeren, who died in 1916.

[79] MT's friend Carola de Crombrugghe de Picquendaele née Van der Bruggen. "Charles du R." probably refers to Charles Du Roy de Blicquy.

[80] Marie du Passage, spouse of Count Paul "Paulo" de Borchgrave d'Altena. "Coupons" means bonds.

[81] After capturing Tabora in German East Africa in September 1916, colonial armed forces of the Belgian Congo (*Force publique*) took German officials and their families into custody, sending them on to France. In retaliation, the German occupation regime in Belgium deported two (not twenty) men, both elderly aristocrats with ties to the Congo, to Holzminden camp. According to the July 15, 1917, *Chicago Tribune*, orders were given to treat them especially harshly. Hippolyte d'Ursel, a former senator and a governor of the National Bank of Belgium, had large interests in lower Congo. Charles-Jean "John" d'Oultremont, grand marshal of the royal court of Belgium and co-creator of the *Compagnie du Katanga*, died soon after returning home from camp, on December 17, 1917.

SATURDAY, JUNE 30

It rained all day long, without ceasing & spoiled a big charity fête at the Deprêts' Chateau de Sterrebeke, where the entrances were 20 frs, besides other expenses.[82] . . .

SUNDAY, JULY 1

Just had a letter & a photo from Dick—he & two friends look quite tidy & even smart. He says he is getting up courage & patience for another winter at Ruhleben.... Alas! At Mons & Tournai no one is allowed to buy any fruit & hardly any vegetables. All the fruit is absorbed by the Boches. Their soldiers, even in Brussels, complain of being so very badly fed, hardly paid & are bitter because the officers want for nothing & have a good time. They say the new governor in Belgium, von Falkenhausen, is a tipler [sic] & consequently signs death warrants very easily, & that more women have been shot here recently....

MONDAY, JULY 2

Saw Father Lecourt[83] about different things. He & Mr. Kattendyck having concluded that living is now 5 times dearer than in normal times, have obtained a great increase for the English Relief Fund, & I have hopes that Sidonie will benefit by it like all the rest. Ours is a grand country for attending to the welfare of its people in all circumstances!

Great talk about Austria not renewing the alliance with Germany, when the present one expires this month; people are longing for the 10th or the 21st, both dates are mentioned.

Von Falkenhausen's drunkenness is also provides much gossip.

... Father Lecourt told me that the Ruhleben camp is just like a bit of England in Germany, quite [well] run & managed by the English themselves.[84]

Mme. W. heard from C[tsse] John d'Oultremont, all the account of how her husband was arrested on Friday, & sent off, with the 19 other notable men, as hostages, to the camp of Holzminden.[85] Cte d'Oul. is 70 years of age, in a bad state of health. He had received, *while he was Grand Maréchal under Leopold II*, from the Emperor of Germany, the grandest decorations & distinctions possible; his wife, on seeing von

[82] The eighteenth-century château of Sterrebeek belonged to Maurice Despret, a Liberal senator and the president of Belgium's second-largest bank, the Banque de Bruxelles.

[83] Remains unidentified.

[84] In 1915 the prisoners took over the kitchen. Each barracks also had a captain to represent them. The prisoners had their own camp magazine, *In Ruhleben Camp*.

[85] Renée de Mérode, who kept a war diary of her own, and was deeply involved in charity work.

der Lancken about this affair, told him she concludes they themselves can't hold all that in high esteem ~~themselves~~ to act thus with one in his condition.

TUESDAY, JULY 3

10 pm. A glorious moonlight night, not yet dark, it being only in reality 9 pm, just such a moon as 35 months ago the day of the declaration of the war to Belgium. I have just come in from a stroll in the garden, I heard the cannon plainly in the far distance & grieved that fellow men are full of hatred & destroying each other still on such a peaceful night.

When will the change come! I often think it wonderful more people don't go mad, if they think as much as I do, of the terrible events. Dieu nous aide! When shall we be delivered from our enemies! 35 months under the odious, grey control!!! What will it feel like to be free!

WEDNESDAY, JULY 4

The best news we've had for a long time! A good Russian victory in Galicia, with 10 thousand prisoners & about 150 officers! God & the Russians be praised! The latter after 4 months inactivity.[86]

Let us hope they "mean it" at last. If only they had fought while we did so on our front! What will Germany do without all she used to get from America, through the neutral countries! I've just read very accurate English statistics on that question. I presume poor Belgium will be super-drained—the people who have fruit in their gardens in the Mons & Tournai districts are not allowed to touch it—it goes to the Boches. How we should suffer if that privation touched us here at the Fougeraie.

THURSDAY, JULY 5

. . . The smaller trees, in the Forest, quite near us, & near the public roads, are being cut down, in broad daylight, by people who help themselves to the wood, and sell it about 30 to 40 frs the stère [cubic metre of wood].

The keepers have no control whatever, are too scarce & having been disarmed by the Germans, the thieves don't fear them in the least.

FRIDAY, JULY 6

. . . The shooting of the English is admirably precise. The Ostend people live in terror. An alarm signal is given when the bombarding begins, & everyone rushes to their

[86] The Russian provisional government launched a large offensive in June 1917 that was initially successful, but the German counteroffensive and increasing mutiny in Russian ranks doomed the campaign by late summer.

cellars, wondering all the time who will survive. All the front doors have to remain open, so that people in the street may take refuge in the cellars. A boche officer was recently killed in front of a door that was closed.

It is well known, at Bruges, that many sub-marines perish—their sailors have a home there & so many never return.

SATURDAY, JULY 7

People <u>insist</u> on hoping the Austrians won't renew their treaty with Germany—it is noticed that the Boche & Austrian officers here in Brussels don't fraternize any longer. . . . I was in the tram with Fernande van den Corput.[87] She had seen Mgr Heylen, Bishop of Namur, at her place in Luxembourg, where she went to be god-mother for the confirmation. She asked him what he really <u>did</u> say, in the pulpit, about the end of the war. He owns he did express his own <u>personal</u> opinion that there won't be another winter campaign, but he doesn't say on what he bases that opinion.

Some say he brought it back from Prague, where he went to the seat of his order of Prémontrés [religious order]. I called on Mme Alb. D'Huart, I hadn't seen her since Freddy's death. He was decorated by his general the day before he died. Her husband & father-in-law have been very exercised about trying to preventing 8 people from being shot to-day, *at Dinant, soi-disant for "espionage."* They had asked the Duc d'Arenberg who is here for the moment to intercede; the result not yet known.[88] Lili's husband Cte Yves de Bourgblanc has refused the 'Légion d'Honneur' because he & his family are still staunch Royalists (white flag & the rest)!!![89] . . .

SUNDAY, JULY 8

. . . The Boches have declared that they buy fruit-stones (cherry, plum-stones etc) at so much a kilo, & that those who deliver 25 kilos, — will be surely able *through them* to procure coals next winter. The fruit stones (or some of their properties) are used for making asphyxiating gas.[90] . . . I hope no one will deliver <u>any</u>. The india-rubber bands round billiard tables have also to be declared. . . . I wonder if we shall lose ours—or how the measure will be applied. The town of Antwerp <u>has</u> to provide

[87] Fernande Van den Corput, née Du Toict.

[88] Engelbert-Marie d'Arenberg had transnational ties like many aristocrats. Raised in Belgium and married to a Belgian aristocrat, he was an officer in the Prussian army; during the war, he served on the staff of the German Seventh Army.

[89] Elisabeth d'Huart, a younger sister of the fallen Alfred d'Huart; in January 1914 she married the Breton aristocrat Yves du Bourblanc, who would be killed at Verdun on October 25, 1917.

[90] Fruit stones were used in the manufacture of charcoal filters for gas masks, not for the gases themselves.

a great quantity of wool—I forget how many kilos. I suppose each locality will be forced in turn.

Mme. Alb. D'Huart has 40 French refugees in her house at Sovet.[91] *She & her family are going there next week, after all sorts of bother for passports, as it is in the étape. She has only 4 rooms to dispose of for her family of 6, & 4 servants.*

MONDAY, JULY 9

I think so much of Linnie & Bertha Quin Harkin when I read the Boche aero-raids on the south of England.[92] We don't yet know particulars of the one on the 7th over the City. There seems to be more than usual political unrest in Berlin—Kaiser at Bethman-Holwegs' [Bethmann Hollweg], Socialists demanding his "buts de guerre" [war aims] etc. . . .

The Boches have ordered all harnesses & saddles to be declared to give up. They have appropriated all that remained at "Old England" & closed the shop for good.[93]

TUESDAY, JULY 10

I wrote nothing, having nothing particular to relate.

WEDNESDAY, JULY 11

Mr. Leeds, a "forty-fiver" who was recently let out from Ruhleben, came to see me, told me Dick was well, rather thin, like all the Ruhlebenites, but one of the "wise" ones of the camp, working hard at languages & his book-binding, & holding himself up morally. There are 3,500 captives there.

The sentinels are very obliging in return of a little grease or money, & even let in English newspapers. . . . [T]he chief German officer is quite a decent fellow, but the "sous-officiers", (like everywhere with Germans) are the worst monsters. The Englishmen who fill the commanding posts there were all living in Germany before the war, no one taken in France or Belgium is in authority. Plenty of food, *sent in from England of course* but they tire (naturally) of everlasting tinned things. As far as food goes they are better off than we are here. Mr. Leeds says the English send the same supplies to the Serbians. The promiscuity is trying, no selection is made, an earl is next to a rough low fellow. Only about 20 per cent make use of their time "healthily" in study or sports, thank God Dick is laborious. . . .

[91] A village northeast of Dinant.

[92] MT's English friends.

[93] Old England (today the Music Instrument Museum) was a department store in central Brussels.

THURSDAY, JULY 12

I think there must have been some fighting off the Belgian coast last night, between 11 & 12 o'clock I got up to listen to the cannon at the open window.[94] Thank God the Russians are getting on. Things in Berlin still very shaky, nothing settled yet. . . . The Abbé C., Pav's [Pavlik] professor, had tea & long conversation with us; he thinks the English don't mean to break through the German front, because the Boches would then devastate Belgium, but that the "percée" [breakthrough] will be made north of Verdun, & the Boches in Belgium be obliged to surrender.

Cannon loud again to-night & during day.

FRIDAY, JULY 13

I heard the cannon <u>very</u> loud last night about 2 o'clock. The wildest rumours of peace all over Brussels to-day. . . .

Mr Josse Allard says he knows (but may not tell his authority) that peace will be signed before 3 months have elapsed.

I wondered (since I saw the Kronprinz had been to see his Pater) if latter meant to abdicate. The report that he does is current everywhere, also that there has been an unsuccessful attempt to kill the Kaiser & Bethman-Holweg [Bethmann Hollweg] while together. How <u>can</u> it all end! I wonder if it will before this book is full.

SATURDAY, JULY 14

I wonder if the French have done anything special on the front for their 14th of July! [French national holiday, Bastille Day]

No German or Dutch papers allowed in Belgium to-day . . . but we heard to-night that Bethmann-Hollweg <u>has</u> retired from office.[95] . . .

What next? . . .

At Antwerp 35 German soldiers threw down their arms, in a public square & cried "Vive la Belgique"! They were surrounded by *other* soldiers & taken off in motors, where? . . .

SUNDAY, JULY 15, & MONDAY, JULY 16

Some neutral "Dips" here last evening said that Michaelis, as successor to Bethman-Hollweg, means the Germans will be wanting peace less than before, or rather that

---

[94] In an offensive known as *Operation Strandfest*, the German Marine Corps Flanders advanced at Lombardzijde on July 10, 1917. The aim was to keep the German-occupied Flemish harbors out of the range of Allied artillery.

[95] Bethmann Hollweg resigned on July 14, 1917, and was replaced by Georg Michaelis.

their ~~wont get it~~ "buts de guerre" [war aims] will be still less acceptable for us!! Wait & see!!! . . .

It is terribly sad that no one can get *a* sufficient quantity of bread, no one being allowed to be supplied with more than the grammes [*sic*] daily, which means perpetual hunger to those who have no potatoes or accessories.

TUESDAY, JULY 17

Everyone is in great expectation concerning the maiden-speech of the new German Chancellor Michaëlis (the first Chancellor with a "bourgeois" name) that is to be made on Thursday. My constant feeling is, that if peace is to come "discussed" & not militarily[, w]h<u>y</u> continue to sacrifice thousands & thousands of men on both sides. May the inspiration of the Holy Ghost come down on all!

It is heartrending to see the poor people pulling cartloads of things far too heavy for human strength; it is <u>so</u> distressing that the poor have been deprived of their old horses & ponies that meant their daily bread. Sadness everywhere one turns!

WEDNESDAY, JULY 18

So Broqueville becomes minister of Foreign Affairs, & Beyens will probably be Belgian Minister in Paris. The change is made <u>now</u>, no doubt, in order that Beyens will have nothing to do with the peace negotiations, for he would not be the man to treat with Germany, after all the revelations he made since 1914 of his impressions at Berlin till the war broke out.[96] . . .

THURSDAY, JULY 19

I am glad the English Royal Family have discarded their ~~German~~ **Boche** [*sic*] names & that the King is now Mr. Windsor.[97] . . .

Someone I know, heard Cardinal Mercier praise English diplomacy on his return from his 2nd trip to Rome. Our English Minister at there Vatican, Howard told him he would get rid of Mgr von Gerlach, the German (or Austrian) "Lecteur du Pape" who had been sent there by his country to endeavor to influence the Pope by making him read the German views. We heard a short time ago that Howard's

---

[96] Baron Eugène Beyens, minister of foreign affairs, instrumental in negotiating the "Declaration of Sainte-Adresse" (February 1916) which bound the Entente to the restoration of Belgian independence, lost his post in August 1917.

[97] Under anti-German pressure, on July 17, 1917, George V relinquished the Hanover family name and declared that the royal family be renamed the House of Windsor after the sovereign's castle at Windsor.

intention <u>had</u> been accomplished, & Mᵍʳ v Gerlach dismissed for having secret wireless apparatus.[98]

FRIDAY, JULY 20, & SATURDAY, 21
FÊTE NATIONALE

On Friday we read Michaëlis's speech—nothing very stirring—I wonder what will result from the council of the "Entente".

All demonstrations were forbidden by the Boches to-day, for the Belgian "fête nationale" [national holiday], but there was a T~eum~ Deum at Ste Gudule, vastly attended, most of the men in <u>top hats</u>, which seems to have been the "mot d'ordre" the Boches having forbidden any signs of union. At Ste Gudule the Brabançonne was played by the organ, & the people cried heartily "Vive le Roi" Leve de Koning. [Long live the King]

Cannon going hard all the afternoon & still now—I wonder if the offensive is for to-morrow! this is the 3rd "fête nationale" in servitude.

When will it end!!! I begin to long for white bread & breakfast rolls (petits pains).

SUNDAY, JULY 22

Have read appreciations of German papers & speeches by the socialists after Michaëlis's speech.

It seems to me he satisfied no one so far. Russia once more makes me very anxious. I had the visit of a young French woman, Mme. Cousin, evacuated from Comines (France) in May, to Waereghem. There were 1900 sent off thus. She lodged some days at the Boulezs, & then found a house.[99] Since then she (& 1100 in all) have been sent further on, to Westmeerbeke, near Westerloo,[100] whence she & her father got a passport for 3 days in Brussels, he having to see a Dr. She gave me comparatively good news of my dear friends at Waereghem—they find food & Anna is stout, but Mme. Cousin fears very hard times for [Waregem] are near. A big Boche soldiers' school (Ecole des Cadets) has been transferred there from Ingelmunster.

MONDAY, JULY 23

This morning, at 7, while I was dressing, 5 Allies' aeroplanes threw bombs somewhere near, probably at Berchem on the aviation camp. Bombarding then commenced

[98] Rudolf Gerlach [not von Gerlach], chaplain to Pope Benedict XV.

[99] Waregem in the Étape of the German Fourth Army. MT lived there in 1888 when she worked for the Boulez family.

[100] Westmeerbeek, a village northeast of Brussels.

immediately & lasted about a quarter of an hour, but ~~not~~ none were brought down, all got away safely as far as we have heard.

What dreadful treachery again in Russia, due to the German agents, with Lenine [Lenin] at their head. I pity poor Kerenski; will he be able to bear the burden, & they say he suffers acutely from a painful disease. I was disappointed about going to town to-day, I had to see the Fords, Mr. Kattendyke & others, but was kept here for poor Pavlick who doesn't seem to be progressing, alas!

TUESDAY, JULY 24

Good news from Carola this morning. She has seen Philip in prison, at Liège, quite cheerful & resigned to the consequences of his baulked attempt to get over the frontier in order to serve his country. Our other friend, who jumped out of the train has, thank God, reached his destination. The celebrated surgeon Meyer, Mme. Errera, wife of the Burgomaster of Uccle, & several others are arrested & "mis au secret" [placed in solitary confinement]. Some say a man they helped to get away betrayed them by writing to thank them; others say they were betrayed by a "coup monté" [a setup] by a Belgian traitor, a paid agent of the Boches.[101] I wonder what can be the number of the Belgians condemned to prison since 1914. Cannon loud to-night, while I write.

WEDNESDAY, JULY 25

Mme. Kattendyke's mother came here to-day, she left England quite recently. She is English born, her husband was Dutch. She told many interesting things, amongst others the absolute calm confidence of the German Ambassador in London, in 1914, that the G's would be in Paris in 10 days from the declaration of war, & that Paris would be razed if the ~~French~~ Allies of France went against Germany. This was before England declared war. . . .

She is very much impressed by the dull, monotonous vegetative life we are compelled to live, & suffers from the lack of interest, news, patriotic excitement & strenuous life she left behind in London. She has only been here a week & wonders how we have borne this painful routine so long. I sometimes feel fit to jump out of my skin for the want of a change & especially yearning to see my friends & England again. She tells of the great enthusiasm in England for a military victory "coûte que coûte" [at all costs] & praises the work of the women.

---

[101] Isabelle Goldschmidt, art historian and wife of Paul Errera, ran a home for French and Belgian civilians expelled from front zones. She occasionally helped soldiers cross into the Netherlands. She was arrested with her associates on July 21. In October 1917, she was sentenced to three months' imprisonment. Gille et al., *Cinquante mois d'occupation allemande*, 3:348–349, 452.

THURSDAY, JULY 26

Nothing to relate.

FRIDAY, JULY 27, 1917

The price of things is getting worse day by day. On an apparatus for inhaling oxygen, that we have just got for Pavlick, there are 2 meters 75 of narrow india-rubber tubes at 18 frs the meter; (=49 frs 50) before the war, they cost about 2 frs a meter. I went to see the Fords. At German civilian went to their house when they were out, left word Alec was to go to his office; he went with Lena; was politely questioned as to what he possesses & has to live upon, the source whence his income derives etc etc, was told he probably may have to answer more questions. . . .

SATURDAY, JULY 28

The boys' holidays began to-day. How excited & anxious we all were 3 years ago, when war was fast approaching—who could have thought, to remain so long! The noise of the cannon has been continual, without ceasing one instant, since last evening, just 24 hours, & we hear it so distinctly. I heard to-day of the death *at war* of young Edouard d'Ursel. R.I.P.[102]

A Boche soldier, who brings errands frequently from Ghistelles, to someone I know, says things are going badly for the Germans in Flanders.[103] What will result from all the disorder in Russia & their retreat without fighting! . . . Dieu nous aide!

SUNDAY, JULY 29

Heavy storms several times to-day. Cannon as loud as ever all last night, it seemed to cease during the morning. I wonder if we are fighting hard now? Young François d'Ursel, 18 years old, is condemned to 6 months imprisonment in a German fortress: his uncle Count Hippolyte d'Ursel, one of the Congo hostages, in the Holzminden camp writes: no sheets, his "voisin de paillasse" [the one he shares a straw-mattress with] is B[m] de Steenhault.[104] Melle Cazé came to tea & we had a nice quiet gossip about the war & our present griefs & anxieties. Poor Edouard d'Ursel was killed, by a German shot, as he was walking one evening to his ammunition factory.

---

[102] Edouard d'Ursel was killed on July 8, 1917, at Dixmude.

[103] Gistel [Ghistelles], eight kilometers south of Ostend.

[104] Possibly Baron Léon de Steenhault de Waerbeeck, burgomaster of Vollezele (west of Brussels) and provincial counselor.

MONDAY, JULY 30

Have just read (from Dutch papers) of the revelation of proofs of a famous assembly of Kaiser, German & Austrian Statesmen, on July 5th, 1914, in which war was decided, quite regardless of following events.[105] I hope Germany will be convinced at last that it was not to defend their country that their millions were killed, but to try to subject others. We have no news yet of where *exactly* the terrible artillery duel of the last days took place, nor of its result. Both sides seem to be shooting, bombarding each other more fiercely than ever near Nieuport. Success would mean either our driving the Germans out of Belgium (or into Holland) or their getting to Dunkirk & Calais.[106] To be or not to be??

TUESDAY, JULY 31

Just 3 years ago that Pavlick & I saw Mlle Nebchaeff [107] off, for Petrograde, by the last train through Germany, & she was stopped at the Russian frontier, war having been declared while she was en route! I don't yet know the particulars of that tragic journey, I think all her luggage was lost, *besides horrors more dreadful*. I am longing more & more for white breakfast rolls, the black war-bread is becoming odious to me. The people I meet that I haven't seen for some time, all seem to be wasting away & drying up—and no wonder, situated as we are & food so scarce, expensive & adulterated. . . .

WEDNESDAY, AUGUST 1

Just 3 years [ago] war was declared to Russia & France. . . . [W]ho could have imagined it would last 3 years! Kitchener said: 2 to 3 years & we all thought he didn't think it would be as long.

There is now an English offensive going on—rumours this evening in Brussels mention our having taken 24 villages, & the famous Wytschaete (White sheet I think the "Tommies" call it.) . . .

Such good news to-day from Sidonie: she is to have 140 frs a month instead of 60. God bless the English government. Deo Gratias!

THURSDAY, AUGUST 2

The first news of the result of the Allies' offensive seems quite favourable for us, even according to the German communiqués.

---

[105] The German "blank check" that assured the Habsburgs of German support in a conflict with Serbia. There was no face-to-face meeting; much of the discussion was held via telegram.

[106] Fighting near Nieuwpoort, on the northern tip of the Western Front (on the Belgian coast).

[107] Remains unidentified.

We have advanced somewhat. How anxiously I await further news! how excited all England must be, where they are [publicly] informed at once.—I had a long letter from the lady "évacuée de Comine" [evacuated from the town of Comines (Komen) on the French-German border] Mme. Germaine Cousin, she had news of present events at Waereghem (I wonder how!) W. is now in the "Étape-d'opération" [staging and operations zone]; all the houses full of troops, who commandeer all they need; the inhabitants allowed one or 2 rooms only in their own houses, forbidden to move out of a certain circle, an aviation ground & pioneers camp quite near the Boulez's, *etc etc* in fact every horror of war—the next step will be evacuation of the inhabitants. How I feel for my dear old friends there! God help them!

FRIDAY, AUGUST 3

Such wretched weather for our offensive, torrents of rain & wind, what mud it must mean on the battle-field! Our results pretty good, we are pushing them back gently. I heard there are 72 German towns in state of siege! That means people are somewhat troublesome! Hindenbourg has promised the Kaiser that the Russian army will have succumbed in 2 months—so for the beginning of October! Had a few words with the curé at St Job this evening—he like myself thinks war can't possibly last much longer, in spite of all the sayings on both sides. I read the "testament de Bissing" an awful piece of hypocrisy, he annexes all Belgium & treats it most brutally, it made my blood boil, & I feel we must have a military victory to save ourselves from the Huns.[108] . . .

SATURDAY, AUGUST 4

3 years ago to-day war was declared to Belgium—it was a lovely moonlight night, & I packed part of the night, in view of our return to Brussels the next day. 3 years we've been thinking of & suffering morally *all the time* from hateful Germans! How much longer????

After reading von Bissing's political will one realizes there is nothing to do but continue till we get a military victory. God help us please to do so soon! A new decree forbids to keep open any workshops (except those for food-stuffs) unless with special Boche permission—Another turn of the ever tightening screw. . . .

[108] Von Bissing's "Political Testament" was a series of texts written in 1915–1916 by the late governor-general, advocating a German and authoritarian regime for Belgium after the war. Von Bissing's son published them in May 1917 to galvanize German war enthusiasm. But the Allies used them to decry German imperialism. An English translation appeared under the title *General Von Bissing's Testament: A Study in German Ideals* (London: Unwin, 1917). In occupied Belgium, copies in Dutch, French, and English did the rounds. MT presumably got hold of one.

SUNDAY, AUGUST 5

Three years ago we went back to town, & lived the <u>awful</u> days of the fighting before Liège & all the horrors we heard of before seeing the Boches in Brussels on the 20th. . . . I remember the state of mind we were in, just living in rooms without arranging them or taking any books or ornaments out of cupboards where they were put away for the summer. I had my bag packed all the time, the valuable pictures were bricked up in the cellars, we were expecting death, in some shape, every moment. The strain was immense . . . & has lasted 3 years! Cannon heard again to-day, weather more favourable. Oh! for the victory that is to deliver us!

MONDAY, AUGUST 6

I went to see the Rinquets & found them both so changed since I saw them in May—so much thinner & more "affaissés" [slumped], like everyone one hasn't seen for a certain time. Even the well to do people suffer from at least semi-starvation. They had just paid [for] a kilo of butter 26 frs, & two small slices of bacon 3 frs 50. Ernest's idea is that peace <u>must</u> soon be made diplomatically, that no government can continue demanding the sacrifices *even* civilians have been making so long already. . . .

TUESDAY, AUGUST 7

I went to the *1ˢᵗ Tuesday* monthly Boche control; we all received a printed notice that we need go no more till further notice etc. Does it merely mean that the men who were in the offices for these affairs are needed on the front? <u>Many many</u> trains of wounded pass through Brussels every night. It seems there was an invasion of German soldiers, from the front, in Ghent these last days; they took possession of all the houses—the same as I heard of Waereghem last week. Villalobar got news to-day of the death of young Jean de Liedekerke, killed in Russia, where he was with armoured motors. I pity his courageous little mother. . . . God help her![109] . . .

WEDNESDAY, AUGUST 8

To-day there was a requiem mass at 10.30, at the Carmes, for Edouard d'Ursel. Isie saw the Belgian flag over the coffin at 10-a.m, but the Boches interfered, & had it taken off before mass commenced.

---

[109] Count Jean de Liedekerke, a volunteer with a Belgian mobile machine-gun unit on the Eastern Front, died in Ternopil, Ukraine, on July 22, 1917.

THURSDAY, AUGUST 9

Heard yesterday that the banks at Roulers were sending away their stock, & people were being evacuated, also from other places between Tourcoing & Courtrai. To-day they say all the places along the coast are being emptied. I think <u>we</u> are trying to get the coast line. What will become of dear old Bruges!

A card from Dick, & a letter from Sidonie, who just had a sad letter from Dick, (in one of his more despondent moods). She asks me to go see her "now that we may travel" & I think of going next Friday, it will do Dick good to know I have seen her & Robert. Villalobar's opinion is that after 2 months more hard fighting, a "diplomatic" peace will be made. (Possible only if Germany gives in & marches out of Belgium!)

FRIDAY, AUGUST 10

Mr. Morel lunched here; told us 100.000 kilos of tomatoes had been sent from Malines to Germany—& such things happen daily—all the grapes from Hoeylaert—etc etc.

He said 900 réfugiés from Moorslede came to places near Malines, that Roulers is being evacuated. I tremble for Bruges & Ghent, & poor dear Valérie! God help us all.

People have all sorts of tricks for smuggling butter; one may carry a loaf of bread, so they cut it in two, cut out the crumb, stuff it with butter, & pack it up again. I am trying to get from Bruges a red blanket I have in my belongings there, in order to have it dyed to make a winter coat. But it is hard to get anything from there, & I fear I shall not succeed. Mr. Morel told me that they used to make 15 million tins of preserves a year at the Soleil, before the war—this year, barely a million & a half, and <u>no</u> jam, because they can't receive any sugar from Tirlemont. Thet tin used to cost 2 frs a kilo, <u>now</u> 33 frs, so the prices of tinned vegetables have risen terribly. . . .

SATURDAY, AUGUST 11, & SUNDAY, AUGUST 12

Had a letter from Dick yesterday. Some 2 or 3 weeks ago he had one from Edith dated March 16th; she says her health is excellent, thank God. Everyone in Brussels is learning English "for when the Allies arrive", no more English dictionaries & few books to be found in shops. The feeling of being for <u>such</u> a long time, surrounded & governed by "the enemy" makes me very depressed at times, it is a sore trial for those who are *in territory* "occupied" by the Boches. . . .

MONDAY, AUGUST 13

We hear the cannon terribly to-night, & have heard it all day—and <u>such</u> heavy showers, the battle field must be an awful sea of mud. So much seems to go against each of our offensives. Mr. Morel heard, through people from Ghent, that the inhabitants are being prepared to evacuate the town at 6 hours notice. I feel quite ill, thinking of poor dear Valérie & Emma, & my old friends at Waereghem, for it will soon be evacuation there I am sure. God help us! and dear old Bruges! and the last few old relics there of dear mother! <u>Where</u> will the people be sent to! they think to Holland. I never realized what war means to civilians. I need God's help more than ever not to become melancholy.

TUESDAY, AUGUST 14

A better day to-day for weather for the offensive. I went to see the Fords. Alec thinks if we can get Roulers & Thourout [Torhout], the Boches will <u>have</u> to quit the coast.

If it were true! Everyone I see after a short time of absence seems so much older & worn, & I feel I make the same impression on others as they do on me—I feel so low at times, all thoughts being sad & sorrowful for others in greater trouble than I am. The evacuating Ghent seems to be general talk, poor dear Valérie! . . .

WEDNESDAY, AUGUST 15

Such a heavy showery Assumption day—the 4th of the war . . . and now it impedes our offensive! of which we read next to nothing in the communiqués. I wonder <u>what</u> we are doing! It seems decided <u>now</u>, at last, that neither English, French or American Socialists will assist at the Stockholm conference, which, *the conference, I mean*, I think is a German manoeuvre to improve <u>their</u> chances of making their conditions of peace. Heard to-night that there is a great appeal, from the Pope, to cease fighting. What will result from it??? Am curious to see what the papers will give concerning it.

THURSDAY, AUGUST 16

From a few lines in this evening's *Belgischer Kurier*, the English seem to have had some advantage in Flanders—we shall see in to-morrow's communiqués. Have just read about the people of Armentières being poisoned by small bullets that burst on the ground & exude poisonous gas. . . . <u>What</u> next! & against civilians!

I am off to-morrow to Antwerp, by the 8.50 train, to return (I hope) on Saturday. More than 3 years [since] I set foot in a railway station or a train!! It will be quite a new sensation—and a Germanised railway too! . . .

FRIDAY, AUGUST 17, SATURDAY, 18, & SUNDAY, 19

I left for Antwerp on Friday, at 8.30, in 3rd class (4 fr 80 single fare, no return tickets available) Women sell the tickets at the station. Train <u>crammed</u>, it always is. Before reaching Malines, I saw the ch ruins of the church of Sempst [Zemst], destroyed during war. Several houses in Antwerp are in the same state, though as they have been more or less pulled down, to make them look tidy, one couldn't tell the cause of their destruction. The harbor is pitiful—grass growing everywhere, & one *tiny* little Dutch steamer, from Dordrecht; lying where formerly all *the* space was tightly packed with ships.... Under the covered wharves, nothing but coal here & there, brought from the interior of Belgium by the canals. Found Sidonie & Bobby well, thank God, latter much improved but both longing wearily for Dick's return. Antwerp looks like a big village, the shops are shabby as here, ham 25 frs the kilo! ... The train packed again for my return yesterday 1.30 from Antwerp, several carriages of *Boche* officers & soldiers, latter evidently bound for the front, to start from Brussels, laden with their parcels. Meantime, <u>we</u> have been doing well in Flanders, & the Pope's message is being discussed<u>???</u>

At Schaerbeek the carriage began to turn, there was a bit of a panic, I got out, & finding no means of entering another, so crammed were all, I got into the open luggage van [car] in spite of Boche admonestations [admonitions] & reached Brussels safely, satisfied that I still knew how to take a train—& even a luggage van.

MONDAY, AUGUST 20

Three years [ago] to-day the Germans entered Brussels! and 17 officers & 50 men & horses slept in this house, *& the greenhouse & stables* one officer in the room I am now writing in—they only stayed one night, fortunately, & hurried away to continue their march early the next morning. And for more than 3 years, we have thought of nothing but the war!!! This evening's German paper announces a big French attack at Verdun! <u>At last</u>, is the offensive going to be general on the French & English front! Opinions & feelings are <u>so</u> various concerning the Pope's message of peace....

TUESDAY, AUGUST 21

Melle Cazé came to see me, she is always so agreeably conversational. She told me poor Eduard d'Ursel had his head shot clean off. He volunteered for a most dangerous service, four soldiers accompanied him, one of whom was killed also.

The *Belgischer Kurier* announces this evening a French success at Verdun, & the offensive on the West Front seems to be very general. God grant it may be decisive! Cannon <u>so</u> <u>loud</u> all last night & early this morning. Count John d'Oultremont has been released from his captivity, they say by the Kaizer's [*sic*] command, who was furious that a man who had dined at his table, should have been treated thus!!!!

WEDNESDAY, AUGUST 22

I wonder what the Kaizer came to Brussels for yesterday! Cannon terribly loud all last night & to-day. We are fighting <u>very</u> hard on all the west front.

Big success in Italy, 7.000 prisoners, very good at Verdun too, 4.000. God grant we may push on sufficiently to have a <u>military</u> triumph over our enemies before winter sets in.

A German woman who knew Mme. F[rantz] Wittouck at the home R de Berlin,[110] & from whom she hadn't heard since the war, wrote her yesterday from Aix-la-Chapelle [Aachen], entreating her to send food: bacon & nourishing eatables, as she is dying of hunger....

J̶E̶U̶D̶I̶ THURSDAY, AUGUST 23, & FRIDAY, AUGUST 24

... I went to see Melle Cazé at Boitsfort,[111] & had a chat with Ctesse Aug. d'Ursel.[112] <u>She</u> says Cte John d'Oultremont was allowed back from Germany, because his wife flaunted his German decorations so much in the face of the Boches, that they finished by being shamed somewhat. There was another requisition of horses, mules, & donkeys to-day, & Mme. W's horse has at last been taken (for 1,600 fr instead of the 2,400 p̶r̶o̶p̶o̶s̶e̶d̶ given a short time ago, when it was returned through Bredo [Bredow], who is now in Germany till Sept 1st)

SATURDAY, AUGUST 25

Two years ago that poor Dick died in Australia, & all I know of it were the few words William wrote me several months later.[113] R.I.P.

Melle Bolo came to see me; she has altered so much, another "victime de la guerre" owing to the difficulty of buying proper food even for those who are not quite poor. <u>What</u> terrible times for the aged & lonely! A rumour in town this evening of our having taken Lens, but such rumours go round constantly while our troops are in the vicinity of different towns....

SUNDAY, AUGUST 26

No gossip to-day....

[110] The late Franz Wittouck and his family at some point lived on rue de Berlin, close to the Paul Wittoucks. The street was renamed rue d'Alsace-Lorraine ten days after the Armistice.

[111] A suburb of Brussels.

[112] Emma de Rouillé, widow of Count Auguste d'Ursel.

[113] Richard "Dick" Thorp, MT's younger brother; William is her elder half-brother.

The Majority in the Reichstag seems most dissatisfied with Michaëlis. I wonder if he will hold on. Orphan children evacuated from Lens are in a convent near here— many of them lost their relatives during the bombardment; one little boy *there* lost a leg & saw his grandfather killed before his eyes. The Prussians want to make an independent Duchy of Alsace-Lorraine—rather late for that move!

MONDAY, AUGUST 27

To-day, between 2 & 5 o'clock (all the time) we heard a continual uninterrupted "feu roulant" [rolling barrage] of cannon in the distance. I think another great battle must be taking place in Flanders, but alas rain set in this afternoon, wind raging too, in fact the worst weather possible for us. The shameful "Conseil des Flandres" [Council of Flanders] is becoming more and more "vaudevillesque" in its pretentions & writings. All the members are sure of an annuity from the Boche Government, money being deposed in a bank to this effect. A patriotic old Belgian Colonel met one of those contemptible traitors in a train the other day, & said publicly to him, in great anger. "Crapule, descendez de ce tram, je ne veux pas me trouver avec vous," ["You scum, get off this tram, I don't want to be in your presence,"] stopped the tram & the traitor, too ashamed to speak, meekly quitted the tram as he was bid. I would like to congratulate the old Colonel.

Dr. Dumon, of the Rue Haute, Bruges, is one of the ignoble traitors of that nauseous farce "Counseil des Flandres!"

TUESDAY, AUGUST 28

Seven years to-day dear mother died![114] R.I.P. I went to mass in town for her, to the anniversary mass of Cte Aug. d'Ursel, who died a year ago. It seems that King Albert & the Queen have left La Panne for another locality in "Belgium" because the English want to work their way along the coast to Ostend & Zee-Brugge. I can't understand how the Boches let Dr. Leboeuf out of Belgium, (to see the Queen?) & in again.[115]

It is rumoured the English are in the suburbs of Lille.

There was a terrible tempest all last night (no sleep) & to-day; great havoc done to trees in the Forest & everywhere, calmer to-night & the moon is shining—I hope to make up for ~~lost~~ sleep lost last night.

WEDNESDAY, AUGUST 29

Heavy squalls all day, so bad again for our progress. . . . Yesterday Micha & Jean went to see the Tirlemont factory. Mr. Baudouin made them each a regal present of 10

---

[114] Annette Townshend Thorp died in Bruges at nr. 2, Oosterlingenplein, aged eighty-five.

[115] Dr. Leboeuf led the field hospital established on August 6, 1914, in the Royal Palace of Brussels under the auspices of Queen Elisabeth; the hospital was allowed to function all through the war, taking care of the heavily mutilated.

kilos of sugar—if they dared to smuggle it. They did so, successfully, though a man, in the Tirlemont station who saw them take leave of Mr. B, & their packets under each arm, knowing it must be sugar, offered them 10 frs a kilo for it, but they refused naturally. Micha let his mother have 5 kilos (for 25 frs) for her to give Lady Phipps, & is going to give the rest as presents. (2 kilos to me good boy, for my friends & poor).

THURSDAY, AUGUST 30

I have had a disappointment. I had hoped to buy 2 middle sized blankets, to have *them* dyed violet, to make a warm winter coat, but the person who proposed to sell them, now wants to keep them for herself. Everybody is having blankets dyed, as there are no more stuffs for making clothes. At Antwerp the Boches (who are already taking the wool of the mattresses) have forbidden to have blankets dyed; in view of taking them themselves, & it is greatly feared that it will very soon [be] forbidden here. I am sadly in want of something warm for winter; three years ago one didn't dream of providing for 1917, nor of the possibility of the war lasting so long.

FRIDAY, AUGUST 31

I sent boots to be soled & heeled—the price now is 16 frs; last October it was 7 f 50, & before the war 3 f 50 to 4 frs. I arranged to have a very old dress dyed & made over; if it were not "the war" it would have been given away long ago, but the veriest rags are now worn to the bitter end. The relations between Spain & Holland, *or rather their ministers* in Brussels, & principally concerning the Relief Committee are worth noting. Le Marquis de Villalobar is very conceited & "swelled headed" "un moi trop glorieux", van Vollenhoven a good all round, or rather, square Dutchman. Villa always, in all things, wants to be the first fiddle (& I put it mildly at that). After a stormy interview with the Dutch members of the Relief in which they claim their right to act as they think proper *& the Marquis declares they shall not & bangs his little hand on the table* Vollenhoven writes a polite bit of Dutch mind to the diminutive Spanish grandee. Latter replies in a friendly, somewhat patronizing manner, tells his young friend that he didn't mean this, that or the other that he is his best friend etc etc. Holland is mollified. . . . Then at the first opportunity, they quarrel again, being nevertheless diplomatically polite in public. They each have their partisans & flatterers, but the Marquis has the greater capacity for digesting overdoses of incense. What comedies one reads in "Society"!!!

SATURDAY, SEPTEMBER 1

Have just read the entire text of Wilson's answer to the Pope's note—I think it splendid, just what we all think I feel.[116] What do Soukhomlinof's (the ex-minister

---

[116] Pope Benedict XV's August 1, 1917, note proposed unilateral disarmament and other unpopular peace proposals. Wilson rejected these claims as did the other Allied nations and Germany.

of War, in Russia) revelations in his trial signify?[117] that Russia really did continue to mobilize when Germany asked her to cease? What of all that was said in the White or Yellow (I forget the colour) books of the beginning of the war?[118] or is this man such a traitor that he wishes now to incriminate Russia & exonerate Germany. I am longing for the Italians to get the Austrians out of Mont St. Gabriele, it will mean, I think, almost getting to Trieste.[119]

Dieu nous aide!

SUNDAY, SEPTEMBER 2

... The Boche papers are raging about Wilson's answer to the Pope—& no wonder! for it contained many awkward truths for them.[120] ...

MONDAY, SEPTEMBER 3

Nothing to write about.

TUESDAY, SEPTEMBER 4

Splendid weather yesterday & to-day, glorious; though not the news of the fall of Riga, given in the Boche papers.[121] Cannon loud all last night on our front. An allies' aeroplane flew over Brussels to-day & dropped papers, I don't yet know what they said. Trains stopped, but no firing, the aeroplane was too high.[122]

The taking of Riga was celebrated by the B's by firing guns etc. I wonder if it means more treachery on the part of the Russians at Riga. . . .

WEDNESDAY, SEPTEMBER 5

What will be the result of the fall of Riga??? Marthe Kervyn du Roy is in town with a passport for a week. She doesn't seem to mind being so near Bruges, says she fears nothing. . . . 500 English prisoners were made to sit down on the Grand

---

[117] Vladimir Sukhomlinov, former minister of war, was tried for high treason and sentenced to hard labor. The Bolsheviks released him in 1918 on account of his age.

[118] The "White Books" and "Yellow Books" detailing the diplomatic run-up to the war.

[119] The Eleventh Battle of the Isonzo in Italy.

[120] Wilson rejected the pope's note with the argument that peace could not be based on a "restitution" of Germany's power.

[121] With the collapse of the Russian offensive, the Germans moved to take control of Riga and other Baltic areas.

[122] The Brussels chronicles do not mention this.

Place, at Bruges; the Boches *then* took away their military caps & gave them other ragged caps. A "Brugeois" was severely punished for having given an Englishman some cigarettes & another for having spoken to a Tommy, who told him to take patience, because in 2 months, we should have all the Flemish coast & the B's would evacuate Flanders.[123] Marthe was waiting the other day for a train to pass at the barrière of the Rue Maréchale.[124] A German motor had to wait too, in it were a German & an English officer. Some of the railway trucks contained the remains of military material, & each time one passed thus loaded, the English officer prisoner took his cigarette out of his mouth & made the military salute.

No houses at Bruges are destroyed by the bombs, they always fall where they are intended to. Food doesn't seem more scarce than here, butter 22 frs (only) a kilo, but there will be no coal for the winter, less than here! What the Tommy said about our having the coast in 2 months, is exactly what Vollenhoven said here last Sunday. Weather glorious & ideal for aviation.

THURSDAY, SEPTEMBER 6
FRIDAY, SEPTEMBER 7

. . . The famous fêtet organized by Villalobar for to-morrow is to be a tremdously [*sic*] splendid affair. He has already received 75 thousand frs for the entrances, which were marked minimum 20 frs. I think the W's sent 5 thousand, & many people sent large sums. The Dietrich's place, Val Duchesse, is a splendid estate, beautifully situated, many ponds.[125] Mme de Beeckman offered me a ticket, but I don't care to go, & Florrie is coming to spend a quiet afternoon with me. The Stockholm conference seems to have become "un enterrement de 1ʳᵉ classe." [a first-class funeral]

SATURDAY, SEPTEMBER 8

A calm, mild, misty day for the Marquis de Villalobar's fête, which was splendid, and a great financial success—they say over 2 hundred thousand francs.

Nearly everyone one hears talking in the street is complaining of the dearness & scarcity of food. Who would have thought that the smallest piece of sugar for instance, could become such an important article. People are making real fortunes by cultivating anything eatable in the a small piece of ground—I heard of

---

[123] The *brugeois* would continue to cheer on Entente POWs, in spite of reminders of punishment.

[124] The railway grade crossing at Maarschalkstraat in Bruges.

[125] The eighteenth-century Château of Val-Duchesse (a former priory) in Auderghem, outside of Brussels, was rebuilt as a sumptuous private residence by the Brussels businessman Charles-Henri Dietrich.

a man getting more than a hundred thousand francs for cabbages on 3 hectares. All the farmers are making piles of money by "accaparements." [hoarding] forestalling?

SUNDAY, SEPTEMBER 9

Another glorious day, sun through a lovely delicate mist. Marthe du R. K. [du Roy Kervyn] returns to St. André to-morrow. She says people at Bruges feel secure so far, & think there is no danger there; ~~though~~ the archives of Ostend have been brought there even, but they hear bombs & cannon all the time. War is making so many thieves; soil produce is robbed everywhere, the other night a hole was made in our hedge & 50 kilos of potatoes stolen from the field. Bands of thieves plunder from the fields, under the very eyes of the authorities, & cart away their booty, the authorities being less in number & unarmed. This occurs in broad daylight; the same thing takes place here in the Forest where trees are cut down all the time.

MONDAY, SEPTEMBER 10

Went to see the Fords today, Alec more optimistic than ever. I asked him if he thought Wilhelm is going to calmly walk down from his throne & make way for the people to make peace with us, according to our declaration: "No peace with the Hohenzollerns." He says the people will dethrone him—I wish they would hurry to do it, before all the men are killed.

Cannon so loud last night—& all day, especially between 4 & 8 pm. Alec says there are so many people dying of want in Germany, that it is forbidden to bury them during the daytime, not to make matters worse.

TUESDAY, SEPTEMBER 11

The cannon continued to be terribly loud & seemed to [be] much nearer (on account of the perfect stillness) all last night, it made my window frames rattle. Will the result make to-morrow's news less dull??? Nothing interesting whatever to-day, but lovely weather; Micha, Serge & I had a two hours ideal walk in the Forest.

WEDNESDAY, SEPTEMBER 12

It is rumoured to-night in Brussels that the English have a success in Flanders, Italians ditto on Mont Gabriel & French in Macedonia. I am longing for to-morrow's papers. Kornilof is going against Kerenski to Petrograde.[126] What will ensue from the Russian confusion??

THURSDAY, SEPTEMBER 13

Heard nothing particular.

FRIDAY, SEPTEMBER 14

Mr. & Mme. Fernand du Roy, their son Henri & 4 servants were arrested last evening *& are in prison at St. Gilles*, it is supposed it is for the *Libre Belgique*.[127]

Mr. Carels' (of Ghent) yacht was at Antwerp & used by the Governor there, for trips on the Scheld [Scheldt]. The other day, 9 gentlemen, speaking German perfectly, went on board, said the Gov. had proposed they should have a sail. They went off, & when far enough to be safe, mastered the German crew & made for the Dutch coast, where they all remained, yacht & all, to the amazement of the Gov. when the next day he wanted to go sailing. One of the 9 gentlemen was Mr. Carels himself & the 8 others his friends.[128] "[P]ayer d'audace" [to show daring] often succeeds with the B[oche]'s.

SATURDAY, SEPTEMBER 15

A year ago to-night I began my diary. We all thought <u>then</u>, that we were near our delivery. Alas! To-day I heard that a German (rather important functionary) told someone of a firm that had to apply for certain business authorisations, that they might continue quietly their work, because for [by] the 30th of September, peace would be made & that the Germans were "d'accord" [in accord] with the English on the subject!!! I should <u>love</u> to believe it, but I fear it is a hoax! Que vivra verra! [Time will tell!]

The Kornilov & Kerenski trouble seems to be resolved in favour of latter. A Swedish Dip., just back from his country through Berlin, told the company here to-day, no one is cheerful in Berlin, everybody looks exhausted. He was at the excellent "Hôtel de de l'Esplanade." No coffee (but *torréaline*)[129] no butter, no fat, no sugar, no potatoes, black bread with honey. He with two friends paid 160 frs *or marks*

---

[126] Lavr Kornilov, commander-in-chief of the Russian army, led a failed coup d'état against Kerensky's government in August 1917.

[127] Baron Fernand du Roy de Blicquy, his wife Gabrielle de Beughem de Houtem, and their son Henri played an important part in the *Libre Belgique* network. Belgian State Archives, Services Patriotiques Papers, dossiers 81 and 193.

[128] The firm Carels Frères manufactured steam engines in Ghent; the yacht probably belonged to Gaston Carels.

[129] Torréaline was a rye substitute for coffee.

for their dinner, following menu: vegetable soup, quite "maigre". [meager] Boiled fish, no kind of sauce, in spite of special offer to pay. On insisting, they also procured duck, & an apple each was their dessert. On the railway between Berlin & Brussels, there <u>was</u> a Restaurant Car, <u>but</u> only <u>one</u> <u>tiny</u> ball of minced meat, with red cabbage. When a second was demanded with offer of payment, it was not possible to obtain it. How must it be with the poor who can't afford anything!

SUNDAY, SEPTEMBER 16

... All one reads in the papers just now, seems to tend to peace; I think that ~~the~~ we Allies appear somewhat mollified about our ideas of making (possibly) a diplomatic peace.... The Voorwaerts [Vorwärts] writes a sensible article on the incapacity of Boche diplomats, chosen specifically for their name, *supposed good* manners or admiration of militarism....

MONDAY, SEPTEMBER 17

Our servant Charles went yesterday to Enghien[130] to get some "precious potatoes;" only had to pay his brother-in-law 1 fr a kilo, lucky man! He says that tram is crammed with potato smugglers, about 30 tons are brought in by it every night, the Germans soldiers who are supposed to search the people let them down very easily & often say "what do we care about potatoes, we know we are doomed to be killed." On the tram last night, 2 G soldiers, trying to desert, dressed as civilians, were caught. Round about Enghien many desert. Recently, two offered someone 200 frs each for an old suit of clothes, no matter how ragged, to get away in, but the bribed man did not accept—the penalties in such cases are immense, & many people object to the chance of being shot.

I hope & pray the rumours of peace may be realised—people are suffering <u>too</u> much....

TUESDAY, SEPTEMBER 18
WEDNESDAY, SEPTEMBER 19

... The rumours of peace going to be negotiated are very confusing.... [A]re they true? or merely sent out by the Boches to favour their own ends? Still, the "Manchester Guardian" writes that Lloyd George referred to it seriously in a public speech & said "Peace is not far off." Michaëlis said the same at Stuttgard [Stuttgart].

... Well, this red covered book has continued in terrible bloodshed—how will it be with its successor???

---

[130] Southwest of Brussels.

Book 3

"WE STILL HEAR THE SAME ETERNAL
CANNON," SEPTEMBER 1917–MARCH 1918

*T*horp's diary for 1917 juxtaposed tales of British heroism with the realization that soldiers were drowning in mud. To fight on or to end the horror by seeking peace: this question, which roiled much of the belligerent world, permeated her diary. Meanwhile, she kept following the news from the fronts and relied on neutral diplomats for information. These were depressing months. The continued bloodshed at the fronts and civilians' deepening misery disheartened her: she ended many a day's entry with the cry "God help us!" The death of her employer Paul Wittouck in November 1917 compounded the gloom.

Another disturbing development was the Russian Revolution. It spoke to her diary's underlying question of resilience versus compromise, for it showed that civilian despair could lead to the overthrow of the existing order. In unoccupied Belgium, King Albert feared that the frightful misery of the occupied population would discredit the Belgian state forever. In smuggled reports, Belgian elites in the occupied country advised him it was time for universal male suffrage.[1] For all that, Belgium's elites did not fear an actual uprising of the Belgian working class; they thought Germany much more receptive to actual revolutionary ideas. So did Thorp. Her diary so far showed no fear of revolt. She noticed the rise of wartime banditry, but she saw it as a product of wartime misery, not as a wholesale rejection of the existing social order. By war's end, however, she would grow considerably more anxious on that score.

[1] Survey of Belgian leaders' opinions. Brussels, Royal Palace Archives, King's Cabinet, Albert I, 1914–1918, Ministry of the Interior, 280bis, "Extraits des opinions exprimées par différentes personnalités de la Belgique occupée sur les principaux problèmes de l'avenir du pays, 1918."

On her fifty-fourth birthday, January 1, 1918, she implored divine intercession for an "honorable" peace. Hopes for such a peace would vanish once the terms of the Treaty of Brest-Litovsk became public in March 1918. Germany's vast territorial gains convinced the other Allies that structural peace—a balance of power on the Continent—required a German defeat. Meanwhile, heavy fighting looked set to resume in the West. Thorp registered the buildup of troops and munitions in preparation for the German Spring Offensive. She wrote about the stream of refugees and evacuees, about the men taken to work behind the German lines, and about the shelling and bombing of civilians. While she was glad her active life saved her from despondency, and continued to be very aware of her own relatively comfortable circumstances at the Wittoucks', she felt painfully for those who suffered, and she dreaded the coming offensive. As she ended her book, she longed for Easter 1918, hoping it would bring redemption.

CONTINUATION OF "LOCAL GOSSIP," 1917

THURSDAY, SEPTEMBER 20

Will this third book be that of the "eleventh hour"? I had so much hoped it for the red cover no 2. This one happens to be partly green . . . hope & the olive branch??? In any case, some of the German papers say that the German answer to the Pope's message (which we shall soon be able to read) agrees to restore the independence of Belgium, & that will probably entice the Allies to take some steps towards peace, or rather the discussion of peace.

. . . So many people will die of sheer starvation if the war doesn't end. This copy book cost 95 centimes, <u>war price</u>!

FRIDAY, SEPTEMBER 21

The *Belgischer Kurier* of this evening gives the first news of an advance of the English, east of Ypres—one kilometer in the Boches depth of trenches . . . so that is the least, let us hope <u>our</u> communiqués to-morrow will be able to announce even more. Articles in the same paper, & continually in all the other Boche papers, on making peace. . . . We are wondering what Michaëlis will say on the matter, on the 27th, at the sitting of the Reichstag. There is a new German poster, <u>terribly</u> <u>severe</u>, telling us even brass nails, door handles, banisters, lightning-conductors, works of art etc etc in copper, brass & bronze are all to be given up to them. . . .

SATURDAY, SEPTEMBER 22

Cannon roaring all the time, & good news for <u>us</u> of the battle that began again in Flanders, on the 20th. God grant the continuation may mean something more decisive than henceforth. I went down town in quest of soap. Very poor stuff, containing hardly any grease, 3 frs 25 the cake of 55 grammes. . . .

Mme. Frantz's [Wittouck] coachman, bringing butter from Petit Bigard in the pony cart, was stopped by 2 Boche soldiers; they poked iron spikes into the cushions & the packet of butter, seized latter & took away the man's "carte d'identité" [identity card]. Jean W[ittouck] witnessed an amazing little scene this morning: A German with a sack wanted to get into the tram Jean was in. The ticket collector would not allow it, pointed to the sack & said: "You have Kartoffelen." [Kartoffeln, potatoes] Ya, said the Boche, let me in & I'll give you some. The collector filled his pockets with a few kilos, & before the Boche could board the tram, rang for it to start; off it went, leaving the German on the road, minus a good many precious potatoes. Bravo! petit Belge! [Bravo! Little Belgian!]

SUNDAY, SEPTEMBER 23

. . .

MONDAY, SEPTEMBER 24

Cannon so loud last night towards midnight & again this evening . . . yet the advance is so limited when we know the result. Mr. Fernand du Roy & his son are out of prison, Mme. d.R. only comes out on Wednesday. A bookbinder who called at their house was also arrested . . . more amazing than all, a boy who was running to catch a tram, who didn't even know the du Roy's, was arrested as they were being taken away in a German motor, & bundled into the motor with them on no presumption whatever. He & the bookbinder have been set free, but 10 days undeserved imprisonment is no joke—especially so [sic] at 6. a.m one is forced to turn out of bed without any possibility of lying down, till the bed is let down again for the night.

TUESDAY, SEPTEMBER 25, & WEDNESDAY, SEPTEMBER 26

Nothing but articles on Peace these days in the German papers; I think it must be to prepare public opinion in Germany to the giving up of Belgium & contenting the Allies in the greatest measure possible. I wonder if the latter will be able to proclaim that their aim is accomplished, that of Germany renouncing militarism to lean upon international law & arbitration, according to Germany's answer to the Pope's message!

THURSDAY, SEPTEMBER 27

Cannon booming very loud all the afternoon, & while I write.[2]

---

[2] Third Ypres battle (Passchendaele).

No German papers have come to Brussels since Tuesday morning—an unheard of thing, so far, under Boche sway. We presume the Socialists & Pacifists in Berlin are making a little excitement, in view of the meeting of the Reichstag this afternoon & Michaëlis' speech. What <u>will</u> it be! The Dutch papers of to-day announce that Villalobar ... is called back by the King.... Amazement & "potins." [gossip] He immediately motored to Mme. Frantz W's to deny the fact & of course to send the denial round! I think someone has been playing a practical joke on the "Peacock."

FRIDAY, SEPTEMBER 28

What is happening at Berlin! ~~No German papers yet~~! and the famous sitting of the Reichstag & Michaëlis' speech, which were to have been yesterday, put off to to-day. Rumour speaks of a revolution. Cannon <u>terribly</u> loud all last night. Mme. Germaine Cousin, the "évacuée de Comines" called on me, from Westmeerbeek. She told me my friends at Waereghem have had to leave their house, the Germans wanting to make a double railway track near their house, half of which is to be pulled down. They have taken all their belongings to Villa Salomé, at Zulte.[3] Waereghem is continually "punished" for men who <u>won't</u> work for the Boches, & for some length of time, no one may stir out of doors except one person in each household, to go shopping....

SATURDAY, SEPTEMBER 29

The poster concerning the artistic bronze & *other* metal articles having to be declared, appeared on the walls to-day, & causes great consternation. The new orders concerning the use of Flemish instead of French in public Banks *& institutions*, townhalls etc etc is also a source of great annoyance & difficulty for many.

... When Prince Rupprecht of Bavaria spent a day & night at Oydonck [Ooidonk], the Ctesse 't K. went to Ghent.... [O]nly Cte 't K. spoke to the Prince, took meals with him, asked to obtain passports for Brussels (but they were never given).[4] ~~Mary~~ Rupprecht had to gaze, during meals, at pictures, of his sister Queen Elizabeth & King Albert, decorated with the Belgian colours—he remarked: I see people are patriotic here. He had about a dozen officers with him, & a whole retinue, cooks etc etc; he had a military band play on the lawn during dinner.

---

[3] The Boulezs left their much-damaged residence in Waregem and went to Villa Salomé, their house in Zulte.

[4] Count Arnold 't Kint de Roodenbeke and his wife, Isabel Francisca de Borja de Silva y Borchgrave d'Altena.

SUNDAY, SEPTEMBER 30, 10.15 PM

A lovely moonlight night, & the cannon ever <u>so</u> <u>loud</u>, making my windows rattle. We didn't hear it during the day. Would to God we could take the Flemish coast & make the Germans go from there! . . .

To-day the weather was simply divine, an ideal day; Isie & Marie Cazé came to see me, all our conversation was of the war & its terrible trials & sufferings. The cannon is <u>so loud</u>, I wonder if it means a battle on sea on the coast of Flanders!

Dieu nous aide!

MONDAY, OCTOBER I

I have just received notice from Caisse des Reports, that the accumulated interest of my coupons, which I haven't been able to touch (being English) since the Germans are here, has been sequestered by them & the sum of 3,343 frs 86, due to me, has been credited to the account of Mr. Einhan??? In his quality of Sequestre.[5] . . . Shall I ever get the money back? It is terrible to be *living* on the side where the enemy triumphs. . . .

TUESDAY, OCTOBER 2

A heavenly autumn day, the last I fear, of a series of fine ones.

WEDNESDAY, OCTOBER 3

. . . I saw 4 poor women, being marched to the police station, by a Boche sous-offc [non-commissioned officer] for carrying potatoes, small quantities. It appears that the confiscated potatoes are sold to the alimentation, the price *is* given to those who arrested the carriers, who, besides losing their precious wares, are fined one mark per kilo, of what they were smuggling.

There is a <u>great</u> <u>scare</u> in every home about the Boches taking away everything in bronze, copper or brass. People are taking down their metal banisters & scheming to save all they can of their things of art.

How terrible it is to live so long in the hands of the enemy! What will it be like to feel oneself free & master of one's self & possessions. An English victory in Mesopotamia! Better there than nowhere. . . .

High wind & rain to-night, I'm afraid the spell of beautiful weather is broken, alas for our front in Flanders! It is very striking to see how <u>thin</u> nearly everyone is, who formerly was plump (myself included) So far people lived on their fat, but I fear many will succumb to exhaustion this winter. . . .

---

[5] Enemy assets were frozen and later seized by the occupying authorities.

THURSDAY OCTOBER 4

... The Germans have stuck up a poster forbidding people to <u>carry</u> <u>about</u>, outside their communes, acorns, beechnuts, horse chestnuts etc. This means of course that the people who go to the trouble of collecting them (& many do, in order to use them as food) will in reality save the Germans the trouble, as <u>they</u> will confiscate them for their own benefit. Very artful! Nothing in the boche *Belgique Communiqués* about our success in Mesopotamia, though the Dutch papers announced it yesterday.[6]

The light & fuel question is a source of anguish to many.... [O]nly a certain amount of gas allowed to each meter, & if people use it to warm water for baths, it will be cut off at once. What will my friends the Fords do? No lamp oil of any kind; horrid, tiny, sort of dirty tallow candles 1 fr & 1 f 25 each, the size of a finger—<u>so hard</u> on the poor who have no gas or electricity! ...

FRIDAY OCTOBER 5

Twelve years to-day dear Lizzie died. R.I.P. I'm sure poor Valérie has been thinking of her also & the great grief we were in. I fear Dear Val suffers much from the constant bombardment near Ghent—there has been a terrible one, that caused a great fire at the Aviation camp at St. Denis Westrem, that was seen for miles around.[7] I went to call on Lena & Alec, he very cheerful & optimistic, as usual, about the war....

SATURDAY, OCTOBER 6

There is heavy fighting round about Poelcapelle, Becelaere etc since the 4th & the Dutch papers say the "real thing" will only come on in 2 or 3 weeks. Oh! if we could only take the coast! Life is getting harder every day—one can't find anything that one wants, I had failures to-day for the size of gloves (& cotton ones only) no underwear to be had for the boys at 2 of our best shops—all is sold out, & the few things that remain are unsuitable or would have been sold long ago.—A man carrying a bronze statue was arrested by the Boches, who meant to confiscate it like the rest of the metal. He had the good idea to say it was a present he was carrying to the Marquis de Villalobar. They worried him a little, but he stuck to his declaration, & saved his statue by depositing it at the Marquis' house.

[6] In Mesopotamia, in the autumn of 1917, the British slowly forced their opponents to retreat.

[7] In 1917, the Imperial German Air Service constructed an airfield on Maaltekouter in Sint-Denijs-Westrem near Ghent. It housed a squadron of Gotha G.IV bombers, the so-called England Geschwader ("England Squadron"), used for strategic bombing of British civilian targets, specifically London (Operation Türkenkreuz).

SUNDAY, OCTOBER 7

Very cold, wind, rain, tempest since noon. So bad I fear, for our fighting in Flanders. In the "jour de guerre"[8], the Boches (they say it is the ~~Prince Arak?~~ *Count Harach chief man of the censorship* who writes it) seem to be preparing the German opinion for their evacuation of the Coast & part of Flanders.[9] The Germans have been making luminous signals every evening these last few days, but of course no one knows what they mean.

No more "communiqués" translated from German & Dutch papers, for the moment—there is a scare of some sort on just now.

MONDAY, OCTOBER 8

It is rumoured our success in Flanders last week is greater than the Boches admit, strategically; a Dutch paper even compared its consequences to those of the battle of the Marne! "Feu roulant" [rolling barrage] again this afternoon.[10] . . . Everybody is very exercised about hiding as much of their metal things as possible; the Germans did all the Rue de Trèves to-day to look them up. . . .

TUESDAY, OCTOBER 9

Fortunately the Communiqués have returned, & told us there was a very excited sitting in the Reichstag last Saturday. They don't seem satisfied with Michaëlis, Helleferich [Helfferich] & their minister of war.[11] Last night was to be a very important meeting also, I am longing for particulars. Marthe Kervyn has come from St. André, & brought my blanket from Bruges, in view of my having it made into a coat. I will see her to-morrow, & hear something of dear old Bruges. It is said that Roulers is completely rased [razed] by our artillery. God grant our objectives may be obtained in Flanders, & the land freed so that we may negotiate.

WEDNESDAY, OCTOBER 10

Had a full day. Down town early for shopping, found underwear for boys, a part here, another there, & so *expensive* 4 tiny skeins of black wool, for mending stockings, not

---

[8] "War Days," a daily chronicle in *La Belgique.*

[9] Count Hans Albrecht von Harrach, head of the Press Bureau of the Government-General, was a close collaborator of Von der Lancken.

[10] The rolling (or creeping) barrage allowed infantry to follow a slow-moving artillery "curtain."

[11] Karl Theodor Helfferich, secretary of the interior, lost his post on October 23. Chancellor Georg Michaelis was ousted a week later.

even 40c before war, now 4 frs, & everything on the same scale. Had a letter from Père Guinet the Provincial of "les oblats de Marie," [religious order] asking to see me at the Basilica, to give me news of the Boulez.[12] His letter was addressed "Miss Thorp" had been opened by the military censorship . . .(one may close letters addressed in Brussels, but not outside) & this ~~was in~~ was in) [*sic*] I called on Martha Kervyn, who had kindly brought my red blanket from Bruges, to make into a coat. She says bombs fall over the place there on moonlight nights; not long ago one fell in their pond *50 meters from the house* at the Château St. André; another damaged Count van den Steen's house. She travelled to Brussels in the evening—the train quite dark as far as Ghent. A German officer had taken her passport to her, last Sunday, in a carriage, through the pouring rain, & had said "Vous pourrez dire qu'il y a, au moins, un gentil Allemand!" ["Now you'll be able to mention at least one kind German!"] All ~~German~~ men, from 16 to 48 years old, born in Belgium of German fathers, even though they are naturalized, have been called up to the military authorities. What now? Marthe said Ada Houvenaghel was threatened to have 40 Germans to put up in her house.[13] What of my few goods & chattels there then? A good thing I've secured the red blanket!

THURSDAY, OCTOBER 11

Ctesse Paolo de B[14] had the visit of a half German Belgian Count who was very "down-hearted" about the state of Germany just now. . . . The burgomaster of Roulers ~~says~~ evacuated here with all his population,[15] says the losses of the Germans in Flanders are immense, that on both sides of the roads into Roulers the dead bodies are heaped up; that the English Artillery is terribly destructive; that division after division of Germans are brought to the front & killed. Soldiers have frequently been heard to say that the English could pierce the front if they liked, but that their tactics consist in killing the most Germans possible ~~without~~ while destroying the least possible of Belgium towns & villages.

FRIDAY, OCTOBER 12
SATURDAY, OCTOBER 13

The Germans are making perquisitions in all the houses to see if the brass & other metals have been delivered. Everyone is busy hiding all they can.

---

[12] Father Antonin Guinet O.M.I., provincial of the Congregation of Missionary Oblates of Mary Immaculate; the Brussels congregation resided in Koekelberg, a suburb of Brussels, site of the basilica (in construction since 1905).

[13] The Houvenaghels were a patrician family of Bruges.

[14] Marie du Passage, spouse of Count Paul "Paulo" de Borchgrave d'Altena.

[15] Civilians left Roeselare (Roulers) because of heavy shelling; British planes bombed the city later that month and a complete evacuation followed in November.

The weather is so stormy, wind & rain in quantity; the battle field in Flanders is like a sea of mud. God help the poor men there! Everybody here is shivering in their homes, not daring to use already the very small provision of coal each one has. We have no "chauffage central" [central heating] going, nothing but a wood fire in the schoolroom in the evening & one in the hall. Not allowed to light our gas-stoves, the allowance being limited too. Many people have to go to bed in the dark—nothing to burn or light where there is no electricity or gas, both threatened to be cut off beyond a certain measure.

SUNDAY, OCTOBER 14

This war means to us a return to the medieval ages in many things.... Country women are spinning the wool from their own sheep, in the measure allowed by the Boches, for everything is "regulated." A well known family in Brussels, fearing to have their mattress wool requisitioned like in the étape & at Antwerp, have sent theirs to be spun, to make clothes for the poor. There is such a scarcity of wool & cotton. They say Bruges is very animated by "cafés chantants, cinemas etc for the benefit of the German troops, & that the greatest quantity available of ("articles de modes" dress, millinery) etc etc is sent there for the "ladies" (quantity not quality, fortunately) who are friendly to the soldiers. Politics in Berlin are very "stretched" between the Socialists & the government. I think the Chancellor & von Cappelle must retire.[16]

MONDAY, OCTOBER 15

... Père G. always believed war would come; he lived several years in French Lorraine.

He says many men in Flanders are working "voluntarily" for the Germans, their great destitution & high wages account for it. Having the *German* soldiers in all the houses & the long absence of their own men cause *many of* the women to be too easily influenced by them, also! When Isie saw Marthe off for Bruges last Saturday at the Gare du Nord, she saw many miserably poor men & women going off as volunteer workers to Germany! alas that the war lasts so long!

TUESDAY, OCTOBER 16

Mr. Wittouck gave us each a ~~piece~~ cake of good soap of "before the war", such a boon! quite soothing to feel && look at. He must have paid it dear. What we buy now, almost its weight in gold, is a horrid compound of pumice stone powder, soda, & no grease at all, & it makes the skin ugly & uncomfortable.

---

[16] Admiral Eduard von Capelle, state secretary for the German navy, banned socialist literature

There is so much robbery everywhere. Darchambaud's shop was robbed, from Sunday to Monday night, of 50 thousand francs worth of furs. I wonder if Maud's fur coat was in it! Will the Germans get to Petrograd, now that they have taken Dago & Oesel?[17] No stirring news these days & the Reichstag adjourned till Dec 15th. Will Michaëlis retire? or will von Cappelen [von Capelle] suffice as scape-goat for all their "gaffes"???

WEDNESDAY, OCTOBER 17

Beautiful weather, & good for our brave Tommies. Heard the cannon that had been silent to us, these last days.

No special news from the front. Mr. de Bestequi, the Mexican diplomat, announced this evening that Mexico had declared war on Germany, but nothing of it in the papers yet.[18]

THURSDAY, OCTOBER 18, & FRIDAY, OCTOBER 19

On Thursday Villalobar gave a big tea-party & cinema of "his" famous fête at Val-Duchesse on Sept 8th. Everyone delighted to see himself & each other on the film. . . .

A terrible trial to the poor is having no light when evening sets in—it is agony to those who don't have gas, as no petroleum or carbur [acetylene gas for lamp fuel] or anything is obtainable. I saw a poor woman who suffers terribly from this idea—I must try to get her a candle.

SATURDAY, OCTOBER 20

Cannon very loud all last evening & night, weather fortunately clear & bright.

Had to buy an umbrella, 41 frs!!!!! only a little good silk remains in a few shops, for umbrellas; no means of finding the ordinary quality—all the medium qualities, in all things have been sold everywhere. . . .

Shops closing every day, having no more goods for sale, & *the windows of* those that are still open tell a pathetic tale of "trying to keep up a good front" with the few articles that remain.

Bacon & fat 30 frs the kilo.

from the fleet in August 1917. In an October Reichstag speech, he accused the left wing of the German Socialist Party of fomenting revolution. His inability to produce evidence alienated the party and led to the dismissal of Michaelis.

[17] The Estonian islands Dago (Hiiumaa) and Oesel (Saaremaa) were taken by German forces in October 1917.

[18] Don Miguel de Béistegui, first secretary of the Mexican legation in Brussels, married to a Belgian.

A few old fashioned air-ships (dirigibles) were flying about this morning, we hadn't seen anything like a zeppelin for a long time.

New bills on the walls call for workers, men & women, to labour at "digging" in France & Belgium (as navvies for making trenches, of course) good wages offered of course; the misery of so many being so great here, it is not astonishing that a certain number can't resist the possibility of getting food.

I made investigations about my lost parcels to Dick. There are generally only a few despatched to Ruhleben, & only make up a small case, which, being light & portable, is, it appears, stolen between its arrival at Spandau station & getting to the camp....

SUNDAY, OCTOBER 21
MONDAY, OCTOBER 22

... To-night's papers announce another attack of Zeppelins on the English coast, on the 19th, so probably the one we saw here on Saturday morning had been to England, alas!

The Allies seem very firm about continuing to fight till they get back Alsace Lorraine—I wonder if ever the Germans will finish by giving it up instead of letting it return to ~~milit~~ France after a military success, which they probably know must come if the war is prolonged. A tailor-made dress in Vienna costs 1,700 frs, wrote Lady Phipps' niece Ctesse Apponyi, asking to have one made here where they are 600 *or 700 frs* instead of the habitual 200 frs or so.[19]

TUESDAY, OCTOBER 23
WEDNESDAY, OCTOBER 24

... I made inquiries to-day about having boots clumped with wooden soles & heels. Wood specially cut & sold for this purpose is sold cheap, 75 c the pair. We shall all have to come to this, leather being "hors de prix," [unaffordable] when it can be found; what there is is about to be requisitioned. I wonder if the Boches will use any more Zepps, after their losses in the recent attack. Fine day to-day, but a terrible gale blowing since sunset.

THURSDAY, OCTOBER 25

This day in 2 months will be the 4th Xmas of this "3 Xmas war" as poor Kitchener prophesied ...

---

[19] US-born heiress Gladys Steuart, the wife of Count Gyula Apponyi de Nagy-Appony.

Thank God for our success on the French front, between Soissons & Laon, 7,500 prisoners! and a small advance for us English, in that terrible "bois de Houthulst" (Vrijbosch) which I read is a formidable German fortress.

Count Jean de Mérode acted upon a good inspiration. . . . He being "Grand Maréchal de la Cour" the Kaiser, on his last visit to Brussels, presented him with his "imperial" bust in bronze, & a dedication. Count de Mérode has just sent it in to the German requisition of metals (artistic or otherwise) & has refused to be paid for the weight of it. I should like to have seen the faces of the Boches who received it. . . .

FRIDAY, OCTOBER 26

A very dismal day, rained all the time. We were rejoicing over the French victory on the Aisne (Soissons-Laon) when this evening came the bad news of the big Italian defeat—30 thousand prisoners made by the Boches & Austrians. Latter never do any good till the Germans arrive to support them. What a pity this has occurred, after the hard times the Italians had! There must be great excitement in Berlin, now the Kaiser is back from Constantinople, concerning how he will act in choosing a successor for Michaëlis—will he turn to the Pan-germanists or to the Reichstag & call them it delegates to be consulted??? Life is very dreary on the whole. . . . I must do what I preach to the poor, & take it only day by day. Dieu nous aide!

SATURDAY, OCTOBER 27

Alas! Alas! for the Italians! to-night the *Belgischer Kurier* says the Centrals have made 60 thousand prisoners! and that the Italian Cabinet has fallen.[20] What will be the result? We are getting on well in Flanders, & the French especially well on the Aisne—but I fear we shall not make 60 thousand prisoners. How long will it all last!

Each day brings fresh hardship. I bought "carbure" [acetylene gas for lamp fuel] to-day, for an old couple, absolutely without any light; it is 7 frs 50 the kilo—the ordinary normal price 65 centimes. I bought a pair of boots for Serge 115 frs, & the tops are in cloth, if entirely in leather, they would have been at least 200 frs. A kilo of leather for soling boots costs 135 frs . . . & now, all the leather, & boots, from all the shops & factories are to be given up to the Germans—so no more boots will be obtainable, except by fraud & in secret, like so many things now, & the price will be????

All the dogs 40 centimeters in height are requisitioned by the Boches, for traction service (maxim guns I presume "mitrailleuses" [machine guns]) & will be kept & paid for only if they are fit for the work required. Imprisonment & fines for those who suppress their dogs to avoid presenting them.

---

[20] The twelfth battle of the Isonzo (Caporetto) was a disaster for the Italian army. Habsburg forces captured nearly 300,000 prisoners, thousands more deserted, and the Italians retreated almost to Venice.

I went again to the Prisoners' Agency about my lost parcels to Ruhleben—no news of them yet.... To-morrow I write to complain to the officer commanding Ruhleben camp.[21]

I think our offensive in Flanders & near Soissons continues—this afternoon the cannon was terribly loud again as I came through the Forest. At the same time I heard the cries & shouts of a German boys' school playing in the Avenues: Otto, Ulrich, Mayer, etc etc & the master's throaty grunting cries too....

How long, how long ...

SUNDAY, OCTOBER 28

This morning a letter from Dick; he has received my September parcel, thank God....

The news from the Italian front is awful; the Austrians talk now of over 80 thousand prisoners.... What consternation there must be amongst the Allies ... & what will the Allies' November Conference say about this new defeat.... It is maddening to see things get worse instead of better. How shall we get out of the trouble! I don't feel confident in a military victory for us....

MONDAY, OCTOBER 29

Last evening, between 9 & 10 o'clock, all lights were put out in Brussels' streets & cafés, the trams stopped & aeroplanes announced, but it appears there was no shooting over Brussels. They made a raid on Antwerp—vague rumours to-day of rather much damage done *there* & people killed & wounded—but we don't yet know. I pray God Sidonie & Bobby are safe! I suppose Brussels was warned, by Antwerp, to make all dark. We never know by the papers, where there have been raids, until they announce "So & so, victims of English cruelty & bombs; so & so had a father, son, uncle or cousin on the Belgian front." All that to in order to make the Belgians hate the English. And the victims are killed by the German firing more than by bombs thrown.

TUESDAY, OCTOBER 30

This evening's *Belgischer Kurier* says that the victims of the aeroplane raid, on Antwerp, last Sunday evening, are 50 killed & 100 wounded.... [I]f it is true, but probably there was much damage, alas! I trust that Sidonie & Bobby are safe, their living near the docks makes me uneasy.

Hertling, the Bavarian, has been named German Chancellor—once again without the Kaiser consulting the Reichstag—they won't like it. I wonder if Italy is going to have a revolution on account of her recent disaster. How & when will this

---

[21] Count Schwerin and his deputy, Colonel von Reichenback, were the commanding officers of Ruhleben in 1917.

terrible nightmare end! Dieu nous aide! I am thankful that my life is a very active one, that takes me away at times, from the ghastly *mental* visions of death & agony.

WEDNESDAY, OCTOBER 31

There is a rumour in town that the bombs that fell on Antwerp last Sunday evening, came from a German aeroplane, & that the Boches accuse of course the English.

To-day German agents went to all the boot-shops & had them closed. Pavlick was buying a pair of boots for 120 frs, & 2 Germans locked the door, & prevented any further business being done, so he had the last pair of boots that was sold there. Mr. Baudoin has returned from Holland & says all is very scarce & tight there also; bread cards in hotels, & one may not get more than the meagre ration. A lovely calm moonlight night, full moon, I fear there will be lives lost again through aero raids. . . .

THURSDAY, NOVEMBER 1, ALL SAINTS

A radiant autumn day.

Cannon very loud, especially in the afternoon, making windows & doors rattle.

FRIDAY, NOVEMBER 2, ALL SOULS

All souls weather, misty & damp. . . .

Hertling <u>has</u> accepted the post of Chancellor in Berlin, in spite of his age & ailments & opposition in certain quarters. The German papers say his is not "annexationist" that his spirit is that of the Pope's note, that he is a Catholic etc etc. Please God he may do some good!

Italy seems us to understand [*sic*] she is not crushed in spirit & will rise in union of all political parties.

SATURDAY, NOVEMBER 3

Mr. W taken seriously ill with broncho-pneumonia. . . . I went to fetch nurse, etc etc. Dieu W. aide!

Cannon <u>very</u> loud to-night; I presume there will be hard fighting in Flanders & France, to keep the Germans at it, & prevent them sending any more soldiers to Italy. Poor Italy! . . .

MONDAY, NOVEMBER 12

Since I wrote last a <u>terrible</u> change has occurred here. Good Mr. Wittouck died on Nov. 9th R.I.P. We buried him this morning. We are in the greatest grief. Our best friend has gone. Dieu nous aide!

And the bad news of the extended Italian defeat & the Anarchy in Russia, with Lenine in Kerensky's place, makes me more miserable than ever.

I have just read the ~~Kaiser~~ Emperor Charles I was nearly drowned in the Isonzo, & that he had a good long dip in the water. Will he recover! Yesterday there was a scandalous meeting of 3 thousand Flamingants at the Alhambra, exciting the assembly against the Belgian government at the Havre. I hear there were (fortunately) counter manifestations, but the Boches have succeeded in stirring up the hatred between the Flemish & the Walloons. Alas! Alas!

TUESDAY, NOVEMBER 13

The house is <u>very</u> sad & silent with its good Master in his grave, Mme. W. & the boys away & packing up in the greatest gloom. I walked to Boitsfort to see Mme. W [Frantz Wittouck], inconsolable. The cannon was going all the time, <u>such</u> slow work on our front, alas! if only <u>we</u> could make a rush like the Austrians in Italy! The Voorwaërts [*Vorwärts*] seems uneasy about the plan of adding a kingdom of Poland to Austria Hungary, & Duchies of Courland & Lithuania to Germany. Lenine's "coup d'état" in Russia results in a peace programme of very sweeping dimensions! Will it have any weight with the Allies! & what will the Centrals say?

WEDNESDAY, NOVEMBER 14

We attended the funeral service for dear Mr. Wittouck, at St. Job, this morning. R.I.P.

A foggy day, bad for our armies. News in to-day's *Belgique* most depressing, concerning Italy. Something too, of Kerensky overpowering Lenine & his Maximalists. I wonder <u>how</u> we, English, French, & Americans can ever get the <u>military</u> victory so much talked about, & I begin to feel we are "cutting off our nose to spite our face." The English who have lived under German sway in Belgium since 1914 can understand that. When the Van den Brandens[22] & Carola go to see their sons, prisoners at Liège, only <u>one</u> person is allowed in, & only for 5 minutes. The other day they saw a woman have her baby, of 3 months old, thrown on a table while she "ein person" [*sic*][23] was allowed in alone to see her husband.

ST. ALBERT THE KINGS FÊTE, THURSDAY, NOVEMBER 15

To-day is the 1,200th day of war! & how many of those I know have not lived to see it! Just a fortnight ago, dear Mr. Wittouck walked to church (all Saints day) with

[22] Possibly Jean Van den Branden, an assistant director at the Solvay firm, whose son, also named Jean, was arrested for attempting to join the Belgian army. He himself incurred a condemnation in 1915, as did his wife; another son had been killed in action in 1914.

[23] A rendering of the German "eine Person," in this case meaning "one visitor only."

Micha & me; it was a beautiful bright day. It is so hard to think we shall never have him with us again! . . .

God help him & his family & all those who loved him! This is my last night at the Fougeraie; we settle in town to-morrow. What other changes will there be, ere we return here!

Will this cruel war be ended? It seems now that Lenine's power was very fleeting & that Kerenski is again at the head of the government. No active news from Flanders. I hear there were demonstrations and Brabançonne at Ste Gudule this morning. How much happier I was this day last year, when I cried "Vive le roi" there with thousands of others!

FRIDAY, NOVEMBER 23

I left the Fougeraie a week ago to-day, Nov 16th. Mr. W's funeral service at the Sablon Church took place on the 17th, & on that day Mme. W & the boys returned to the house. I was too busy to write anything here of the war, & am still too sad & unsettled on account of our great, immense loss. . . . God help us all!

This last week the Maximalists in Russia *with Lenine* have got the upper hand, & want to make peace with Germany—whose creatures & agents they have been all the time. Clémencau [Clemenceau][24] has become Chef de [Head of] Cabinet in Paris, & preaches "unlimited war"! Lloyd George got into a scrape in England for the speech he made in Paris, & out of it by a satisfactory one he made to defend himself on his return to London. The best news is an English victory this week south & south west of Cambrai—so far, 8 thousand prisoners of which 180 officers & lots of cannon etc. This was specially due to the work of the tanks & was a surprise party for the Boches, who didn't expect anything in that part of the front.[25] . . .

The house is so sad & empty without its good master—the soul of the family has departed, alas! I never knew anyone so deeply & sincerely regretted. R.I.P.

I had a long letter, last Saturday, from Mary d'Alcantara, by . . . a specially favoured opportunity. . . . [*sic*] She wants sugar so badly for the children, but no means of getting her any. Fortunately she is able to get certain essential articles of food to dear Valérie once a week, what a boon! The German foreign affairs man here, Count Moltke, wanted to buy an old fashioned picture frame, from our neighbor, Gonthier, who didn't want to part with it, but bargained that he would sell it if Moltke got to Brussels a painting that was at Bruges. After saying it was impossible, M. arrived at G's door, the same night, at 11.30, in a motor, with the picture rolled up safely. M was very pale & upset, said he had been through a perfect hell of fire & bombs bursting over Ghent on his way back from Bruges, where he went himself to get the picture. Poor dear Valérie & Emma! what they must endure!

[24] Georges Clemenceau, prime minister of France from 1917 to 1920.

[25] In the Battle of Cambrai, for the first time, tanks were used (relatively) successfully.

SATURDAY, NOVEMBER 24

The particulars concerning the battle of Cambrai point to the success of the attack being due this time to the tanks; their cry was "each tank must do its duty" & they did.

... Yesterday 2 German sub-officers came to this house, to inspect the water-pipes. Which are <u>not</u> in brass—they didn't attempt to take stock of anything else. When will we regain our liberty!!

TUESDAY, NOVEMBER 27

Different people coming from Germany say that the people there have become quite indifferent to German military success—that the only thing they demand is: "peace." Still, in spite of Lenin's proposals of armistice, we realise quite well that the G. government <u>can't</u> further them, they are too advanced, & if taken "au sérieux" would probably increase the revolutionary spirit in Germany.

A diplomat just back from Berlin says that the women are stopped in the streets & stripped of their boots, if in leather. People in the region of Mons, are walking about with two overcoats & the most clothing possible, in order to keep it from the Boches, who are requisitioning clothing over there....

I wonder if in France & England with the Allies, people realise what everything costs here.... <u>When</u> shall <u>we</u> have normal prices again for anything? The misery of the poor is <u>intense</u>, & they tell me how happy & satisfied they were "avant la guerre" when they could get sufficient work. Everyone bears the mark of starvation & privation.

WEDNESDAY, NOVEMBER 28

Mr. van Vollenhoven has just dined here & told us: "that the Sultan of Turkey has sent him a special messenger from Constantinople, to ask him, to procure for him (the Sultan) through The Hague, & from London: 40 pairs of trousers, 12 ~~pairs~~ sets of winter under garments, & 12 sets of summer ditto. The patterns were brought, & the order executed in London, & the underwear is already on its way to Constantinople. All that in defiance of the Black List!!! Vollenhoven thinks the war will last another 2 years! & then not end in a military victory. If so, why shouldn't it end now? He says <u>he</u> has settled affairs so that no more of the Allies' aeroplanes will bombard Brussels or Antwerp. I asked him if the Boches had promised also not to do so, as they did at Antwerp in ~~Octo~~September, when there were 50 killed & 100 wounded.... He didn't like to admit the Boches did it, but I asked if the English had owned to it & he could not answer to that question. I told him we are all convinced it <u>was</u> the Boches, since they haven't (according to their never failing custom) published the list of the "victims of the English, with the names of their respective relatives in the Belgian army" in order to excite hatred against England. To-day I had to go the "Meldeamt" to announce my return to the winter residence—the German was polite & I also. How many more times shall I have to go to them about change of residence!!! Oh! if they could change <u>theirs</u> before the summer!

THURSDAY, NOVEMBER 29

This afternoon we went to visit *"l'ecole professionnelle du Cardinal Mercier 31. Bd Lambermont, dirigeé par les Aumôniers du travail,* with the Abbé Reyn, the founder, at the head. What a <u>good</u> man he is! He has 50 French war orphan boys housed & fed there for the moment, & a lot of trouble they give him. He had just received the news that 3 of his priests, Aumôniers du travail [Labor Chaplains], at Seraing, have been arrested & imprisoned by the Germans; one was already in their clutches. . . .

FRIDAY, NOVEMBER 30

This morning Mr. Ashman, the English race horse breeder, of St. Denis (Ghent)[26] called on me to give me news of the Boulez, & we had a pleasant chat. The Boches, (those who belong to the jockey club like him) granted him the great favour of a passport to Brussels, for business with other members of the J.C. [Jockey Club] & they sometimes treat him a little less rigorously than usual. The Governor of Ghent, Von Something[27] goes to see his horses now & then, & says "Quand vos compatriotes arriveront-ils"! ["When will your countrymen [the British] arrive?"] When indeed??? Ashmans' place is near the aviation camp & he is treated to a near sight of bursting bombs. Food in Ghent somewhat cheaper than here, eggs 75 centimes instead of 1 f 05, potatoes (smuggled) less also.

SATURDAY, DECEMBER 1

Villalobar & Vollenhoven were both here to-day—they both think that the events in Russia will force the Allies to make peace also—& Lord Landsdowne's letter in the *Daily Telegraph*? or *Chronicle?* is the given in the Dutch papers, is the subject of all conversations this evening in Brussels.[28] His theories seem to have veered round immensely to making peace on milder conditions than supposed so far in England, but of course his opinions are personal. In any case, I wonder what will happen, if all the German & Austrian army from the East front, & all their prisoners released from Russia come to increase the forces against us!!! And alas, the Boches write this

---

[26] George Ashman ran a well-known racing stable at Sint-Denijs-Westrem near Ghent.

[27] Oberstleutnant Georg von Wick from Hannover.

[28] Lord Landsdowne's open letter advocated a negotiated peace.

evening of having retaken some of our newly won villages near Cambrai and 4000 prisoners. Alas! Alas!

SUNDAY, DECEMBER 2

I went to Zuen early, with the boys, for a service for their Father. At Petit Bigard, & even here in town, the cannon was very loud all last night, & the sky in the distance was quite red they say.

The news arrived to-day that Elizabeth de Bourblanc's husband *Count* Yves, was killed near Verdun. Poor girl! he went to war when they were married only 4 months, & she has a little daughter. He had already been all but suffocated by asphyxiating gas, saw those around him die from it. He was the Frenchman, an obstinate Breton Legitimist, who refused the Legion of Honour, because he would not accept it from a Republic.

MONDAY, DECEMBER 3

There seems to be a general feeling, in Brussels even with those who were absolutely "jusq'au-boutistes" [those who championed fighting war until the end] that the war must cease *shortly* by a discussed peace, now that Russia asks for peace. The fear is that Germany & Austria, having all their army & prisoners back from Russia, would certainly make a huge offensive against the West front & that we should not be able to resist. Mme. W, after Society gossip on the subject, feels quite confident that I need not purchase more than 2 dozen tablets of soap (that I have an opportunity of buying) so sure does she feel that peace is very near. I fear we shall want more soap than that before the end comes! The Marquis de Villalobar said yesterday that "*il avait en poche une paix superbe pour nous*" ["he [the German Emperor] was offering a very advantageous peace for us,"] when he went, 2 years ago, after the Kaiser's proposal last December, to offer it to the Allies—who rejected it without examining it. He thinks it won't be as advantageous for us now. . . .

That Lenine & all his clique are simply paid Boche agents is a well known fact— Von der Lancken said, in Brussels, some time ago, that one day's war was an expensive business for Germany, & that Lenine cost them less daily than the war.

Carola has had the Boches in her house to make an inventory of all her furniture, which they threaten to sell by auction, because she will not pay a fine of 5 thousand marks because Philip attempted to cross the frontier & is now in prison.[29] She doesn't know how her affair will end, but vows she would rather be sold up than pay. Her cousin Mme. de Crombrugghe, at Moere, had a bomb pass through the walls of

---

[29] Philippe de Crombrugghe de Picquendaele, son of MT's friend Carola née Van der Bruggen. Their Brussels residence was in the elegant rue de Crayer, off avenue Louise.

her drawing-room while seated in it; she was not hurt, ~~but~~ merely displaced violently, but the walls were shattered.³⁰

No particulars of Cte. De Bourblanc's death, simply a telegram from Broqueville to Villalobar: "Mort glorieusement pour la Patrie devant Verdun." [Died gloriously for the Fatherland before Verdun] Poor Elisabeth, without her parents or own family on the other side! God help her! It snowed last night & this morning, the streets were white & sloshy.

TUESDAY DECEMBER 4
WEDNESDAY DECEMBER 5
THURSDAY DECEMBER 6

I have just been dining beside the Marquis de Villalobar; he is going [to] return to Oydonck [Ooidonk] soon, & will take them news of me. He says the English, "his dearly beloved English, who all have something that makes them specially loveable" will, in a year after peace, be saying: "The Germans are not so bad after all!!! I didn't agree with him there. . . .

FRIDAY, DECEMBER 7

. . . Vollenhoven dined here again, we had a little talk; he, like myself, fears the masses of released Germans *from Russia* will be rushed at us, if peace is signed between them. No one can really imagine how events may turn now.

Darchambaud is selling off all his goods rapidly, as an "arrêté" is coming out, that like for the boots, the Boches take ("buy") 9 tenths of all the shops contain, leaving 1 tenth for our wants. I ordered materials for two suits, to be made next summer for Micha & Serge.

SATURDAY, DECEMBER 8
SUNDAY, DECEMBER 9

A month to-day poor Mr. W. died. We all went to the cemetery. R.I.P. A new German "arrêté" has caused all lights to be hidden when it gets dark. The very few street lamps that are lit are darkened by blue paint, tram lights ditto, none may be seen in houses, in fact the same state of light as *has been* in London this long time. It is really dangerous to be out after dark & I am glad not to have to leave the house.

---

³⁰ Valentine de Nieulant Pottelsberghe, wife of Albert de Crombrugghe de Looringhe. Their château "Le bon séjour" was in Moere, near Ostend, only ten kilometers from the front. The occupying forces placed a "Max" railroad gun (nicknamed "Langer Max") on the grounds. The château was bombed repeatedly.

Vollenhoven told me on Friday, that "living" in Holland is almost as bad as here, cards for everything & hardly any coal. His mother is obliged to forsake the big rooms *of her house* & live in a small one, in order to save firing; that the Dutch people are furious to see their potatoes being sent to Germany in order to get coal in return.

MONDAY, DECEMBER 10

All the shop windows, fanlights of doors *etc* are darkened; we can hardly see a tram passing on the Bd; all the lights are dark blue. To-day, further sale of goods at linen-drapers forbidden, & by Dec. 22nd, they have to give to the Boches an inventory of all that remains in their shops; the Boches then relieve them of 9/10 of everything, at the cost price *of July, 1914*, plus a little for their expenses & interest since then, I think the greatest percentage is 2%. . . . Our life here & the continual depressing news is . . . enervating, to say the least, & yet we, in this house, have so much to thank God for, & ought never to complain.

TUESDAY, DECEMBER 11

We had a meeting of the "Assistance Discrète" this morning, about making money again. We spent a million francs this last year for the entire work. Now it is to be a "Tombola Alimentaire," [charity event] nothing but eatables as prizes, & the first prize (gros lot) a pig. Let us hope it will be a "<u>fat</u> lot"! I think this will catch on well, everybody being famished more or less. The tickets are only 10c each. I have got many shops to put them up for sale, & on the 23rd, the "Boches" have allowed us to have them sold publicly in the streets, by <u>boys</u> & girls; they don't always allow boys to sell; we don't know why. I shall lose a lot of money if Russia won't recognize the former "dettes d'Etat," [state bonds] but the Dutch papers seem hopeful, & can't see how Russia could find it good policy to ignore those loans.

WEDNESDAY, DECEMBER 12
THURSDAY, DECEMBER 13

Yesterday we read the Allies took Jerusalem.[31] Deo Gratias! It is <u>good</u> to know Christian flags are floating there at last! Even the German papers own it is a great moral & historical success for us. How I should like to be there for Xmas! the 4th War Xmas, not foreseen by Kitchener who spoke of a 3 Xmas war. . . .

---

[31] General Edmund Allenby's British forces, aided by Arab allies, entered Jerusalem after a long campaign.

FRIDAY, DECEMBER 14
SATURDAY, DECEMBER 15

... The British Relief Fund (during War) is a grand & generous institution. I know, for a fact, that many English women, employed in Belgian families, being not paid, or very underpaid on account of war, are getting 50 or 60 frs a month in order to get extra food & necessaries, the food being very poor & scarce in many families of the upper classes.

MONDAY, DECEMBER 17

Count John d'Oultremont died quite suddenly this morning, exactly 8 years, (to an hour) after his Lord & Master, King Leopold II. I remember *it was in 1909*, I was at Bruges, it was a dull, gloomy day; Mary d'Alcantara came to see me & Willie Moore saw us as we were crossing the Grand Place.... How tame & easy all was then! ... Mary d'Alcantara arrived in town to-day, like a "bolt from the blue," with an 8 days' passport. How glad she must be! 18 months she hasn't been to Brussels! I shall see her to-morrow.

The streets are <u>so dark</u>, after dark, that people are being stopped & asked to give up their furs, boots, money etc, in fact some are almost stripped, after being requested not to be alarmed. We think the Boches will forbid us to go out, after 7. pm, at the end of this month. Every evening, & all the time, luminous signals are being made in the sky, & no one can make them out. It looks like sheet lightning, flashes here & there, & sometimes a great flashlight. Are they exercising merely?

I went to visit a mother & daughter for the A.D. [Assistance Discrète], well to do people who had a business & their own house at Wenduyne.[32] Just 3 years ago, they had to leave, with 40 minutes notice, & have lost all they possessed there; the poor girl suffers with heart trouble resulting from all their emotions— & so many thousands have a similar story to tell; alas!

Dieu nous aide!

TUESDAY, DECEMBER 18

I was <u>so glad</u> to see Mary d'Alcantara to-day, & hear news of her part of the world. She came on business for "La Dentelle."[33] They are all trying to keep up their spirits, doing good work all round. For some things *(in shopping)* they appear to be better off than we here, & in others less so. Between 4 & 5 hundred oak trees have been cut in the wood at Oydonck [Ooidonk]. Bombs have fallen quite near....

[32] Wenduine, on the Belgian coast, now in the front zone.
[33] The CRB Lace Committee.

THURSDAY, DECEMBER 20

I haven't something special to write every day, so that explains the days between. The poor suffer so much through want of light & coal . . . it is heartrending! The town sells them a small quantity, but *more than* half the time there is no fire in their dreary rooms, & no light after dark for those who haven't gas. . . .

FRIDAY, DECEMBER 21

This morning I had the pleasure of seeing the Xmas number of the *Illustrated London News* someone had lent Mary d'Alc.—a precious treat. I then went with her to Mme. de Hem's, to have her portrait somewhat altered.[34] While she posed, we "at last" were able to talk a bit seriously (for there are always people wanting to see her) & we agreed upon my sending through her, to dear Valérie, all the little reserve of sugar I have & a long letter. The Marquis motors her home on Monday, so all is facilitated, & dear Val will have a little surprise for this sad Xmas. I thank God for this opportunity of sending her something; how grieved I am to know she is so miserable.

MONDAY, DECEMBER 24

4th Xmas of the War, not foreseen by Kitchener

Serge ill all day, I didn't stir from the house. . . . I have to forego my midnight mass; I think of that of Xmas Eve, in Bruges 1909, with W.M. [Willie Moore]; & of all the poor fellows in the trenches. God grant they will be back in their homes long before next Xmas Eve, but how many of those alive now, will be missing alas!
      . . . I trust dear Val is in possession of my parcel & letter.

THURSDAY, DECEMBER 27

On Xmas day, at our Xmas tree party, I had a chat with the Marquis de Villalobar. He & Mary took 2 hours in his motor, to reach Ghent, there, he gave her the car for ¾ of an hour to do her errands, so I . . . think & hope she left my parcel etc at dear Val's immediately. Villalobar gave me news of Oydonck [Ooidonk]. He thinks the war can't last much longer, that all nations, even England will want peace, but of course the Lloyd George & Clémenceau [Clemenceau] Ministries must fall first. . . . He claims that war will always exist (not this one of course) but that fighting to the bitter end, in order that there never will be another, is (a or an?) utopia, since the first brothers of creation fought & one killed the other.

[34] Louise de Hem, a society portraitist with an art nouveau studio and townhouse of her own design in Brussels.

I went to the cemetery yesterday, with Mme. W, to her husband's grave, all under the snow. . . [W]e heard the cannon very plainly out there. The Fords called to-day, Alec as British to the backbone as ever, raging against those, especially the English, who begin to think the war has lasted long enough. He quite believes in Lloyd George, & that the Americans are going to change the aspect of all things, & doesn't seem to fear there might be a big German offensive on the front before they can arrive.

I was told to-day that 14 railway tracks are being made from Maria-Aeltre to the English front in Flanders, cut through everything, regardless of houses & property, all to get the Boche troops the quicker to the front.[35]

Dieu nous aide!

SATURDAY, DECEMBER 29

Have just dined with Mr. van den Pol (Vollenhoven's cousin) a nice Dutchman on the Belgian Relief Committee. He told us the following <u>true</u> story; he had it from a German officer who witnessed the scene. After the first English success at Cambrai, about 2 thousand brave English cavalrymen made a rush at the Boches. They were all cut down by the German artillery, except about 13, who reached the German lines & were made prisoners. When they were given bread to eat, one of them "<u>coolly</u> demanded: "if there was not any marmalade to be had . . ." & they gave him some! so flabbergasted were the Boches at such an attitude from a man who had been through <u>such</u> an ordeal, in fact they own they felt they wanted to salute <u>such</u> self-possession.

Mr. Van den Pol also told us that 2000 Englishmen were, alas! drowned lately in the mud & water that hides the craters made by the mines & bombs, in an inundated battle-field.

Mme. W had the visit of Mahmout Khan, the Persian minister here, just back from Switzerland, where he met his brother, fresh from Petrograde, where latter had been minister these last 23 years, till Lenine came to rule, when he would remain no longer. He says that England caused the fall of the Czar, by interfering to give Russia a constitution, but that the Revolution went naturally to lengths never imagined possible, & with a result exactly opposite to what was hoped for. <u>I</u> say: How had the Czar & Court acted to make England want to interfere? Qui vivra verra! [Time will tell]

1918

Two years ago to-day I started my diary. Never thought then I should continue to-day. . . . We still hear the same eternal cannon . . . & <u>how</u> much longer? . . .

[35] Maria-Aalter, midway between Ghent and Bruges.

TUESDAY, JANUARY 1

My 4th war Birthday, alas! Had a sweet letter from poor Dick at Ruhleben, he means to be courageous still in this new year. God help him! . . . Saw in the *Belgique* that Mme W's cousin, old M. Gouremikine, ex-premier in Russia, his wife & son in law, have been murdered by "des malfaiteurs" [evil-doers] at his estate in Caucasus.[36] We all agreed not to breathe a word of it to Mme W to-day, that she might not be grieved on New Year's day, but I dread having to tell her tomorrow, as she will live in greater fear than ever, of danger to her other friends & relatives in disturbed Russia. No news of the war, except rumors of a near & terrible Boche offensive at Chemin des Dames & Verdun.

What does 1918 reserve for us? God grant an honorable peace & security for the future, & the healing of as many wounded hearts & bodies.

THURSDAY, JANUARY 3

We hear <u>so</u> <u>little</u> concerning the war, & hardly any "side-tales" since poor Mr. W's death, he used to see different men at club & elsewhere, who had things to relate, & he told us then at meals—which are now, alas, very dull & uninteresting.

At noon to-day, the first time for many months, there was an aeroplane fight over Brussels, hard firing about half an hour, but it didn't seem to create much interest. I don't think the Allies' aeros came to throw bombs anywhere, probably only to pursue or reconnoitre, for we heard no explosions. So far, we haven't heard if there were any victims. We are wondering if it is true the Allies are going to "converse" among themselves on the conditions of peace between Germany & Russia, in order to give an answer of some sort to the Bolshevists. . . . I am anxious to know. Some people are sanguine about good peace being the result???

SATURDAY, JANUARY 5

. . . The soap, book, thread, dress questions, besides food and <u>all the rest</u>, are agonies. We went to the rehearsal of some children's performance for a charity—tableaux vivants & dances. The Boches only allowed them to take place, on condition that something in Flemish should be recited or sung at the same time . . . so a singer had to be called upon to do so, but she only consented on condition she sang not in Flemish alone, but in French also. <u>How</u> the Boches work to make one half of Belgium hate the other! . . .

---

[36] Ivan Goremykin, conservative prime minister of Russia in 1914–1916, was killed by a street mob in Sochi on December 24, 1917.

MONDAY, JANUARY 7 (RUSSIAN MASS)

This morning I assisted at the funeral mass for Count Yves de Bourblanc (poor Elizabeth d'Huart's husband) killed for his country, before Verdun, on October 25th, 1917.

There were many present, praying devotedly. The Belgian flag & French colors on the sarcophagus. The Brabançonne was played after the service (I wonder if the Marseillaise would have been instead, if the poor young hero hadn't been a staunch Royalist . . .).

It thawed at last, all day, town gloomy & muddy. Confusion between the Bolshevists & the Boches, who don't agree at all for the moment about the conditions of peace.

TUESDAY, JANUARY 8

There were a few people to dinner; the most interesting was Mahmout Khan, the Persian minister, a good looking, very intelligent & well informed man, who had lived in a great number of capitals, & gleaned abundantly for his mind. His brother was minister of Persia at Petrograd for over 20 years but couldn't stand Lenine & Trotsky, so the 2 brothers met recently, in Switzerland.[37] The Petrograd Persian told this one that the Allies had mounted a "coup d'Etat," to dethrone the Czar, (who was an impossible man to deal with in politics, & owing to this absolute lack of decision & personal opinion was constantly preventing the Allies doing the right thing) for the end of March 1914 but that the Revolutionaries stole a march on them [preempted them], & did away with all the dynasty. The Allies merely meant to have a Russian Czar with a character of his own, & not a Republic—then happened all we know.

WEDNESDAY, JANUARY 9

We are very astounded by the moderation of Lloyd George's speech of the 5th, first read in the Dutch papers—the peace seems written all over it.[38] . . . God grant it will meet with "men of good will" and . . . good faith in Germany. I am anxious to see the German impressions it has caused.

Heavy snow to-day, deeper than we have had in Brussels for many years; how many people will die of cold this severe winter! And in this country where coal is so plentiful! All because the Boches have made it impossible by all their restrictions, requisitions of every means of conveyance etc. for it to be sold. Even with money

---

[37] The Persian envoys remain unidentified.

[38] British Prime Minister David Lloyd George addressed trade union delegates on January 5, 1918, suggesting reparations, an independent Poland, and the need for continued British sacrifice. The Dutch papers may have presented the speech as more conciliatory than it was.

to offer, it is not to be bought, except here and there by chance, at <u>exorbitant</u> prices. Cannon terribly loud all day.

FRIDAY, JANUARY 11

The Marquis de Villalobar, l'abbé Reyn [&] a few others dined here to-night. I had a great discussion with Villalobar, my democracy against his "aristocracy." He said King George told him himself (when?) that Lloyd George is a scoundrel. . . . He— Vill—hates Republics, on parting he said "We will continue our discussion, next time" & I answered "I accept the challenge." He told us that Von der Lancken has returned from Berlin "écoeuré" [disgusted] of all the harm he heard the Boches still mean to do to the Belgians, in the way of requisitions, tightening the screw in every manner. I wonder if Von den Lancken isn't a real Boche hypocrite? . . . some people here say he is practically the governor of Belgium, & not at all Von Falkenhausen who is really only here for form's sake! It seems we are threatened again to have to give up our mattresses, like at Antwerp, Malines, & many other places. The Abbé Reyn told us that at Malines the Boches <u>took</u> a mattress from under the corpse of a poor man whose wife was very ill. Cardinal Mercier couldn't believe it, but went on the spot & saw it was true.

The Marquis always speaks of his love for the <u>old</u> England, as it was years ago; says also that he is quite Belgian in his feelings; that it is very fine for Wilson, & Lloyd George to make glorious speeches instead of obtaining an end to the sufferings of the Belgians, who prevented Europe being conquered immediately by the Germans. I replied that if the Allies had not & did not still hold out, Belgium would have finally to submit for good to German domination in one shape or another, but to that he won't agree; says that Germany will not prevent Belgium's total independence. . . .

I read Wilson's speech to-day, & the 14 articles of America's conditions of peace. What will result from the two fine speeches of this last week![39]

I am reading "Germany's swelled head" by *the Hungarian* Emile Reich, translated into French by H. Mansvic. *In French: la vanité Allemande.*[40] So much of it is very interesting just now, & I really think it true that the English never understood the conceit of the Germans.

SUNDAY, JANUARY 13

The Russian New Year's Eve . . .

I wonder if for next New Year they will have adopted our Gregorian Calendar?

[39] On January 8, US President Woodrow Wilson presented Congress with his vision of a postwar settlement, the so-called Fourteen Points.

[40] Emil Reich, a Hungarian-born publicist, had settled in England. His 1907 book was translated and reissued in 1914 to wide success.

Villalobar spoke also last Friday about the wicked things the Boches mean to do to Belgians: take all the money from the Banks, destroy all the factories not working for Germany etc. etc. Melle Cazé says we can't, here in Brabant, form an idea of the havoc & desolation that she saw in the north of France. . . . I wonder though, if the idea that America might use reprisals in the States against the Germans there, (at least in what concerns money) will not prevent such excesses here. It seems the poster about the requisition of mattresses is to appear shortly. . . what a shame! The only comfort left to people dying of hunger & cold.

MONDAY, JANUARY 14

M. de Kondriaffsky had the Germans 3 times in his house looking after his "copper & brass."[41] They sounded the ceilings to see if anything was hidden there. They perceived a photo of the Czar in one of the rooms, began talking of Petrograde, where one of them had been, & pointing to the Czar's picture said: "We shall help to bring him back!" . . .

WEDNESDAY, JANUARY 16

Private news came to Mme W. from her Russian friends—most of them ruined during the last two months by the awful revolution, their estates burned, the "richissime" Count Nostitz asking for a loan of money, instead of being able to finance all her family as she had hoped.[42] No particulars yet concerning the murder of the old Gouremikine couple & their son-in-law, but an account Mme Gouremikine gave in a letter of the very narrow escape they already had a short time ago through thieves visiting at night, the villa where they were boarding. They are all in a terrible plight. No news yet of the outcome of the assembly of the Kaiser & all his big wigs.

FRIDAY, JANUARY 18

I went to see the Rinquets & noticed that at "La Bascule" on the Ch^ssée de Waterloo, a real coal market is held.[43] Rows of carts, wagons, barrows of coal, all having come from Charleroi stand there & wait (not long) for buyers, at 325 francs the ton (one thousand kilos, so 32 fs 50 for a hundred kilos!!) and this is a country where coal is plentiful—thank the Boches, who have taken away, one may say all means of

---

[41] De Kondriaffsky remains unidentified.

[42] General Count Grigori Ivanovitch Nostitz, chief of Nicholas II's Imperial Guard, former military attaché in Berlin and Paris, and, in 1917, the tsar's personal representative at the Inter-Allied Conference.

[43] "La Bascule," a neighborhood in Ixelles.

conveyance for this dear coal is drawn from Charleroi by agonising, old, mere skin & bone horses, or by men & women. Hence the scarcity & price of coal in Brussels....

MONDAY, JANUARY 21

The cannon has been <u>terribly</u> loud these last 3 days & nights; to-day we heard it <u>very clearly</u> in town even, in spite of noise of trams & traffic. <u>What</u> is happening? Is it the forerunner of another offensive? Yesterday a notice was posted up to the effect that: "Flanders is proclaimed (by the Flamingants, d'accord [in accord] with the Boches) an independent country!!" With Flemish ministers for all offices! Vollenhoven & Mr. & Mme Van der Pol dined here, & Vollen. said this new departure placed him in a difficult position with regard to the Belgian authorities at the Havre & that he may have to have recourse to the so-called new authorities, which he doesn't want (naturally) to recognize; he said: "what shall I say to them if they come to call on me?" I suggested he should tell them they have mistaken the address, & the place they want to go to is a review of one of the music halls down town! It is <u>such</u> buffoonery, & really will be matter for derision & laughter later on in history, but of course official people here will be placed in difficult circumstances when needing to have recourse to any legal functionaries.

Weather much milder. The Dutchmen told me it is very funny to see, at the Hague, so many smart English officers & soldiers & also German military, allowed to be there, from the different German camps, whence they were released.[44] I wonder if poor Dick on the list for Holland, will be one of the chosen....

FRIDAY, JANUARY 25

The cannon has been <u>roaring</u> all the week, louder than ever, "on dit" [they say] that Ostend is greatly damaged by the Allies' fire, & that refugees are arriving thence in different places. The Boches have, of course, kept the civilians there the longest possible, as a protection to themselves, & especially to their sub-marine base. We read now, that the strikes & revolt in Austria last week were really serious, caused by the German signs of Pangermanism breaking out again during the negotiations at Brest Litovsk.[45]

---

[44] Civilian and military prisoners of war were exchanged through the neutral Netherlands. Prisoner release negotiations took place between Germany and Britain at The Hague. The agreements reached allowed for prisoners over the age of forty-five and other invalids to be exchanged on a one-for-one exchange model.

[45] Hardship on the home fronts led to strikes to protest "imperialist" war aims in Vienna, but also in Berlin.

Have just read von Hertling's & Czernin's speeches in answer to Lloyd George & Wilson. I think & <u>hope</u> they may further peace.[46]

Dieu le veuille [May God grant it]

MONDAY, JANUARY 28

The weather is simply <u>ideal</u> these days, 10 to 12 degrees, & beautiful sun. Will it hasten our? Or the German? offensive which seems to be imminent, but we don't know which of the two. The Germans, we presume, to steal a march on the Americans. We no longer hear the cannon; last week it was simply awful all the time. . . .

Nearly everybody thinks we are "en route" for peace, after Czernin's answer to Wilson's speech, & latter is to comment [on] Czernin's this week at Washington. If it is to be a diplomatic peace, God grant it will come at once, before more loss of life! Dieu nous aide!

WEDNESDAY, JANUARY 30

I was reassured yesterday about my letter to Edith . . . possibly reaching her, in spite of its length, in due time. I hope it will. The Voorwaerts [*Vorwärts*] of to-day says there are 300.000 men on strike in Berlin alone! What will be the result?

Vollenhoven spoke to the Boches about the mattress question. They declare <u>every</u> <u>one</u> shall be given up, even from under the sick & dying, from hospitals etc. etc. Such grief on this score from the poor sick I visited to-day! . . . I advise them to-day to have a German doctor to witness their misery, to see if the acute suffering of the aged will not melt them to making exceptions for that kind.

SATURDAY, FEBRUARY 2

This fact of the Germans taking the wool of every mattress is most distressing. . . . German aeroplanes are flying more frequently over Brussels. How I grieve for all the people they have killed in England & in Paris! Many people who had not applied to "War works" (*oeuvres de guerre*) for assistance, are obliged to do so now, after such long privations & almost starvation. The Boches are always appealing to men wanting work, especially navvies, to go to work for them near the front; glaring different coloured posters all over the town, offering great advantages to the men & their families. Not surprising if many succumb to the allurement, alas!

[46] The Central Powers replied to Wilson (and Lloyd George) in late January with a somewhat noncommittal statement that agreed with many of the ideas "in principle" but calling for a conference to detail the claims.

WEDNESDAY, FEBRUARY 6

Had a card from dear Valérie to-day, not dated, but stamped on 4th inst [of this month]; she mentioned the "hint" I had given her in my last: spoke of "having fait le versement en question à la Deutches [*sic*] Bank" . . . ["having wired money with the Deutsche Bank"] We are obliged to have recourse to some such [ruse], as post-cards (never letters) are allowed only on German business in the Étape, and even then many don't reach Valérie or are returned to me—just as the fit takes Censor. The great "question du jour" is the mattresses. People are trying to hide their wool, some even bottle it! Stuff it in bottles & bury it! I am told the wool of a good sized mattress can be squeezed into 50 bottles. Here we are going to lie on our mattresses till they are taken from under us.

FRIDAY, FEBRUARY 8

I called on Mme Etienne Visart, & we had a <u>long</u> gossip. She told me all about the "persecution" she & her family *suffered* while . . . in their town where her home is. [*sic*] She & Suzanne were 10 days in the town prison, "au secret;" she was fined a thousand marks for having her watch at "Allies time;" her house was taken at a day's notice; her husband & son went to Germany (they don't till now, know the reason) where they remained 13 months, & only came back on Nov 7th 1917. They have suffered greatly morally. It all came from Mme V. having discharged a *Belgian* maid who got engaged to a German, & used to stay over at night. Fortunately Fräulein Strasser, the German governess they had for 18 years, came & gave evidence in their favour & put her in contact here with a decent German functionary who helped her to obtain the return of her captives.

SUNDAY, FEBRUARY 10

"Mattresses" are the general topic of conversation in Brussels; every one asks each other "what of them?" Some people are hiding as much wool as possible, only deliv-ering a certain quantity, others are giving up all, & many are already "sur la paille." [sleeping on straw]

  . . . Tomorrow there is to be a great counter-manifestation against the "Flamingants" (the activists). They had a bad time of it at Antwerp last Sunday, but the Boche papers give out quite the contrary. Young people are preparing to make it hot for them in here in the streets to-morrow. No moon to-night, but the usual German light signals we always see now on dark nights.

MONDAY, FEBRUARY 11

After peace between Germany & Ukraine, it is announced to-day at Petrograd. I am curious to know the conditions. . . . The Flamingants did not dare show themselves at the Hôtel de Ville to-day, so all the people who were out to "counter-manifest" were deprived of their sport, but nevertheless were "un peu là" [somewhat present] all the same, & made the usual noise. Micha & Jean were stopped by a German civil "authorized" spy, had to give him their identification cards & appear before him this afternoon. He made them wait a long time, then cross-questioned Micha a great deal, threatened him with St. Gilles[47] several times if he didn't answer to this, that & the other, & sent him home at 7 pm with further threats of <u>what</u>? is in store for him [*sic*] . . .

TUESDAY, FEBRUARY 12

To-day when I went to see a poor old couple, the woman was in tears, her husband had just taken their 2 mattresses, their greatest comfort, to the Germans. This is such a cruel blow to the old & infirm! It seems the diplomats have informed the Germans, that their fury against those who consider the "Flamingants" as traitors to their country ought to be somewhat calmed by the counter-manifestations that true Belgians are making everywhere. So far, nothing has resulted from Micha & Jean's cross-examinations by the Boches yesterday.

Sewing cotton [thread] is so scarce, that at the Union Patriotique des Femmes Belges, Melle van den Plas told me, the other day, that though they still receive materials from America, they fear they will have to suspend the women's work, for want of cotton.

I hear Brussels is overrun by mice, there being hardly any more cats. I suppose [the] latter have been <u>eaten</u>, everyone being so hungry. At a fête de charité [charity event] the A.D. [Assistance Discrète] is organizing for Easter week, we think of adding "cats for sale" to our flower stall as flowers alone would be a failure, everyone wanting now something very useful or "eatable" for their money. . . . *At last some news of Edith, Dick having received a letter from her dated Nov. 27th. I wonder if mine then is safely on its way!*

THURSDAY, FEBRUARY 14

. . . One sees everywhere now, second hand boots, placed in windows of shops that never sold boots, fruit shops etc, marked 150–175 fs, & horrid common things they are, tops in stuff [lower quality woven fabric] & merely a little leather at the tips. I feel quite like a "nouvelle riche"[48] because I am wearing a fine pair of <u>all leather</u> English mountain boots I bought at Lausanne, in 1911, to wear at Caux &

---

[47] The prison at Saint-Gilles (a district of Brussels) where the occupation authorities brought resisting civilians.

[48] The "nouveaux riches" of wartime were a staple of resentful jokes, cartoons, and even musicals.

since then had them put away as too coarse & heavy for town wear. Who could have thought I would be proud of them *some day* in the Brussels streets! They are a great boon, would cost here more than 258 fs, even if they could be got, which is doubtful.

FRIDAY, FEBRUARY 15

<u>Many</u> German troops are coming here from the Russian front, now that it is officially agreed there is to be no more fighting there. I hear <u>all</u> the hotels near the stations are to be ready to put up 3 thousand officers, & that quantities of houses are to be requisitioned for soldiers. It is true that the governor, von Falkenhausen has informed Cardinal Mercier that all the church bells are to be given up to the Germans—also the brass *church* organ pipes; the *bronze* gates of the Palais de Justice have been taken—all that for ammunition. There is a rumor Brussels is to be declared in state of siege, since the 3 barristers of the Court of appeal have been sent to Germany. We have to give in the wool of our mattresses on Monday.

SUNDAY, FEBRUARY 17

Last night was my first on my "war mattress" in oat husks, (balles d'avoine) quite tolerable, though of course not comfortable like wool. Our wool has to be given to the Boches to-morrow, & then we shall have their perquisition to see if they can't discover any more. . . . Mme W. has bought a cow (for 4,500 fs) that we may be sure of our milk, because every dairy has to give it up to a "centrale" for making butter, & we can only obtain a small quantity of skimmed milk. Cow has to be placed under the Dutch or Spanish flag, otherwise the milk would be confiscated on its road to town. . . .

WEDNESDAY, FEBRUARY 20

. . . This morning Micha & Jean both received a notice from the Prussians, that they are fined 3 thousand marks each, for having been arrested last Monday week during the anti-flamingant manifestation. A <u>nice little</u> sum for so <u>great</u> an offence!!!

THURSDAY, FEBRUARY 21

On Tuesday a Belgian aeroplane flew very low in a street near here, the airman got quite close to his father's house a painter Mr waved his handkerchief to his father & called out: Bonjour Papa; the father responded, rushed to a window on the other side of the room, & saw the aero already high up in the air.

Several German flyers were up at the same time, I saw one, but there was no shooting so it is presumed the Belgian came down in a swoop & went up so rapidly that it hadn't time to be discovered. [49] Alec F. [Ford] was told to-day by a reticent man who never <u>would</u> impart news of any kind, that we have pierced the front at Verdun.

SUNDAY, FEBRUARY 24

1300th day of War!

To think we have been to bed & got up thirteen hundred times since the war began!!! & how much longer??? Nothing special to relate. We are living in expectation of "an offensive" either on our side or the Germans'. They are marching to Petrograd; and what when they get there? The different towns, Brussels, Antwerp, Ghent, have sent protestations to Germany, signed by their Senators & Representatives of all parties, against the Flamingant activist movement. The people manifested against it everywhere; fortunately every one wasn't sentenced to 3 thousand marks fine, like Micha & Jean!

TUESDAY, FEBRUARY 26

Mme Duvivier, from Spa, called on me to-day, before she gets shut up in Spa; in a day or two, no one there will be allowed to go out of a circle of 3 kilometers. It is to be the German head-quarters for Hindenburg, the Kaiser & all the "grosses légumes," [bigwigs] in view of the offensive.[50] All the convalescents & ambulances have been sent away to Gembloux; great preparations are being made by masses of work-men: trenches, placing of telegraphs & telephone wires etc etc—no more communi-cation with the outer world from there, for fear of news getting known. I hear that in different parts, the Belgians who are compelled to work for the Boches are building "crematory furnaces" in prev[iew] of the numerous corpses after the offensive.[51]

---

[49] On February 18, the aviator Willy Coppens, Belgium's leading fighting ace, made for Brussels, flying very low over the house of his parents (the painter Omer Coppens and his wife), quite close to the Wittoucks' city residence. Coppens's parents recognized him and waved; residents came out to cheer. Louis Gille, Alphonse Ooms and Paul Delandsheere, *Cinquante mois d'occupation allemande* (Brussels: Albert Dewit, 1919), 4:89–90.

[50] That month, German GHQ had moved to the town of Spa to prepare the Spring Offensive.

[51] Cremation had become legal in most German states before the war, and engineers had developed blueprints for mobile crematoria to use near battlefields. In the event, however, very few of the German war dead were cremated. MT's note, though apocryphal, is typical of civilian discourse, which used distaste for cremation—still illegal in Belgium and opposed especially by Catholics—to revile Germany. Some chronicles even claimed that German bat-tlefield corpses were used for industrial purposes.

Just read Chancellor von Herlting's [*sic*; Hertling] "pacifist speech" how will it be understood by the Allies???[52]

THURSDAY, FEBRUARY 28

M. Morel told us he <u>saw</u>, at the Deutsches [*sic*] Bank, a cheque for 300.000 fs, to be sent to Russia, to Lenine! . . . It makes one wonder about all the goings on that take place under the cover of mutual hostility between Germany & the Bolchevists!

Many women are now spinning (on the sly) their mattress wool they were able to hide from the requisition. When spun, it sells more than a hundred fs a kilo. *Small spinning machines are being offered for sale.* . . . M. Morel told me that all the papers & stock the belligerents have in the Banks are going, or have gone to Berlin, so . . . farewell my little bundle at the Caisse des Reports! May we meet again though, soon!

SATURDAY, FEBRUARY 2 [*sic*; MARCH 2]

To-day a <u>rare great</u> pleasure! Received a bit of writing from May & Maud . . . full of love & affection for me & Isie, it did me a lot of good. Edith & May have corresponded. So happy that <u>Maud</u> has found her real vocation![53] & trust her future will bring her the reward of her present labours. Mme W. bought to-day a hundred kilos of flour, for a thousand fs., so ten fs a kilo, & glad to get it even at that price. *(It must be hidden as no one may possess any.)* Alas! winter has returned; snow & icy north wind, & nothing cheering in news of the war to warm our hearts a little. It doesn't seem as if von Hertling's recent speech will convert—or pervert—the Allies to an arranged peace.

MONDAY, FEBRUARY 4 [*sic*; MARCH 4]

Peace signed yesterday, between Russia & the Centrals, and <u>what</u> a peace!!! The Germans speak of it gloriously, as if it were due to their victories! Is it not easy to walk into a country that has ceased to defend itself? And how glorious to treat with <u>such</u> men as Lenine, Trotsky & their adherents!!!

WEDNESDAY, FEBRUARY 6 [*sic*; MARCH 6]

The German Socialist papers consider the conditions of the peace with Russia as scandalous as the Allies themselves consider them—& quite understand that the latter can't think, for a moment, of an arranged peace, of that sort, for themselves. Their articles might have been written by us, so well do they agree with our views.

---

[52] Von Hertling addressed the Reichstag about Wilson's points but stated that negotiations required more Allied respect for Germany's requirements.

[53] Maud Bainbridge.

FRIDAY, MARCH 8

I had a card from poor Dick, he says a batch of Englishmen have left Ruhleben, for Holland, & he wishes <u>ardently</u>, he could be one of the next. How I pray he may! I fear the poor fellow may become neurasthenic, after having borne up so grandly for three years. Dieu nous aide! We had 2 <u>lamblike</u> German soldiers to visit the house for wool. They simply felt all the mattresses, found no wool, & did not open a cupboard or a drawer—so different to many other instances, where the seekers remained for hours, opened everything, even cardboard boxes & bandboxes. We had no unnecessary vexation whatever, & I heard the butler offering them a glass of wine as they were leaving the house. Pavlick met Van Vollenhoven at a lunch at Lady Phipps. He announces the Kaiser & staff were arriving to-day at Spa; that the German offensive will begin in a fortnight; that never has offensive been prepared with greater care in all minute particulars; that the Boches think it will go well for them & that peace, the "peace of Spa!!!" will soon be signed....

Qui vivra verra! [Time will tell] But that it will be the fiercest battle ever known in history ... [*sic*] How I wish we were already at Easter! ...

MONDAY, MARCH II

[This entry contains a newspaper clipping, which Thorp entitled "Model of our current vexations!!!" It reports the German ban of February 28, 1918, on stuffing mattresses with straw or chaff on pain of fines or prison sentences; the ban advised civilians to use paper instead.]

The Boches are again taking away thousands of young men, even boys 14 years old, to work for them near their "ligne de feu." [Firing-line] Many have been taken at Mons, & 500 the other day from Peruwelz, of which 3 brothers of a girl I know. One of these three has already been a compulsory labourer in Germany, & has been home now some little time.

Eggs are somewhat cheaper, 85 centimes instead of 1 f 25-. This morning this sensational arrêté in the paper [this refers to the ban reported in the newspaper clipping]; it comes out now, after nearly all the wool has been delivered, & people have bought the newly forbidden stuffings, which were sold publicly. I wonder if we shall have to give them up again! How ironic to suggest <u>paper</u>! stuffing; paper is as scarce as food, people pick up the scraps they find in the streets to light their fires.

TUESDAY, MARCH 12

... It is so pathetic to see how the shop windows try to put on a little springlike gaiety, with next to nothing of old odds & ends. I am quite <u>longing</u> to have some decent new clothes, & well fitting boots, not the ordinary kind I had to buy last, two years ago. When? Oh when??? I heard to-day that plucky English airmen set down & take up "passengers" on some of the big solitary commons in Belgium, & that plans for rebuilding a big financial establishment had thus been taken away to "the other side" not of the water, but to Le Hâvre.[54]

FRIDAY, MARCH 15

... Last Saturday, at 8 a.m. an <u>awful</u> explosion was heard & felt even in Brussels—it was 700 wagons of ammunition exploded by an [*sic*] Allies' bombs from an aero. I forgot to write that last Sunday was read in all the churches, a splendid protestation of Cardinal Mercier, against the German ordering all church bells & organ pipes to be given up to them (to make ammunition—for killing our men). It was so grand & awe-inspiring regarding the sacrilege it signifies that people are wondering if the Boches will ever dare commit it. . . .

It is <u>galling</u> to see huge *and numerous* cartloads of sacks of wool, from our mattresses, being conveyed to stations by the Germans. . . . We are wondering every day if we shall hear that the <u>great</u> offensive has commenced. Mme Myriam R. went to the Hague (I ignore by what favour) & assisted at a ball given at the English Legation there for the English officers let out of German camps. Oh! If poor Dick could get out of his cage at Ruhleben! This book has lasted nearly 6 months, tant mieux for the scarcity of paper; but each time I begin a new one I ardently hope it will see the end of the war. Since poor M. W's death I hear less little stories worth noting down. . . .

[54] MT is probably referring to reports on civilian conditions and plans for reconstruction that were smuggled out to the government in exile at Le Havre.

Book 4

"HOLY MARY PRAY FOR US!"

MARCH–OCTOBER 1918

Thorp started her fourth notebook without allowing herself to hope it would be the last. At the same time, she battled despair, although the German Spring Offensive sorely tried her nerves. Uncharacteristically, she no longer wrote every day. She seesawed between worry and hope. She rejoiced to hear that on April 22, Saint George's Day, a British detachment had attacked the German submarine base at Zeebrugge. In reality, the raid created only a temporary hindrance, but its panache lifted the Allied mood, as it did hers. Meanwhile, she worried about her loved ones across the world. To quell anxiety, Thorp kept busy with her volunteer duties. But relief work meant less than ever in the face of deepening misery, and she knew it. A fifth war winter, she wrote, would kill a great many civilians and ruin the health of many more. How long would the war last? News of German successes on the Marne shook her. More than ever, she sought solace in faith, whether popular devotion or high church observance: one day, she visited a Lourdes grotto in a working-class neighborhood; on another, she attended Mass celebrated by Cardinal Mercier. And she worked on. Through June, she provided aid to English POWs in a camp near Brussels. Meanwhile, to her relief, her nephew, Dick, had been released from Ruhleben camp and taken to Holland. But events on the front remained worrisome. She did take heart from signs of war-weariness within the Central Powers such as the German Independent Socialists' criticism of the war and Austrian food riots. Signs of desperation did not escape her. Vienna-bound trainloads of Belgian potatoes were falsely marked as Ukrainian to make Austrian civilians believe that the eastern conquests would save them from starvation. She scoffed at the Flemish activists' appeal to German militarist opinion.

*From mid-July, things turned definitively: the fifth German offensive in the West col-
lapsed. In Brussels, civilians celebrated the Belgian national holiday of July 21 in a hopeful
mood quite different from that of the preceding year; the military police barely retaliated.[1]
Thorp rejoiced. But she also took stock of the permanent damage war had brought. In early
August, she looked back: in 1914, she wrote, the thought of four years of misery would have
been inconceivable. The long ordeal showed in the faces of the destitute people she visited.
Six weeks later, she noted that it was the second anniversary of the diary she had started in
September 1916 in hopes of seeing the war end soon. But this time she did allow herself to
hope for a speedy end: the Hindenburg Line had been broken, the Americans had scored a
victory at Saint Mihiel, and German troops were weary of the war. Before long, Brussels
street scenes marked the imminent end of occupation. And on this note, Thorp closed her
fourth book, hoping that the next one would document a happier time.*

MONDAY, MARCH 18

How will the world be when I come to the end of this book? Each time I begin one
I pray it may be the last. . . . The cannon so incessant yesterday & the day before &
the weather so ideal & springlike, but the imminent offensive takes all the joy out of
it alas! To-day was "the day of penance & prayer" demanded by the bishops, preparatory to St. Joseph's feast to-morrow, patron of Belgium. May the numberless prayers
from tortured hearts be soon heard! I called on the Marquise de Beauffort.[2] . . . [S]he
told me 2 thousand trees have been cut down at Oydonck [Ooidonk].

WEDNESDAY, MARCH 20

The atmosphere we live in gets more despairing every day, & we need more & more
God's help to retain our confidence & cheerfulness. To-day I know another band of
farm-horses coming in to the Germans; how many thousands have we not already
seen taken away from the land; it always grieves me so much. So many people, indirectly victims of the war, through grief & hunger & misery, are dying constantly,
or going mad. . . .

How lucky I am to be spared the anxiety of getting food, & to enjoy perfect
health! I cannot sufficiently thank God for these & so many favours. . . .

FRIDAY, MARCH 22

They say the great German offensive began to-day on different sections of the front.
Dieu nous aide! Sidonie wrote me yesterday they (the Dutch Consul) told her that

---

[1] Louis Gille, Alphonse Ooms and Paul Delandsheere, *Cinquante mois d'occupation allemande*
(Brussels: Albert Dewit, 1919), 4:264–265.

[2] Anne de Romrée de Vichenet, one of the patrons of the Discreet Assistance.

there might be a chance for English women & children to get to England. She is on the list. To-day I consulted Father Lecourt & W. Kattendyke *who says there might be an exchange with German women from the conquered colonies*—they both think she would have more advantages there than here—& Dick & she wish for the change—I like his patriotism, he appreciates all that is English, Ruhleben has made a staunch Britisher of him, & he wants wife & boy to be "Anglicised."

They say there are new rumours of peace, (Germany giving in) since the last war council, but I can't believe it, wish I could. . . . I spoke to a man from Deynze, who was taken as a chômeur to work in the trenches before Verdun, nearly 2 years ago. After 14 months he was wounded, lost the 4 fingers of his right hand, he is now our neighbor at the hospital annex next door.[3] He & others told me they suffered <u>terribly</u> from hunger, which caused the illness of many who were not wounded, but had to come to the hospital in Brussels to be nursed & fed.

10 pm. <u>Bad</u> news—let us hope it is exaggerated. The Marquis & Van Vollenhoven both announced (official from the Germans) that the offensive began yesterday & that the Germans have driven <u>us</u> back 20 kilometers deep on 80 kilometers in length, between La Fère & Cambrai. . . . God grant it may be simply an effect of <u>our</u> strategy, but oh! Our hearts are heavy to-night!

SATURDAY, MARCH 23

Alas! Alas! This morning's *Belgischer Kurier* announced they had taken 16 thousand English prisoners, 200 cannon etc. This evening's announces 25 thousand prisoners, 400 cannon, etc. etc. I am in great grievous dismay. . . . What will follow? . . . I had a letter from poor Dick, with 3 passages painted thickly out by the censor; it concerns a "promenade militaire" that was proposed to the prisoners, & in which he refused to participate.[4] I am so anxious & troubled about all our poor men in the front. This defeat will be so demoralizing. . . .

SUNDAY, MARCH 24

This evening's latest <u>German</u> news: 25 thousand prisoners, 400 cannon etc etc, the center of the English front driven back from Péronne, left wing resisting well, right wing retreating methodically . . . how I long for tomorrow's results!!!! *God grant us a successful counter-attack! To-morrow is the Annunciation!!!!* The Germans praise the brave fighting of the English. 5 thousand terribly mutilated & wounded soldiers have already arrived at Hal,[5] & they say some of the German nurses are mere girls of

---

[3] Repatriated deportees who received medical care in hospitals across town took their meals in a former hotel on Boulevard de Waterloo 24, close to the Wittoucks'.

[4] "Promenade militaire," marching the men through town in military formation.

[5] The town of Halle near Brussels. After being wounded, the German author Ernst Jünger was evacuated to the Halle Lazarett in September 1918.

15 & 16. The Marquis lunched at Petit Bigard; he said he thinks this terrible offensive means the near end of the war. . . .

German soldiers often oblige Belgians by bringing them errands & messages from their country friends (& get paid for it). One bought Bertha some butter from her brother at Beernem yesterday, says eggs there cost 25 centimes (they can't be sold out of the locality) here they are 95 c to-day.

MONDAY, MARCH 25, ANNUNCIATION

News no better for us to-night, alas! The Germans are rapidly moving forward towards Amiens. . . . To-morrow holiday, bell-ringing & national rejoicing in Germany for their victory. . . . Shall we stop them in time on their march! I feel heart-broken, & grieve for our poor men—& all lost lives. And what will be the end! God grant us his help before it is too late! I try to imagine how people look & feel in England to-night.

It is awful to be here, passive & useless, except by my poor prayers. It is colder too, & weather changed since yesterday—moonlight, but rather cloudy. Each one of my thoughts is supplication to Heaven for those in danger, and for our victory, malgré tout. [in spite of everything]

TUESDAY, MARCH 26

Another terribly anxious day. . . . They are nearing Albert, or rather were yesterday. Notre Dame de Brébières grant they may be checked there! (Where they have already destroyed the beautiful Basilica in 1915.)⁶

There were salvos of artillery, & aeroplanes flying here to-day to celebrate their victory—and heavy hearts full of grief, and ardent prayers that we may see a silver lining to the cloud. I have a feeling (but hardly dare write it) that we may bar the way in time. . . .

WEDNESDAY, MARCH 27

The Germans announce to-day that they have taken Albert. Where & when shall we stop them! On dit [It is said] that Haig was in England when the offensive began, & that there was no proper direction at the onset. He is at his post now, they say— please God there may be a favourable change. What must we think of the great cannon that is methodically bombarding Paris from such a distance, 120 kilometers???⁷

⁶ The basilica in Albert was shelled in January 1915, causing a Madonna and child statue to fall to a horizontal position on its roof. The "Leaning Virgin" became a symbol for all troops fighting on the Somme in 1916. The German army recaptured Albert in March 1918; the basilica was destroyed by British artillery in April 1918.

⁷ German heavy artillery pounded Paris from March 23, 1918; roughly 250 people died and hundreds more were injured.

Had a card from Dick, of 21st inst [of this month]; on the 20th he received a letter from Edith, of Jan. 23rd (her happiest birthday, she says, Deo Gratias). She expects to be in Paris in the middle of April, with the American Red Cross, address c/o N.Y. Herald offices, Paris. God grant all may be well for her, & a safe passage.

MAUNDAY THURSDAY, MARCH 28

... Albert d' Huart ... told me that though André de Broqueville is severely wounded in the head, the Drs. hope to save him. He didn't know if André is at Maud's ambulance. Wind & rain to-night; after a bitter cold dry wind all day. God help all our brave men, and make them victorious—and may the souls of all those who are killed go to God immediately. R.I.P.

SATURDAY, MARCH 30, EASTER EVE

I had an extra letter from Dick to-day, dated 23rd inst. [of this month] (with special permission of his censor) to give me the contents of Edith's letter to him. We conclude she is engaged, but 7 lines of her letter were painted out; I presume they gave name, whereabouts probably with the American army in France, of the fiancé so we ignore the most interesting particulars. . . . Patience & let us hope all will run smoothly, & that Edith will have a safe passage, if she is to be in Paris for middle of April. . . .

EASTER MONDAY, APRIL 1

My Easter was made happier by the hopeful news of Edith—& also that I was able to . . . open my heart to her, also to Maud & May, thanks to a meeting at our luncheon party here *yesterday*—& I hope to get answers in due time.[8] Deo gratias! . . .

WEDNESDAY, APRIL 3

Thank God, the news is better. The Germans are stopped for the moment on their way to Amiens. God grant they never get there! The wounded brought to different places in Belgium, very numerous. A hundred English at Hal, & alas! We may not go to them. It is said that chloroform is scarce with the Germans, & that they operate their men only with it, and ours without. . . . W. Kattendyke offered them 3 bottles, which they refused. Though there is a terrible lack of infirmarians, a body of Red Cross Belgian women who offered their services were not accepted. All I hear of the thousands of victims makes my blood run cold. I can only pray . . . & try to keep my nerves calm. I think constantly of Edith being possibly on the ocean, & in

[8] MT probably refers to Villalobar's help in smuggling out letters to her friends.

danger. . . . My letter to her starts to-morrow; that to May & Maud on its way since Monday. How I long for answers.

Another mean trick of the Boches: At the Central Post office, every indication of "guichets" [counters] & general information, formerly in French, has been torn down, the Flemish & German remaining. Till now they had tolerated the French, but no longer. The result is great confusion, the generality of people understanding French only, don't know where to apply. I am so grateful to the Marquis de Villalobar for the . . . comfort he gave me on Easter Sunday.

SATURDAY, APRIL 6

Yesterday Florrie & I went to the Basilique & to the Grotto of N. D. de Lourdes.[9] . . .

These days of the resuming of the offensive are mortally anxious ones. . . . So far the Germans are not gaining ground. . . .

SUNDAY, APRIL 7

The Kattendykes & Mme. K.'s sister M[elle] Boreel lunched here with others to-day. M[elle] B. has lived in London these 2½ last years, & came over 3 months ago because her mother was very ill. She told me the particulars of her coming from London to the Hook of Holland; 3 whole days at anchor on the boat at Gravesend, till there was no more danger of proceeding, unable to write to friends; then 27 hours passage; *there were* 9 boats conveyed by "contre-torpilleurs," [anti-torpedo craft, i.e., destroyers] which spin round the boats all the time. She used to work at the Canteen in Euston Station; all the soldiers were always full of life & go & jokes; the only time she saw them & the English public in dismay, was on the day of Kitchener's death, when even the people were weeping in the public conveyances—(like myself on hearing the news here at the corner of the Rue du Trône). Mr. K. [Kattendyk] said it is true his 3 bottles of chloroform were refused "officially" by the Boches for the wounded, but he sent them in another manner, likewise a tram & motor full of medicines, surgical appliances, brandy etc, to Mons, where there are, alas! about 1,500 English wounded. He is trying to get his wife['s] "permission," to see our men at Hal, says he would spoil even her going if he tried to let me go too, but that if any English come here, he'll do his best to let me be allowed to approach them (invoking my grey hair & Croix rouge [Red Cross] certificate as I told him). He had seen in Antwerp, a Miss Olliver (who used to live at Bruges) on trial after 8 months imprisonment for helping young men to pass the frontier. She was sentenced to 11 months prison, he hopes to get her off the rest.[10]

[9] The Basilica at Koekelberg, under construction; and a grotto dedicated to Our Lady of Lourdes, built in 1915 in the Pannenhuis neighborhood north of central Brussels and dedicated by Cardinal Mercier. It became, during the war, a center of intense popular devotion; thousands of pilgrims implored salvation for their men at the front.

[10] Probably the Englishwoman Olive Olliver, born in Bruges in March 1886.

Mr. K. had heard from an eye witness at Mons, how hard to suffering our men are; one having his hand operated without any aenest*h*etic [*sic*], when asked if he would like anything, merely said, yes, give me a smoke, & was quite satisfied with his cigarette, while the operation continued. I think constantly of the terrible fighting going on just-now, on the road to Amiens ... quite near Mary's place,[11] which I fear may suffer terribly, after having sheltered the English staff so long. Dieu nous aide!

TUESDAY, APRIL 9

3 of my parcels to Dick at Ruhleben sent in 1917, did not reach him, the contents having surely reached Boche tummies. I put in complaints of course, some time ago now, & to my surprise, I have just received a notice that the sum of 24 fs will be refunded me here, at the Prisoners Agency, by the Ruhleben camp. . . .

Everyone in Belgium lives in perpetual terror of their servants, & dares not dismiss them, for fear of being, (with or without reasons) denounced to the Germans as having laid themselves open to their fines & penalties, either for hiding things requisitioned, receiving letters etc etc. Anonymous letters often make things discovered [*sic*], but sometimes are only a hoax, & mean nothing but revenge.

The great newspaper excitement of the day is Clemenceau's saying of Czernin's declaration "Il en a menti" [*sic*; "he has lied"[12]] As soon as I read that *(Cz's speech)* I changed my rather favourable opinion of Czernin & thought him hypocritical. The Germans don't seem to be advancing much towards Amiens, thank God; fasse-t-Il [may He grant] they may not! . . .

THURSDAY, APRIL 11

I took some money to Totote D'Orel[13] who is collecting to buy articles of absolute necessity (combs, toothbrushes etc) for some of the 900 wounded English soldiers at Mons. How I wish I could get to them! . . . A camp for Belgian prisoners is being made at Diest—no one could understand why—till it was rumoured a great aviation camp is to be made close by.[14] . . . I got my 24 fs from the Ruhleben camp for . . . missing parcels.[15] . . .

[11] Mary d'Alcantara's estate at Querrieu.

[12] Count Czernin had stated, in an April 2 speech, that France had agreed to enter into peace discussions with Austria; Clemenceau had called it a lie.

[13] Remains unidentified.

[14] At Schaffen, a village close to Diest (northeast of Brussels), the imperial Luftstreitkräfte constructed an airfield. The civil internment camp at Diest opened in March 1918 and held mostly Belgian and French internees.

[15] The prisoners of Ruhleben managed camp finances, including, in some cases, restitution for lost parcels.

We are told Spa is quite gay with the Kaiser & his suite, many elegant officers' wives, quite a little German court, having a good time & gambling at
Roulette etc.

SUNDAY, APRIL 14

Armentières has fallen—another failure for us, alas! But let us hope it is only par-
tial, for since Friday the Germans don't seem to get much further. To-day has been
a most bleak, dull, gruesome Sunday, to match our bad spirits. The thought of all the
lost lives quite crushes me. . . . To-night we have to put our clocks on an hour, to rise
to-morrow with our summer time. How will it be with the war when we put them
back an hour six months hence! Where is Edith now!

TUESDAY, APRIL 16

General amazement! Czernin is retiring from office. Surely something to do with
Clémenceau's [sic] "Il en a menti" [sic] & emperor Charles' letter to his brother-
in-law (some time ago) saying France was justified in claiming Alsace-Lorraine.
Now, the Austrian cannon on our front pretend to deny it.[16] Thank God! no further
advance of the Germans at Armentières. What is to be expected next? To-day the
philanthropist Mr Solvay is 80 years old, in honour of which he treats every school
child of Brussels to a roll, a biscuit, & a stick of chocolate—such a boon in these time
of "lean kine";[17] even well to do children don't despise it.[18] . . .

THURSDAY, APRIL 18

Not a ray of sunshine since Friday; these are dull, drab days of terrible anguish;
the Germans are killing our men & taking our positions on the Lys & Poelcapelle
& Langemarck. . . . Will Ypres be encircled & taken? & the Belgian front on the
Yser! . . .

SUNDAY, APRIL 21

. . . Alec & Lena [Ford] called yesterday, he as sanguine as ever & as determined
as ever to bear up cheerfully, even if the war is to last years yet. If it does, the
people, at least in Belgium, will die of starvation, even though it be but one year
longer. . . .

---

[16] Austrian Škoda cannon were in heavy use on the Western Front.

[17] Genesis 41:20: "And the lean and ill-favored kine [cows] did eat up the first seven fat kine."

[18] The entrepreneur and philanthropist Ernest Solvay.

The constitution of the people is being weakened so terribly, & it is written on all the faces. Ellen Rinquet told me on Friday that their midday meal, for her & Ernest, cost them 15 fs, simply a small quantity of meat & potatoes. I received from Mme W 5 kilos of sugar for my friends & poor, took Ernest ½ kilo for his midday coffee, so delighted.

WEDNESDAY, APRIL 24

The Boche paper to-night gives the first news (as always of course) of an attempt of the English to land at Zee-Brugge & *blow up everything*—40 Englishmen really landed, but of course, like in all Boche versions, did no harm but to themselves.... I will await <u>our</u> version. I wonder if the Allies realise <u>how</u> famished everyone is here, except the very rich who don't mind what they have to pay for food. People are just wearing away for want of nourishment; <u>no one</u> has a sufficient ration of bread *even* & everyone's constitution is being undermined, <u>many</u> dying of want. Alas! till when? . . .

THURSDAY, APRIL 25

We've heard a little more of the brave attack of the English at Zee-Brugge—the *Belgischer Kurier* gave something of Sir Eric Geddes' speech on the subject. Happily we did some damage to the Boche submarine base, in honour of St. George's Day! On the early morn of the 23rd.

The Fougeraie is let for 3 months to someone who won't be expelled by the Germans,[19] so we hope to go there ourselves in August! I went to see Langasken's paintings of Belgian soldiers in the camp of Gottingen & Munsterlager—such pathetic figures & faces & attitudes.[20] . . .

FRIDAY, APRIL 26

Deo gratias! I had a card from Dick this morning, written on the 22nd, saying he was leaving Ruhleben for Holland yesterday evening, the 25th, so he is probably still en route, as I presume they don't let their prisoners travel rapidly.[21] What a relief, poor boy! & <u>how</u> I thank God for granting our prayers for this great grace! . . .

---

[19] This seems to be the first time the family rented out their summer residence for the summer, suggesting both (relative) financial hardship and fear of being dispossessed.

[20] The Belgian painter Maurice Langaskens, a POW at Göttingen, Sennelager, and Münsterlager camps, painted and drew his fellow prisoners.

[21] Once released from Ruhleben, prisoners traveled to the Netherlands by train. There they waited for transfer home or the end of the war.

MONDAY, APRIL 29

... Alas! Mount Kemmel seems to have been taken—but we will again "wait & see", for the Zee-Brugge marvellous affair means trumps to us, & the first Boche version gave the contrary impression. What a glorious record for the British marine!

The Kaiser is said to have said to Mme Peltzer-Graux, in whose villa he is at Spa, that she must not worry too much about it because the war will be over by August, when she can occupy it herself! ... Famine extends every day; I saw Melle Legros & Maria Scholler these last days; they have no potatoes for several weeks, can't find any, even at 3 fs a kilo. Rice is 15 fs a kilo, meat dearer & dearer, (27 fs a kilo) eggs one franc. How grateful I am to divine Providence that I am spared the "food trouble!" but I pity, from my heart, my friends that I see wearing literally away with care to se-cure the insufficient meagre provisions they can only get for heavy prices. It is indeed a terrible thing for a country to be so short of bread, and potatoes & all farinaceous aliments [grains]. Dieu nous aide!

Last Friday afternoon Melle Cazé was not well, & went to bed. At her window little Jacques d' Ursel was playing with a bit of looking-glass, making the sun rays reverberate on the passersby. Suddenly a knock at her door, her room is on the 2nd floor, & in rushed a German officer, furious because the looking glass had been re-flected on him—told them it was not "permis" [not permitted] to treat a German officer thus, that he supposed they didn't know what "German officer" means. So he is awaiting to be summoned to learn his lesson. Oh Prussian militarism! ...

WEDNSEDAY, MAY 1

I had to-day Dick's last letter from Ruhleben, written April 24th, & he was to leave on the 25th, for Scheveningue [Scheveningen], he thinks, Hotel Bristol.[22] I trust he has survived safely & is already benefitting by his comparative freedom. Deo gratias! And when shall I have news of Edith! Details about the heroic feat of our sailors at Zee-Brugge have reached us. I never dare mention Zee-Brugge to M. Jean Cousin, whose masterpiece of engineering it was, his glory, & never really served but the Germans in this war. I often wonder also how the 1st of May passed for the Socialists in belligerent countries. Bulgaria & Turkey seem like [they are] going to quarrel over their spoils. No news of the presumed counter revolution at Petrograd, & no Boche bluff tonight from the Western front.

FRIDAY, MAY 3

The Kaiser has been in Brussels, *& there was great banqueting at von Falkenhausen's (the governor general) for the big* Germany *swells;* The Austrian, Count von Falkenstein,

---

[22] Scheveningen, a seaside town in Holland, received a great deal of former prisoners of war, both civilian and military. The British Red Cross provided employment for them.

who is like Austria's representative here, was not even warned of the fact, & is, in consequence, very vexed with the Boches.[23] A lady I know sees him sometimes, (on account of her relatives in Vienna) & the impression is that Austria is not so friendly "au fond" [actually] as the imperial telegram tries to make out. The advance at Kemmel is stopped, Deo gratias! Meat now 30 fs a kilo; many people accustomed to keeping a servant are doing without now, can't afford to feed them, & also prefer doing their own work to running the risk of being denounced to the Germans on false grounds, & being fined in consequence. It has become quite a common occurrence, unfortunately, for servants & many others to make accusations as a means of vengeance, & no end of people have thus got into trouble with our "gentle invaders." There must be a <u>terrible</u> lack of workmen in Germany for the Boches to make the <u>varied</u> appeals they do to all trades here: most suggestive pictures, exhortations to men wanting good salaries, advantages for their wives & families etc, etc, the coloured pictures especially are most eloquent. I hear there will shortly be an "Arrêté" forbidding all carpenters, joiners & workmen in wood to ply their trade here in Belgium. I wrote to-day my first post-card to Dick at Scheveningue, to Hotel Bristol, the presumed address from rumours before he left Ruhleben.

God help him & us all! & Edith wherever she may be; I am <u>so</u> anxious about her.

SUNDAY, MAY 5

While the Kaiser was here recently, he had the Doyen of Ste. Gudule [the Dean of the Collegiate Church of Sainte-Gudule] warned that he wished to visit the churches. The Doyen gave the keys to the beadle, to admit the K. at the hour indicated. The beadle declined the honour! & gave the keys to the chair-setter (la chaisière) who was alone to receive the K, & who, after admitting him, took no further notice of him, but went to pray before the altar of the Blessed Sacrament. The K.'s visit to the church was a very short one. . . . The old Count & C[tsse] De Baillet[24] have at last been let out of prison, but the latter made an unpardonable "faux pas." During her trial, when asked how she received foreign correspondence found in her house, she stupidly said: through the Marquis de Villalobar. Latter was reproached with this by the Germans, chiefly by Von der Lancken, who spoke of reporting him to his (Spanish) government. Villa. got angry, said *it is perfectly true and* pray do report me "for as I pass here for being too Boche, it will rehabilitate me in the eyes of the Allies." A splendidly diplomatic answer.[25]

[23] Wilhelm II visited Bruges (in the aftermath of the Zeebrugge Raid) and Brussels in late April and early May 1918.

[24] Possibly Count Ferdinand de Baillet Latour, senator and honorary governor of the province of Antwerp, and his wife, Caroline née d'Oultremont.

[25] Villalobar passed for being a "Germanophile" but was mainly a conservative, on good terms with German aristocrats. Prentiss Gray of the CRB noted his friendly personal relationship with von der Lancken.

He asked Villa . . . the other day what we, the Allies, think just now of the Boche offensive on the West; V. answered "Que vous piétinez;" [that you are not getting anywhere] & when Villa enquired some day after of V d Lanker [Von der Lancken], how they were getting on, he replied "nous piétinons" [we are getting nowhere] as they own to it. M. van de Pol, the Dutchman & others dined here this evening. M. Fernand du Roy[26] had *official* business the other day with a German doctor, who had just heard that the airman von Richthofen had fallen in the English lines; this German said: he is well there, the English are gentlemen & will do their best for him.[27] Du Roy remarked they don't speak like that of us in their papers, he replied, no! we are obliged to write about "les sales Anglais" & all the rest, but we think & know they are gentlemen.

Eggs are to-day 1 f 15 each. The shops are heart-breaking to behold, & *in the sense they* sell the most varied second hand articles one can imagine—old boots & shoes, old adulterated food-stuffs, tiny quantities of rare haberdashery, brushes, soap, etc etc. . . .

FRIDAY MAY 10

I've just heard, from Père Guinet, that poor dear old Mme Boulez had an apoplectic stroke 2 [?] months ago, & received the last sacraments; is now nursed by Anna & a nun, somewhat better, but alas! he writes also that there are 14 railway tracks established in what was their garden. . . . [at Waregem]

Thus end there the remembrances of my youth! What an extra calamity for poor Anna, if her mother dies before the end of the war, all their affairs will be more confused than ever. . . .

We heard that at Petrograd the scarcity & exorbitant prices of everything are just the same as here. The many that will die of sheer exhaustion & misery if war lasts another winter! I who lack for little materially, *but suffer much morally, separated from all friends, no news, & knowing they* must *be in trouble*, thank God, have every day to strive to take courage to bear the burden the best possible, so what of the poor starved people one sees everywhere! I wonder if the Allies really know what is endured in Belgium, except by the immensely rich.

TUESDAY, MAY 14

I've just written a letter (by favour!!!) to Dick & one to Edith. No news yet of Dick since he is at Sch. & no answer from Edith to my letters of January to

[26] Possibly Baron Fernand du Roy de Blicquy.

[27] Manfred Von Richthofen, the German flying ace known as the "Red Baron," was actually killed on April 21, 1918—but he had been able to land his plane while fatally wounded, which

N.Y. [New York] of Easter to P. [Paris] <u>How</u> I hope those will reach them! God grant it! . . .

WHIT SUNDAY, MAY 19

1385 day of War.

During the week Mme Poncin came to ask for help for a wounded soldier. In future, she will always warn me when an English or Allied soldier dies at the military hospital that I may attend the funeral. Her son hears of it because he is employed at the Ixelles Town Hall. . . . No news yet from Dick since he is at Scheveningue—& none from Edith—so anxious. We are having torrid midsummer weather these last days, & are going towards the full moon. . . . A German offensive is said to be very imminent. Ladies' boots marked now 200 fs the pair, & only ready made, stuff tops, & the least little bit of leather at tips. Starvation more & more general, it is heart-breaking to visit the poor, & see them <u>so</u> painfully altered each time one goes.

No matter what one gives, it is as but a mouthful, <u>everything</u> one can buy being so monstrously dear. The shortage of bread & complete lack of potatoes are a terrible source of prolonged misery & exhaustion. What will it be if we have a 5th winter of war! The strain is too long, & those who survive will be ruined in health.

WHIT MONDAY, MAY 20, 1918

Isie & I were standing in a <u>very</u> overcrowded tram. A gentleman got up to give us his seat, saying: Madams, had I heard immediately you were English, I should have offered you my seat immediately. I thanked him for "his homage to my country." I know all the decent Belgians (those who do mind about their country not being germanised) have a proper feeling for all they owe to England.

TUESDAY, MAY 21

Isie, Inès[28] & I went to the Allies' tombs in the Ixelles Cemetery.[29] All our men who die at the military Hospital are buried there: English, French, Italians, Indians, Russians & some Belgians. The tombs are very nicely kept, flowers growing all round. Each cross is painted in the soldier's colours & bears his flag. I took flowers &

---

explains the false rumor. His father, Albrecht, was military commander of the occupied city of Aalst in the Étape.

[28] Baroness Inès Pycke de Peteghem.

[29] There are thirteen First World War Commonwealth Graves in the Ixelles Communal Cemetery.

placed them cross-shaped, on the tomb of Captain Harry Rawson, 16th Regiment Royal Scots, 33 years old. He was buried there last month (April). Near him lies the poor English soldier who died on arriving at the Gare du Nord & was so terribly wounded & disfigured. He had nothing on him to identify him by, & his little red cross, with the Union Jack painted in the corner simply bears the inscription "Soldat Anglais inconnu." [Unknown English soldier]

I lingered there, & prayed for him & for them all, in the name of those who loved them at home, & made a nice cross of flowers on the tomb of the poor "Inconnu." [Unknown] God grant they are all happy with Him! And to think of the thousands who have no tomb at all . . . & no one will know of their noble end.

FRIDAY, MAY 24, 10.30 PM.

I've just returned from the Ixelles cemetery; I followed the corpse of a poor English soldier, Barnes, 30 years old, who died before reaching the hospital.[30] Half a dozen people, who are accustomed to follow the funerals of the Allies' soldiers were there, & M. Gahan, the protestant minister, who said prayers after the body was lowered. Isie met me at the cemetery. We all threw earth on the poor fellow's coffin, & I the flowers I had taken for him. . . . A German soldier was there also, assisted at the little ceremony at the tomb, in the most correct military attitude. I thought perhaps his presence was due to regulations, but M. Gahan says no, it was pure sympathy. There are 2 English soldiers at the military hospital, Gahan says they are made comfortable & well looked after, 5 meals a day. What a pity I can't get to them *but it seems the Dutch Legation sees them & does all it can.*

FRIDAY, MAY 24, EVENING. DEO GRATIAS!

Just had a letter from Miss Edith Thomas, of March 30th.[31] Edith [Dodson] had just left, & had the comfort, at the last moment, of receiving my long letter of January. . . . God grant she has reached her destiny safely & may get my letters of March 31st & of May 20th—& I get answers.

---

[30] Lance Corporal Charles Edward Barnes of the Lancashire Fusiliers died on May 22, 1918, at age twenty-eight.

[31] Edith M. Thomas, a well-known writer for popular literary magazines such as *Harper's* (R. H. Walker, "THOMAS, Edith Matilda (Aug. 12, 1854-Sept. 13, 1925)," in *Notable American Women: 1607–1950*, eds. E. James, J. James & P. Boyer [Cambridge, MA: Harvard University Press, 1971], 2:444–445, http://search.credoreference.com.dist.lib.usu.edu/content/entry/hup-nawi/thomas_edith_matilda_aug_12_1854_sept_13_1925/0.)

MONDAY, MAY 27

Oh! <u>how</u> painful it is to live under German sway, deprived of our liberty, and <u>so</u> long! To-day I wanted to send to Antwerp, by carter (Messageries van Gend)[32] an old costume, & was informed they are not allowed to send any sort of clothes without permission of the German authorities, so I took the dress out of the parcel, & will send it by a friend who goes by train. Oh! How maddening to be thwarted on all sides!!! Almost every shop window is filled with second (& 3rd till 10th) hand articles of every description, prices of which are simply fabulous. People must be emptying their lumber rooms [storeroom for odds and ends] & getting rich on the proceeds. . . .

WEDNESDAY, MAY 29

. . . Yesterday Isie ran in to me, in great grief; had just heard that Inès's brother, Etienne Pycke, had been killed accidentally—& they thought he was safe for 2 months, at a course of instruction. R.I.P.[33] God help those who mourn for him! I called on Lena & Alex [Ford] to tell them Hughie got their message (of January) about Easter week![34] Thanks to my letter reaching Edith in time. Now I long to know more of her & something of Dick—nothing yet since he is in Holland, except what Sidonie's sister has been able to write her from Dordrecht. The Boches announce 25 thousand prisoners at the Chemin des Dames, but I don't feel very upset, don't fear the illustrious! Fritz's army.

FRIDAY, MAY 31

. . . Inès Reyntiens[35] & a friend, coming back from a stay in the country, spied some English soldiers working near the hangar [shed] at Evere.[36] They talked to a German

---

[32] A mail service.

[33] Baron Étienne Pycke de Peteghem, b. 1898, a war volunteer, died of wounds in Calais on May 7, 1918.

[34] Hughie is Alec and Lena's son, Hugh Alexander Ford, British consul in Boston.

[35] Inès Reyntiens, daughter of Major Robert Reyntiens, former aide-de-camp to King Leopold II, and Anita de Errazu y de Rublo de Tejada, a Mexican heiress. In 1922, she married the US diplomat Hugh Gibson, who during the war had been secretary to the US Legation in Brussels.

[36] From late May 1918, about twenty-five British prisoners captured near Kemmel were held at Evere, near Brussels, to "protect" and work on the German airfield there. Reports spoke of poor conditions, noting they were held in a thirty-square-foot wooden cage. Civilians came to cheer them and throw gift packages over the barbed wire. This led to the closing of the camp on July 8, 1918. Gille et al., *Cinquante mois d'occupation allemande*, 4:250; *Sydney Morning Herald*, September 13, 1918.

soldier in charge of them, & got him to give them a bottle of milk they had with them & their sponges, combs, & brushes, in fact all they had with them.

The Germans are on the Marne. *45 thousand prisoners.* God grant Foch may obtain his second miracle there! Van Vollen. says the Boches think, or <u>say</u> they think they are going to have a definite victory. If they get at about 40 kilometers from Paris, they will bombard it for all they are worth, in order to terrorise, & at the same time try & push on to the coast by Amiens. God help us! Holy Mary pray for us! . . .

Bought braces [suspenders] for Serge 16 fs 50, & war braces at that, just a mere make-shift. Micha ill with high fever, I trust it won't be serious; no means of getting a single lemon to make him drinks, no alcohol for cleaning thermometer—we live without so many things we thought were essentials.

Please God may to-night's fighting be in our favour!

MARDI, JUNE 4

This morning Mme P. ~~Poncin~~ came to tell me that this evening, at 6 o'clock she was going with a German Countess (an artist-painter *sympathetic to us*) up to see the 30 English soldiers imprisoned near the "Hangar d'Evere." I gave her 30 fs to buy cigarettes for them, *one gets very little now for that sum alas!* & to-morrow, she will come & tell me how she found them situated. No one can understand why they are there, unless it is to protect the aviation shed from being bombarded by the Allies. . . .

I heard (from Dutch source) this evening that the offensive on the Marne is not the real one, but merely a diversion; that the great final German apotheosis may be expected towards the end of the month, when the military attachés of the neutral countries will (a thing unheard of heretofore) be invited by Germany to assist at the performance!!! . . . Wait & see! Happily "l'homme propose et Dieu dispose!" Mon Dieu je vous supplie de disposer! ["Man proposes, but God disposes." My Lord, I beseech you to dispose!]

THURSDAY, JUNE 7

. . . Mme Poncin went to see about the English prisoners; no means of approaching them, they are confined behind several rows of barbed wire. Many people go out of sympathy, to look at them & try to throw them small parcels. My cigarettes reached them safely, thrown over all the obstacles by a smart little boy, who achieves this feat for a few coppers.[37] It seems it was a treat, tobacco being scarce. ~~The~~ one [*sic*] same Englishman walks as near as possible to the limit of the enclosure & picks up all the small boy throws over, while the sentry's back is turned. Mme Poncin saw

---

[37] This was dangerous. In October, near Charleroi, a girl of ten, Yvonne Vieslet, would be shot by a German sentry for having handed food to a French POW.

the 25 Tommies then turn out each smoking a cigarette & giving her the military salute. . . .

FRIDAY, JUNE 9, FEAST OF THE SACRED-HEART

The feast of the Sacred Heart was celebrated most devoutly all over Belgium to-day. . . . I assisted at Cardinal Mercier's High Mass, at 10 o'clock, at Ste. Gudule. Crowds of people, not a chair to be had, I sat on the steps of a confessional. The Cardinal went into the pulpit after mass, & recited a splendid act of consecration to the Sacred-Heart surrounded by the great multitude that followed it with touching piety. No political demonstration—the Rue du Bois Sauvage was barred by police, to avoid any ovation being made to the Cardinal on his leaving the Church—Brussels doesn't want to pay any more fines to the gentle "Pouvoir occupant," [occupying power] for cheering our beloved Cardinal.

So Broqueville is replaced by Cooreman as Prime Minister—I wonder what is the real reason of the change![38] . . .

SATURDAY, JUNE 8

Isie, Inès[39] & I went this evening to the aviation ground at Evere. Unfortunately there were so many German sentinels & soldiers about, that we had no chance of throwing our parcels to the English prisoners. Besides they were not walking about, we merely saw a few heads looking out of the door of one of the wooden huts. A lady in the tram said she had seen them, earlier in the afternoon, cleaning out the officers' rooms. We decided to speak to a smart, decorated [illegible, in margin] officer, who came out of the camp, & was waiting for a tram to town.

He was a gentleman, spoke English perfectly, was surprised to hear there were English prisoners in the enclosure (I presume he had simply alighted there from a flight), took us into an office, gave orders that our parcels should be remitted to our men & a receipt for same be given us. I asked him if he was a flying man or a navy man. He replied: I am a flying navy man. He was most courteous, saluted us in grand style & went off on the tram. I then got a receipt, but merely from an employé, who said my dozen towels & Isies' cigarettes would be given to the men to-morrow. I trust they will. I must ask Vollenhoven if he (the Dutch) can do anything for those

[38] In April 1918, Prime Minister Charles de Broqueville had suggested to King Albert that his right to personally command the Belgian army was not absolute. This step, taken in the middle of the German Spring Offensive, may have been the result of French pressure, given the king's reluctance to commit his army to counteroffensives. Albert indignantly rejected the prime minister's suggestion; the resulting breach ultimately led to De Broqueville's replacement by Gérard Cooreman, a minor and compliant politician.

[39] Inès Pycke de Peteghem.

isolated men; I fear they don't get parcels or letters from England! What a pity it is we can't go near them! . . .

TUESDAY, JUNE 11

I went up to the Basilica to give in a note for Mme B [Boulez] & Anna. The trams for there, & in every direction in fact, are <u>odious</u>, especially the closed [ones] on account of their being so <u>terribly</u> crammed, since people are allowed to stand inside. Trams only run in the proportion of the half of in normal times [*sic*], hence the suffocation & discomfort. The shops get more nauseous to behold every day, worse than second hand articles of <u>all descriptions</u> stuffed in the windows for sale, foodstuffs (such as they are!!!) old boots, false teeth etc etc, everything is offered for sale. . . .

THURSDAY, JUNE 13

. . . Just before 6 this evening, Serge & I got to the Evere aviation ground & saw the English prisoners pick up the parcels the "smart" little boy threw over to them when the sentinel was not looking. I gave him my packet of 3 packs of cards etc, but he said it was heavy, so I took it to the German office there. I had the pleasure of seeing that my parcel of last Saturday, & others daily from many people, <u>are</u> remitted to our men & reception of some receipted by: Maddison, or Banks or others & often the "sincere thanks" of 25 British Tommies. I am satisfied that the best way is to give parcels in for them; & not throw them. Maddison was allowed the other day to speak to Miss Trainer (whom I met there this evening) to tell her to get the people to deposit parcels instead of throwing, as the result might be "palisades" to prevent the view on to the road. And alas! while we were there (many people this evening) angry looking officers came & surveyed & measured the space between the enclosure & the road, & I fear the poor Tommies will soon lose the view of the road & the heights beyond the canal. Such a pity!!!

The German I had to speak to about the parcels, a full smiling faced [*sic*] big fellow had learned English at Frankfurt-on-Mein [Frankfurt-on-Main], suggested I should procure a football for our men to play on Sundays. He assures me they get their parcels & letters from England & may write home like in other camps. There is *one fellow* quite a boy about 15 they say, taken prisoner at Kemmel. I heard that Maddison, the other day, was taken to a dentist's in Brussels, between 2 soldiers; they stopped at a little cabaret in the village of Evere on their return & all the women present kissed him, which brought tears to his eyes. I am told they say they are not badly off & that they play football with the Boches on Sundays (teach it them I presume). I am <u>so</u> relieved to know they are faring better than I feared. I hear there are other English prisoners at Pipe's motor factory at

Anderlecht.[40] All these Britishers are located where the Germans fear our bombs & I suppose let it get known to the English where the men are.

FRIDAY, JUNE 14

At last! News of Dick. I got information through a letter written to the Dutch Legation, but not to me. He is still looking for occupation, received some of our cards after a long delay, writes 3 a week to us, none arrive. Heard from Sidonie, that she got a card from him yesterday, written May 2nd, just after his arrival in Holland. . . . His funds are getting low too. Godmother [MT refers to herself] will have to finance, but 100 fs given here for him only means 50 he would receive there, the change being, alas! so low.

I trust we shall get further news, & pray he may find occupation. . . . I saw Martha du Roy's 2 boys, in from Bruges *St André* for a fortnight by special grace solicited since Xmas. The poor children live there in a perpetual fright, mostly in the cellar at night, on account of awful bombs & continual explosions all around.

MONDAY, JUNE 17

I had a great pleasure yesterday. Juan d'Alcantara, in town with a passport for 10 days (he hadn't stirred for more than 2 years) came to tea with me & we had a long gossip, & hope for another on Thursday. He brought me nice photos of Mary, himself, & boys. He told me 2 thousand trees have been felled *by the Boches* at Oydonck but that his father-in-law doesn't like it talked about. At the "British Section"[41] I saw this morning a young man from Termonde [Dendermonde, East Flanders, in the Étape], who came to see M. Kattendyck about the English prisoners there. A thousand come every week, & after three weeks are drafted off to Germany.[42] They suffer a great deal, alas!!! Miss Trainer came to see me about our 25 Tommies at Evere; a friend of hers spoke to one (Brinks I think) in a tram, he was going, between 2 soldiers, to have a bad hand attended to at a hospital. He asked for toothbrushes for them all (they are going to get them from a subscription), said they are very hungry,

[40] The Usines Pipe, a 1902 automobile manufacturing plant in Anderlecht, was taken over by the German military in February 1917 to repair automobiles. At war's end, the owners, the brothers Goldschmidt (one of whom had been sent to prison in Germany), found it stripped of all equipment.

[41] The department at the Dutch Legation dedicated to the interests of British nationals in occupied Belgium.

[42] With the large number of prisoners taken in the Spring Offensive, the German army put many prisoners into smaller work camps in occupied territory. Conditions deteriorated rapidly for these men.

they only get soup (so called soup) & 400 grammes of bread a day, <u>never</u> potatoes or vegetables, & *twice a week 50 grammes of meat.* . . .

TUESDAY, JUNE 18

This morning I relieved my mind concerning the Tommies at Pipe's factory, where the Germans repair their motors. I prowled round the place, & got information & finally arrived in the tiny bit of an office left to the Belgian firm. The head "employé" & another man told me the 9 or 10 Englishmen who come to work there, on & off, do so voluntarily are well paid & lack for nothing. We don't condemn them as traitors, because we suppose they have good motives for having "a look in." . . .

WEDNESDAY, JUNE 19

Miss Cronin, the Irish girl who lives near the aviation sheds at Evere, called on me to-day, to tell me the 25 Tommies, Maddison, Banks, Sexton etc have all been sent back to Ghent, but the Commander says 50 others are to arrive at the end of the week—so they will get the 25 toothbrushes. It seems the 25 Tommies were covered with vermin, poor men, on arriving here, & Miss Cronin was able to beg shirts for them from the people at Evere, & they got soaps & brushes & were taken to the public baths. They said they were pleased to be here, but wanted more bread—& couldn't realize the scarcity & immense price of eatables & all things. Miss C will warn me when another batch of men arrive there; fortunately the commander is a decent fellow & tells her what they want mostly. They got a lot of things from different sides, I hope the[y] have been able to take them away with them.

SUNDAY, JUNE 23

. . . I bought a copy-book to follow this one for my diary, Book 5th; instead of costing about 50 centimes (in normal times) I had to pay 5 fs 50 (all fives!) I saw a fair sized box of sardines marked <u>25</u> fs, yesterday, in the R. de Namur, 10 times the usual price. Boche authorities here in the worst of humours, have told the legations they don't mean to tolerate any more private correspondence in the diplomatic valises! Poor me!!! Will the famine & revolt in Austria make any change in the general situation?

Mme W's passport for Holland flatly refused (after fond hopes raised) because the W. family are noted as Anti-Boche, since Micha & Jean were fined each 3 thousand marks, for having participated in the anti-flamingant demonstration.

TUESDAY JUNE 25

[This entry carries a clipping from *La Belgique*, June 25, 1918. It reproduces the "Appeal to the German Nation" by the activist Council of Flanders on June 20, 1918. This appeal, launched after the German Western Front offensives of March 21—June

12, stated that Germany's victory was assured, that the Council had never doubted its "German brethren," and hoped they would not forget "the kindred nation of Flanders," whose real enemy was the Belgian state. Thorp commented: "Haase's speech of June 26th in the Reichstag shows <u>what</u> humbug they consider all this, just as we do; perfidious humbug."[43]]

This article is the sort of perfidious rubbish the Flamingants (to flatter their Boche masters & serve their Boche ends) bring out now & then. It simply makes me sick & desirous of seeing such "sycophants" get what they deserve when we shall again breathe a free air. . . . Lynching would be too good for them, & how the Germans themselves must scorn them.! What of the Poles being forced to give up <u>their</u> national language? To all those who know Flanders & the Flemish, it is laughable to read "how they have been sacrificed." The Flemish themselves are <u>astounded</u> to read they have been so badly treated! What hypocrisy & lies!!! . . .

SUNDAY, JUNE 30

. . . They say Belgium is to get a little more food—may it come speedily! Even a few pieces of sugar are considered a nice little present by those I give them to.

MONDAY, JULY 1

This morning an "Interned's" post card from Dick, of June 14th, says "all is excessively well with him & that the previous day, the 13th (St. Anthony)" he had a long letter from Edith, "all well with her." Deo gratias! I trust he has found occupation. Sorry he gives me no particulars whatever of Edith! Patience, patience!

TUESDAY, JULY 2

Had a good letter from Sidonie; she has heard three times from Dick; her sister & family have been to see him; he is very well, & has, thank God, found occupation, not grandly paid, but helps him to be independent. She & he have the same great desire for her & [Bobby] to join him, I hope it will be possible. I had a talk with the painter, M. Ottevaere, in his studio; he told me of the <u>immense</u> kindness & generosity with which he & his family were treated as refugees in England, in 1917–18.[44] He is most enthusiastic about the English, says he has made lasting

---

[43] The activist leadership feared German wishes for a negotiated peace, which would mean restoring Belgium; they therefore sided with the Ludendorff forces and hoped for a clear military victory for Germany. In Belgium, this desperate appeal further isolated the activists; in Germany, it made a bad impression. In the Reichstag, the Independent Socialist Hugo Haase stated to wide acclaim that activism was an artificial outgrowth of military occupation.

[44] The Brussels painter Henri Ottevaere.

friends in England, they are all to come to visit him here. He <u>deplores</u> that some (many) Belgians, abused the liberal hospitality offered them; he himself has quite "cut" [refused to see socially] one of his former Belgian friends who was to blame in this contemptible respect. . . .

THURSDAY, JULY 5 [4]

. . . I was asked yesterday 25 fs for soleing & heeling my boots; I said no, & am having the soles & heels of old galoches nailed on, & this even is quite a luxury, no india-rubber to be had. Pieces of old india-rubber tyres *hidden away from the requisitions* are sold very dear for nailing on boots, already some weeks ago I paid 5 fs for a piece for heels only. Such depression everywhere for want of food, and now train-loads of our new potatoes are being sent to Austria, with "Oukraine" painted on the wagons to make believe in Austria they come from there. Here, the alimentation is selling about ½ a kilo of potatoes per person now & then, & vegetables are hardly seen for sale, when they are, the price is fabulous. To-night we read the Sultan of Turkey is dead. Will that influence the war in any manner? We live in hourly expectation of another German offensive.[45]

TUESDAY, JULY 9

I went to see people in the slums, no one can realize the *degree of* starvation, disease, & misery without going into the homes of the poor. I don't know on what they live, or rather, just keep from dying. Tuberculosis everywhere. A little medicine that cost a few centimes at chemist's before the war, 5 fs 3 weeks ago, now 8 fs. I saw choc-olate marked 60 fs the pound (1/2 kilo) 2 to 3 fs before war; one can do without it, of course but necessary & essential eatables are on the same scale. Every day prices increase; & there must be plenty of "nouveaux riches," the "accapareurs" [hoarders] to buy those expensive things. Little tiny cakes, made without flour (which is not allowed to be sold) marked this morning in the slummy Rue Haute [in the poor Marolles district of Brussels] 90 centimes. . . .

THURSDAY, JULY 11

Yesterday I had a registered card from Dick, it came in 5 days, written July 5th. He is well & as satisfied as is possible *with his situation*; board & lodging paid by our admirable English government, & his employment, though small salary, fills up the gaps.[46] . . .

---

[45] The fifth German offensive drive on the Western Front of that year would start on July 15, on the Champagne-Marne front.

[46] Although the British Red Cross provided former prisoners with jobs, civilian internees in Holland had a harder time finding work than former soldiers.

To-day the "Flamingants," supported by the Boches are making a demonstration for the victory of the Flemish over the French, at the "Battle of the Golden Spurs, Courtrai in 1302." Public administration services like on Sunday! . . . What humbug! All to endeavour to destroy the <u>Belgian</u> feeling in favour of Flamingantisme—What reptiles!

SATURDAY, JULY 13

We have had a good quantity of coal brought in, for the winter provision, at nearly 250 fs the ton (thousand kilos). For several days it created quite a sensation on the Boulevard, because each time it came in about 20 carts, of the queerest aspect, small, low, high, drawn by 1 or 2 donkies, a horse here & there, each conveyance accompanied by 2 or 3 men, to push it when necessary to help the more than half starved animals. Coal is always accompanied by "Urchins" who stand with their thievish eyes for ever on watch,—to run off each with a prize (a handful of coal, <u>such</u> a prize now!)

. . . At all the Post-Offices, every indication in French has been torn down; they used to be neatly presented in French & Flemish but <u>now</u>, as Brussels means Flanders for the Flamingants so dearly cherished by the Boches, everyone <u>has</u> to understand Flemish. The result is I (& others) ask no end of explanations as to which is the wicket for stamps etc etc, & I remarked yesterday to the employé, in front of a Boche officer, how very happy it is we may still make enquiries in French. Von Hertling in his speech to introduce Von Hintze, Kuhlman's successor, seems most anxious to make believe he is not the Pangermanist he was said to be, but a docile follower of his, Hertling's politics, & makes another attempt to tell us how much they want peace and justly fear our economic war in the future.[47]

WEDNESDAY, JULY 17

Had lunch to-day next to the Marquis de Villalobar, he makes me hope still for news of Edith. . . . We had asked the Boches this morning how their offensive (commenced on the 15th east & west of Reims) was getting on. They shirked the answer & changed the topic of conversation, which quite fits in with the tone of their communiqués, so it is well for us so far. The Americans seem to be counter-attacking properly.[48] M. Kattendyke also lunched with us; he knows the "parley" at the Hague about the exchange of prisoners is over, but no decision yet as to if it will mean a departure for English women or not. We hear the cannon very clearly to-day; I think

---

[47] Foreign Minister Paul von Hintze.

[48] Over 300,000 US soldiers joined existing Allied units in the early summer of 1918; the Armistice found 1.5 million Americans stationed at the Western Front.

it comes from the coast of Flanders; it has been heard even since the offensive began on Monday. . . .

Last Monday evening there were 5 aeroplanes over the town; one came to grief in the Chaussée de Haecht, fell into a house, causing death & injury; the pilot was killed & the second man badly hurt. A crowd assembled at once, but <u>nothing</u> is *ever* mentioned in the local papers of anything of this kind, the Boches won't allow it. I suppose that this time they won't really be able to say "c'est la faute des Anglais." [The English are to blame].

SUNDAY, JULY 21
FÊTE NATIONALE BELGE. [BELGIAN NATIONAL HOLIDAY]

We are rejoicing over the victory of the French, in their offensive between Soissons & Château Thierry, more than 17 thousand prisoners etc. Deo gratias! & the German offensive of the 15th on either side of Reims is a real failure. Villalobar said yesterday, he thinks war will be over in 2 months! I wonder if he thinks the Boches will give in! or that we shall have military victory! . . . Mme Van der Bruggen is very troubled just now, condemned to 3 thousand marks for having hidden articles that were requisitioned, wool, brass etc & even works of art that were not comprised in the requisitions & that she had hidden for safety—all confiscated, & the fine besides, hard lines [bad luck]!!!

FRIDAY, JULY 26

On the 24th, I had a registered card from Dick, dated 17th. Thank God all is as well with him as possible. From what he says I infer Edith may perhaps be at Rouen. He is very anxious that Sidonie & Bobby should join him, as he thinks he will be exchanged to England, & wants them to go with him. . . .

SUNDAY, JULY 28

Had another registered card from Dick yesterday, it came in 5 days. He is going to live at the Hague, Rue Tollens 48. Edith is at <u>Tours</u> [in western France];[49] he might have said so at once. He hopes to be exchanged to England in 2 or 3 months, & that Sidonie will get to Holland in time to accompany him.[50] . . .

---

[49] Tours served as headquarters for the American Red Cross, in which Edith was serving.

[50] In England, former internees were taken to special reception camps to be medically checked. Prisoners from Holland, such as Dick, were sent to a camp in Ripon South.

La Fougeraie

THURSDAY, AUGUST 1

1459th day of War. 4 years to-day!

We came here on Monday. Such a relief! Glorious weather. Cannon <u>intense</u> &
<u>loud</u> every night, it makes me wonder what the result may be each night, &—pray
for the victims & a speedy victory. Who could have dreamt, 4 years ago, that we
should live in misery all that time! Even 4 months seemed then an appalling dura-
tion. I began yesterday my series of Wednesdays at AD [the Assistance Discrète].
<u>Such</u> a change for the worse on nearly all the poor faces I hadn't seen for 2 or 3
weeks. Cruel privation is telling more each day. We are so thankful for our advance
between Soissons & Reims! God grant it may continue. The prospect of the misery
next winter is slow death to so many.

SATURDAY, AUGUST 3

An eventful day! Deo gratias! Had a long letter from Edith, written on June 1st. News
good! And Soissons is reoccupied by the French. When shall we all be reunited.
May's son, John Townshend Rennard, the one year old baby I knew in N.Y. now
26 and . . . doing his duty.[51] God grant E[dith]'s fiancé may reach France safely, and
make her the good husband I always pray for.[52]

FRIDAY, AUGUST 9

I've just come back from Waterloo-St. Jean, where I took Jeanne Maisonneuve on
her way back to Genappe station, *she will have* a 2 hours walk from the Gordon
Monument; she preferred returning thus to Houtain, having been delayed 3 hours
this morning by train waiting for an engine capable of taking the train up the hill
at Groenendael.[53] Looking over the Waterloo plain, what a Lilliputian concern the
battle seems now in comparison to our tragic Armageddon! On reaching home
Micha announced [to] me a success on the English front, from the Boche paper; they
admit to having lost men & cannon, so I hope it is a good stroke for us. Mme W. was
called to the Boches yesterday, & informed she might, at last, have her passport to
Holland, for 1 month, instead of the 3 she demanded, on 7 conditions, 3 of which were:

1. She must deposit a caution of one million francs! (unheard of so far!)
2. This million would only be returned her 6 months after!!! her return home and . . .

[51] John Townshend Rennard was MT's American cousin.

[52] Either Edith's fiancé did not survive the war or their romance failed. She never married.

[53] Houtain-le-Val, a village south of Brussels, site of the Moerkerke family's château.

3. She would have to forego it if she were heard to say the least thing against the Boches in Holland. . . .

One can imagine <u>how</u> the spies would have beset her; (we think they pocket 12% on all the fines they cause to accrue to their masters) it would be too easy to fall into such a snare, so of course the passport will be refused by Mme W.

Jeanne M. [Maisonneuve] & many think the war will end in September, by Germany giving in; it is said they have drawn 450 thousand men off the West front to send to the East. M. Franqui, the alimentation man is arrested for having refused to give our "Relief for Belgium" food to a tribe of German children brought over here to some country-place to be fed. Had he not refused, he would not have kept his trust with the Allies' contract, so he is quite on the right side—although he did marry his niece last year.

THURSDAY, AUGUST 15

Since war: 5th Assumption Day.

. . . All the time now, we hear the buzz of German aeroplanes over our heads, & cannon nearly all the time, loud to-day again. I think fighting is at a stand, well for the moment. Thank God for our advance—may it be resumed soon.

FRIDAY, AUGUST 16

Yesterday, 5th Assumption of War, Isie & Marie Cazé spent the afternoon here at Fougeraie. We recalled Aug. 15th—1914—a dull day of <u>anguish</u>, when I fell upon May Bullen *& her dollies* & Marquis De Beauffort, on the B.[d], (he was in from Antwerp to buy horses!!!) & Dick & Bobby came to see me—haven't seen Dick since. What will happen ere next Assumption! God grant the tragedy will be ended! During the night at midnight I got up to look at the luminous signals being made (I think at the Observatoire, about every 2 minutes, a sort of fusée [flare] that developed at a certain height in the air & lit up all the country around, & my room. The cannon was thundering terribly as it did all day yesterday, & so loud, it seemed nearer than ever, but we know it is not. I wonder if it means a new offensive!

SUNDAY, AUGUST 18

Miss Butcher & Miss Dyne, of the British Institute[54] have been arrested yesterday by the Germans & taken to Louvain, & a perquisition has been made, but nothing found, in Miss Ahern's room, Avenue Louise. They say it is concerning a [one]

---

[54] The British Institute and Home for Governesses and Servants, Rue de Vienne 26 in Brussels (Ixelles). Butcher and Dyne were indeed arrested, interrogated, and released.

or some English prisoners, who have escaped from somewhere, I don't know from where. I trust Misses B. & D. will be released; poor Miss Cavell was their friend.[55]

Elise Stevens & her daughters were waiting for a tram at place du Trône on Wednesday. A smart looking elderly German officer walked right <u>on to them</u>, & was furious because they did not get out of his way. Dialogue in German, which Mme S. speaks admirably: "Why don't you get out of my way?—There is plenty of space for you—Don't you see I am a German officer?—Don't you see I am a lady?—you have no respect for a German officer!—you have none for a lady." Thereupon he walked away a few paces, then came back, took Elise's name & address & told her she would hear from him, so she is expecting a "mauvais quart d'heure." [a bad time]

The Germans who are here in office & administration work, after having been long at the front, are being sent back there unexpectedly & Austrians are replacing them here, because the latter don't like fighting against us in the West; they say they only want to fight in Italy. Yesterday I had butter 42 fs a kilo! A card from Gee Greaves, Dick's friend at Ruhleben, to whom he asked me to write. The poor fellow was "detained" in August 1914, so 7 months before Dick, & hasn't had his luck to get exchanged—28 years old, single, home Birmingham. I wrote him another cheering letter to-day....

TUESDAY, AUGUST 20

... 4 years today the Germans marched into Brussels & the room I do my writing in was occupied by a German officer, like the whole of the Fougeraie, but only for one night as they were in such a hurry to get to Paris!!! I saw a few shrimps, the only thing at a fishmonger's, marked 3 fs the 100 grammes, so 3 fs a kilo! We used to get them at Bruges, in summer at 60 c a kilo!

My card in reply to the one I received from Bruges, from Ada Houvenaghel, was returned & marked "not allowed through"—yet she was able to write to me!

FRIDAY, AUGUST 23

Yesterday was a blazing hot day, the hottest of this summer. I thought of our poor soldiers—some surely dying of effects of the heat; God help them! Cannon were loud last night & this morning, makes our windows & doors rattle. We are getting on a little every day, have taken Lassigny, after much fighting. Marie Cazé said, while studying the map of our front with me, that as long as we haven't taken La Fère (her town) & Laon, the Boches won't be driven far back, these places being on high ground, were fortified & keys to all the rear....

---

[55] Just before her execution, Cavell wrote to Butcher asking her to care for a young girl she had taken under her protection. After Cavell's death, Miss Butcher came to the US Legation for comfort.

SUNDAY, AUGUST 25

Three years to-day poor Dick died. R.I.P.[56]

On dit [they say] that 20 English people are arrested now & in prison at Louvain, concerning two English prisoners that are said to have escaped (I don't yet know from where) I heard also that in the room of the Miss Little (was it at the British Institute??) who is "wanted" by the Germans, was found an English prisoner's suit of clothes, I don't know if it was military or not. I'm afraid all this might prevent the much longed for train for English being allowed; poor Sidonie who is dying to get away! I was told to-day that "commerce ne marche plus aussi bien" [business is not as good as it used to be] the trafficking in different foods, because people think the end of the war is near! Would it were true!

THURSDAY, AUGUST 29

8 years yesterday dear mother died R.I.P. & the 5th anniversary during the war! We hear on all sides that the Germans are very demoralised, a story was told yesterday of how some soldiers threatened their officer with their bayonnettes because he remonstrated with them for indiscipline, the officer himself told the tale. A gentleman who had been at Sedan after the French defeat in 1870 says the aspect of the Germans & all things, at Beaumont whence he came, was exactly the same a few days ago. Every day we advance, God grant it may continue! It is said the Germans are making bridges over the Meuse, & fortifying Andenne....

When one takes one's bread & butter to eat at "goûter" [five o'clock tea] at a friend's, it is quite a generous action to share it with those who have a few grammes less than one's self. I enjoy giving a great pleasure to my friends by saving them some of the fruit I get; really no one is able to buy any, it is so scarce everywhere; I have never known it so; a few grapes or a nectarine or a peach is a royal present to make now. Scarcity & cost of everything is excessive, for instance, one brings home, to serve again, the small pieces of paper & string that have wrapped up any small parcel, both are so scarce....

TUESDAY, SEPTEMBER 3

To-day I was called *by a printed form* to the German Military Police Station, 51 Rue du Commerce—we all wondered why, as I have nothing on my conscience Germanally. I was politely received by a civil man, & I was shown a letter I had written to Sidonie on August 18th, & asked to explain what I meant by: "J'ai reçu par extraordinaire une carte de Bruges." [I have exceptionally received a card from

---

[56] MT's brother.

Bruges] It meant simply that I was surprised at getting a post-card from Bruges, as the post so seldom works—and the poor German Censor had thought I might have been fool enough to write thus, had I received it by private means. Poor thing! The man I had to talk to seemed to look upon the fuss as great humbug, & agreed with me, by a knowing look, when I said: Vous ne devez pas vous amuser beaucoup à de telles bêtises, vous pourriez faire mieux. [It must not be very pleasant for you to have to deal with such nonsense, there are better ways for you to spend your time]. The decent man promised to send my delayed letter on to Sidonie immediately. Coming back in the tram I was amused by a Frenchman holding jocular conversation with a friend, & calling out at each stop: "Péronne, Cambrai, Berlin, Berlin, we're nearly at Berlin!"

Now Péronne is cleared of the Boches, what will be their next move! I wonder if they will attack again! Clemenceau, in a speech given in to-day's Dutch papers says the war will be over by New Year! I don't quite see it yet, but will live in hope. Qui vivra verra! Dieu nous aide. [Time will tell. God help us.]

WEDNESDAY, SEPTEMBER 4, 11.30 PM

The Marquis . . . called here just now. . . . The Hindenbourg line is pierced on several points. . . . Von der Lancken is "très-noir" [in a very dark mood]. The Marquis is being subjected to certain little worries & bothers . . . has difficulty in getting his valise off as usual. We shall probably have a gradually worse time here as things get worse for our gentle invaders! We have made 10 thousand prisoners in one day. Heard the cannon loud all the time. . . .

THURSDAY, SEPTEMBER 5

German news to-night in the *Bruxellois* that the whole German front, from Ypres to Reims, is retreating, on to the Hindenbourg line. Bravo! and a long manifesto from Hindenbourg to the Army! which very clumsily tells all the world how very demoralised, (much more than we realised) the German army must be. I heard on reliable German authority, that in Belgium alone, 62 thousand men (especially young men) had deserted during the month of July *but that seems almost too many to be true, though there must be many nevertheless.* What will happen after the Hindenbourg line is reached!!!

FRIDAY, SEPTEMBER 6

Called on Ellen this afternoon. She had paid a sack of 100 kilos of potatoes 250 fs *and glad to find them* (formerly 4 to 6 fs!) & with the greatest difficulty, after failing in five shops, had been able to buy a little pork fat, at 48 fs the kilo, in order to fry her meat, no butter being available. To-day a German inquired at 21. B^d. De W. [Boulevard de Waterloo] if the house was inhabited, . . . the house next door is taken for a general. I suppose there will be a new Boche rush for houses now they are coming back on us.

TUESDAY, SEPTEMBER II

This evening at 6 o'clock, the train for English women (the 1st since Xmas 1915) was formed at the Gare du Nord, & 99 English women took their seats. They have to spend the night in the station; the train starts to-morrow at 4.30 for Holland, and a boat from Flessingue [Flushing] or Rotterdam is to take them to England. This departure is solely for English women & children in the "Grand-Bruxelles," [Greater Brussels] Miss Ahern being domiciled at Petit Bigard, a few meters out of the circuit, was allowed to go by special favour. Poor Sidonie will be so disappointed, but I hope there will soon be other departures for women living out of Brussels.

I was called to the Meldeamt this morning (all the English were) to state if yes or no I wished to go to England! So I presume that by degrees all those who wish to go will be allowed to. . . .

SATURDAY, SEPTEMBER 15

Two years ago to-day I started my diary. Never thought then I should continue to-day. . . . *[W]e still hear the same eternal cannon* & <u>how</u> much longer? . . . We are rejoicing over the American victory at St. Mihiel, 12 thousand prisoners, although the Boches say they had retreated unknown to us!!! On Friday, Mme W. had an interview with the military (very militarist) head man of some department, General von Winterfeldt, in order that her sister Mme Bunting should be allowed to enter Belgium, from Sebastopol—is allowed to hope.[57] Mme W. related their conversation, she gave the von W. a few "good ones for his knob" [a piece of her mind] concerning the Boche friendship for the Bolchevistes, etc etc etc.

Was told of the 90 to 100 English who left early on Thursday morning, (arrived at Gare du Nord at 6 pm on Wednesday) had <u>all</u> their papers of identification taken from them by the Germans; had to get rid of all their food before reaching Dutch frontier; were not allowed to take any jewellery; luggage 45 kilos & persons carefully searched before starting etc. Only 250 fs allowed to be taken, & that not in German money. Mr Kattendyke kindly arranged for warm drink to be given them several times during the night-watch in the station.

---

[57] Generalmajor Hans Karl Detloff Von Winterfeldt, head of the General Staff of the Government-General, published a report on the occupation administration after the war.

SUNDAY, SEPTEMBER 22

I am very preoccupied about Sidonie's departure, & doing all I can to get her off by the train (the 2nd) for Holland, which is daily expected to go. The difficulty is she is not residing in Brussels. No end of bother about an exception being made etc. Hope I shall succeed. . . . This last week we have rejoiced in the advance of the Yanks at St. Mihiel, and an English victory, 10.000 prisoners & 60 cannons near St. Quentin, and a big advance into Serbia by the Serbians & French. I have seen the model of the flag of the Sacred Heart borne by the Belgian soldiers on the recommendation of General Foch, he & his army near the French one. We have great trust in the Sacred Heart for the official return of the French government to faith. . . .

A lady told me yesterday a German officer had shown her a map, with a line drawn from Antwerp to Namur—all the part of Belgium on the left of the line is shortly to be in the Étape. Yesterday we received, through Jeanne Maisonneuve, & from Houtain, 42 kilos of honey, at 18 fs the kilo. This price not considered too high in present circumstances.

THURSDAY, SEPTEMBER 26

Rejoicing over our victories in Macedonia & Palestine!!! German soldiers are getting very weary of the war, we often hear stories to this effect. The last is that 800 soldiers entrained at Soignies for Valenciennes, discharged all their cartridges shooting out of the windows as soon as the train moved out of the station.

Last Monday I had a talk with M. Kattendyke at the Legation about getting S & B. [Sidonie and Bobby] off by the next train for English women, & I hope it will be soon; I have made all arrangements for her arriving here in time. I hear all the doings of every English man & woman here are known to our government; the proof is case of *Agnes Gaffney*[58] who may probably have been "wanted" when she landed at Boston, Lincs [Lincolnshire], & she may have to pay dear for being fast & coquetting with a "gentle invader" here; he saw her off with great solicitude!!! *it created a great scandal!!!* I sat nearly an hour & a half yesterday at the "Pass Central" to get Serge's identification card, & heard a conversation between two "femmes en cheveux" [hatless, i.e., working-class women]; one had just returned from working for the Boches, in Bavaria, for 8 months, & was telling the other all about it. She made quite a cheerful description, said such price & such articles of food cheaper than here ... described German women as "grosses femmes lourdes, de la belle toilette, mais aucun chic pour la porter etc etc," [big heavy women, with beautiful clothes but no sense of how to wear them] it amused me to hear opinions thus expressed. The "Étape" has neared Brussels[;] even Ruysbroeck is in the Étape commerciale now.[59]

---

[58] MT filled in the name later. Agnes Gaffney remains unidentified.

[59] The village of Ruisbroek, southwest of Brussels.

MONDAY, SEPTEMBER 30

The news, from every front is excellent, Deo Gratias! We are getting on splendidly everywhere. The Marquis & Vollenhoven both say, they think all will go so rapidly now, that we may have peace for Xmas, the Marquis even speaks of all being over in October. In any case the Germans are very dismal, & Von der Lancken in a humour that makes him quite unapproachable for those who have to deal with him. The Voorwaarts [*Vorwärts*] speaks of a near Socialist government, & it is thought that may be the solution for Germany, "acculée" [cornered] as she will be if Bulgaria, Turkey & Austria cry off very soon. . . .

Dieu nous aide!

Vive le Sacré-Coeur!

THURSDAY, OCTOBER 3

Yesterday evening we heard of our entering St. Quentin & the complete surrender of Bulgaria, (Deo Gratias!) though in the silly Boche *Belgique* of this morning, they speak of what Bulgaria may still achieve if German & Austrian help come in time!!! The Belgians & English together getting on splendidly in Flanders. This evening our taking Armentières & Lens. Cannon very loud all day, & aeroplanes flying very low, I wonder what that means. To-morrow, First Friday may the Sacred Heart be with us more than ever. What will happen now in the German government! Shall we be able to make peace with a democratic one soon! Dieu le veuille!

FRIDAY, OCTOBER 5

This evening we heard that we have taken Damas [Damascus]. . . . How glorious these daily successes which we quite expect now every evening! God grant they will continue to the near end. I saw heavy cases of money, which had been brought from Lille, being taken into a bank, at the top of the Treurenberg.[60] Heard that thousands of men from Lille, from 16 to 60 years old, are being marched to Brussels by stages of 30 kilometers a day, & that many die from exhaustion on the road, after having lived in their cellars for so long, & been deprived of essential necessaries. . . .

SUNDAY, OCTOBER 6

Notre Dame du Rosaire [Our Lady of the Rosary]!

Is peace near at last?????? This afternoon I treated myself & Isie to "real tea" for tea, (I still have a few leaves left; it costs now 220 fs a kilo!) on the strength of

---

[60] The Brussels banking district.

our successive victories. Then with the evening paper came the astounding news of Prince Max de Bade's message to Wilson, & the acceptation, by all our enemies, of all latter's conditions of peace as basis of negotiations. We can't yet believe it may be a speedy end to the tragedy, & are now longing to know the Allies' answer. Rumours running riot of the Allies being in Ostend, of Bruges in flames, of King Albert being wounded etc etc. Refugees from Roubaix having had to camp here are quite cheerful because they say peace is so near. . . .

The Germans went to every house in the elegant quartiers to enquire how many horses might be accommodated in the stables. The block of fine houses on avenue Louise between Rues de Florence & Defacqz has been requisitioned—inhabitants ordered to evacuate their residences by to-morrow night. Exhausted ragged German soldiers are arriving numerous with their convoys & cattle & being put up here & there. What shall we hear to-morrow! What will Wilson's answer be to Max Bade!

TUESDAY, OCTOBER 8

We are awaiting with immense anxiety Wilson's reply to Max de Bade's message. . . .

Men Refugees are coming into Brussels from Roubaix & other places in the North of France, where boys & men are being sent out to tramp to Brussels. B^{ron} Edgar van der Gracht was ordered out of Thielt, with 24 hours notice; the boys & men of the town to follow his departure very closely. The Germans roared to him that they would not have him there when the Allies entered. In the Ghent station, he saw several big guns coming in from Ostend, which is also being evacuated. Germans are going even to small houses here to see how many men may be accommodated, Carola had them investigating a day or two ago. Douai is now on fire, in company with Cambrai & Roulers. Let us hope it means all extra to be made good by the Boches when accounts are settled. . . .

THURSDAY, OCTOBER 10

1529th day of war.

We are simply dazed to-day by all we hear. . . . This morning we read Wilson's answer to Max de Bade's message, & eagerly awaited latter's reply. This evening we hear that since noon all Brussels is in the greatest state of excitement, that Brussels is to be quite clear of Boches by the 27th inst [of this month], & that they are all to be out of Belgium by Nov. 5th!!! This is repeated by people coming from the Société Générale[61] & everyone is crazy with delight, still I can't understand from what authority it proceeds, as it doesn't seem possible that Wilson's note, dated 9th

[61] The Comité National met in the offices of the Société Générale, Belgium's main investment bank.

Oct, could have been answered by noon to-day. . . . Yesterday great preparations were being made in many houses requisitioned for Prince Rupprecht de Bavière & others, the inhabitants having been turned out with a few hours notice—now they say all is cancelled. . . .

Prices of foodstuffs falling rapidly: yesterday dried peas at Delhaize's[62] 12 fs, to-day 1 f 50. Cabbages on Ste Croix market 20 c a kilo—unheard of for ever so long etc.

All the men from 16 to 60 in places in Flanders have been moved on elsewhere, but we can't get to know if the Germans have kept them under their control or let them all go their own way once out of their locality.

~~Bron Edgar van der Gracht was ordered out of Thielt last Saturday,~~ Yesterday a Boche civilian spy presented himself to me at the B.^d^ [Boulevard de Waterloo] with a soi-disant note from a Belgian prisoner he had picked up in the station at Ghent!!! He showed me the note which said: "Celui qui trouve ceci est prié de dire 21. Bd de Waterloo, que je suis prisonnier depuis le 2 Octobre. Joseph Decelle." ["Whoever finds this should go and tell the inhabitants of Boulevard de Waterloo 21 that I have been made prisoner on October 2. Joseph Decelle."]

I told him very plainly we knew no one of that name, & he insinuated that perhaps one of our boys was at the Front & used a false name. I replied that none of them were in that case & coldly showed him the door. What can that mean? Probably he thought he was on some scent or other.

1531 DAY OF WAR!!! SATURDAY OCTOBER 12

This morning a Boche soldier, (a socialist *to judge from the expression of his opinions*) came to take stock of the premises here at the Fougeraie, & announced [to] us: one or two officers to put up, ten soldiers & 25 horses. Every place in the neighbour-hood is to be filled with the Boche cavalry retreating from Tournai, the result of the fall of Lille which is hourly expected. An eye-witness told me of a scene that took place at the Place Rouppe, about 11 this morning.[63] About 30 English prisoners were brought there, from the gare du Midi, to be sent towards Waterloo—no one knows why. In a very short time a crowd of about 10 thousand sympathetic Belgians surrounded them, cheered them, brought them food of all kinds, tobacco, money, plundered the adjacent fruit barrows to load them with grapes etc. My narrator saw a lady give them her pocket book with all it contained, to share between them. The mob was enthusiastically delirious, neither German or Belgian police were heeded. Everyone was singing the Brabançonne, the Marseillaise, & in the midst of it all, 3 of the Tommies made their escape. When the tram started, people crowded on it, even on the roof. At one of the stops, in front of a pork-butcher's, the shop-keeper

---

[62] A chain of grocery stores.

[63] In central Brussels.

& his wife brought out something to give them, & a gentleman rushed in & returned with 2 hams & heaps of sausages for the Tommies. They were shorn of all their buttons, my narrator showed me one he had got from them. He remarked that there will be no mastering the people in their enthusiasm when the Allies do arrive. May it be soon!

SATURDAY, OCTOBER 12, 11 PM.

So it true! Peace!!!

... Gaston d' Ansembourg[64] & the Spanish minister from the Hague came in like a whirlwind & announced it was Peace, that Max de Bade's answer to Wilson was "all right". During dinner Von der Lancken phoned the same news to Villalobar, whereupon the whole party set to embracing each other, & young d'Ansembourg started waltzing about with a chair—I presume all the girls had previously found partners....

SUNDAY, OCTOBER 13

1532nd day of War.

Germany's answer has come, she yields to all Wilson wishes. There is to be evacuation of Belgium & France—and when will fighting cease??? It is thought Brussels will be chosen for the signing of peace. Every day will bring its vital interest. It is presumed King Albert may be here for his fête, on Nov. 15th. The Germans have told the men who worked for them in their separate Walloon administration at Namur, that they may go with them to Germany if they like, but the *Flemish* Activists have been informed <u>they</u> may <u>not</u> go to Germany—so the traitors will be justly punished.[65] It is said that an Englishman went to the Meldeamt & asked Eicholz when the train for the English was to be organised, & he replied: "Trains for English!!! Trains for us first!" From the pulpit, at mass this morning, calm was recommended to the people—& it is to be hoped the evacuation will bring no local complications through fighting & murdering Germans amongst the lower classes.

So this 4th Book closes with the end of hostilities, & No. 5 begins with a new period—God grant it may be better & a happier one for the world in general—"pour Sa gloire et notre sanctification." [for His glory and our redemption]

---

[64] Count Gaston de Marchant et d'Ansembourg, who owned a château in the Grand Duchy of Luxemburg.

[65] A revenge fantasy: the occupation forces made no difference between their Walloon and Flemish collaborators. Refugee Flemish activists and their families were housed in the spa town of Bad Salzuflen, east of Bielefeld.

Book 5

"THE BOOK OF PEACE!!!"

OCTOBER 1918–JANUARY 1919

P *erhaps the most interesting part of Thorp's diary is the end. The months from October 1918 until she stopped writing in January 1919 saw the war's slow collapse and immediate aftermath. While the world knew that peace was coming as early as mid-October 1918, the belligerents did not sign the Armistice on the Western Front until November 11. Thorp's notes give a good sense of this temporal rhythm. She documented the easing of prices for some goods, the rising feelings of hope, the fear of a devastating German retreat, and the sense of endless waiting for the war's real end. In November, she nervously described scenes of German revolutionary fervor; like many civilians, she was struck by the German rank and file's growing insubordination as the retreat became a reality. With peace, Thorp turned her eyes to the dynamics among Belgians. She relished the imminent punishment of those she considered cowards and collaborators. But there was also a new note of worry about social revolution.*

The day after the Armistice, the empty time of waiting behind her, Thorp felt the course of events to make sense again. She could look forward to traveling once more, and she finally heard from friends and family. Her young pupils went to tour the trenches; with presumably unintended irony, she expressed her fear that they would catch a cold. They brought back accounts of devastation as well as trophies of war. Still, amid this peacetime complacency, Thorp could not forget the price of the war. She fretted about the immense work of rebuilding; like many others, she wanted the Germans to pay for the damage. And she reflected on her personal losses—including the loss of time spent with those she loved. That, precisely, was why she had kept a diary: to record time that could never again be recovered.

BOOK 5: THE BOOK OF PEACE!!!
La Fougeraie

MONDAY, OCTOBER 14

1533rd day of War

The cannon as loud as ever all last night and to-day. <u>When</u> shall we feel re-lieved about the loss of life! Anxiously awaiting the latest news every evening in the *Belgischer Kurier,* which gives it the first. I talked to a group of "compulsory" French men refugees from Lille & Roubaix. They told me all the men from 15 to 60 were called out, & marshalled out of the towns, on foot, in bands of 500, escorted, (once well out of the town) by 4 or 5 armed German soldiers (police) per band. Every half hour or hour they were told they would find a train at the next village, & thus the first day of their tramp passed. At 6 pm they were billeted at the inhabitants of the place they had come to, & very well received everywhere, & so on for the 5, 6 or 7 days they took to reach Brussels. One young fellow from Lille told me the town had already suffered much from the bombardments. They all seemed quite neat & cheerful, in hopes of returning home very soon. In Brussels they are fed & housed by special committees & some of the inhabitants.[1] Nearly all the Boche soldiers were walking about with trunks, portmanteaus or parcels, there is a general though unof-ficial exodus already, & at night the traffic & movement are more intense. 3 Boches came here to-day to inspect our stabling for their 25 horses, we may expect them any minute. . . .

This is the copy-book that cost 5 fs 50! at a wholesale stationer's in June. Let us hope prices of everything will have become more normal before it is filled.

WEDNESDAY, OCTOBER 16

1535th day of War.

People who have important industrial interests in Belgium just now (mines, sugar-factories containing from 20 million francs of sequestered merchandise!) are exceedingly anxious about the present state of affairs. Wilson's answer to the Germans was known to-day, & he says (naturally) that <u>we</u> *the allies* must ourselves regulate the mode of the German evacuation etc, & <u>not</u> treat them as if we hadn't military & strategical superiority. It is now feared here, that as we are advancing rap-idly everywhere & the Boches having to retreat ditto, they will destroy everything

---

[1] By October 23, greater Brussels housed an estimated 130,000 evacuees from France and Flanders. Louis Gille, Alphonse Ooms and Paul Delandsheere, *Cinquante mois d'occupation allemande* (Brussels: Albert Dewit, 1919), 4:October 4, 8, 13, 15, and 23, 1918.

as they pass. It is true they will have to pay damages, but money could not repair the havoc that would be inflicted on Belgium. Still, I have every confidence in our military & political leaders, & think the Germans will be <u>forced</u> to yield to all we stipulate.

I am dying to know the result of to-day's sitting in the Reichstag. I have a feeling Wilhelm will be morally compelled to abdicate. How will Max de Bade clear himself of the letter he wrote in January to Hohenlohe, so different to what he proclaimed to be his opinion on becoming chancellor—in the letter Belgium had to be kept as a pledge etc etc, not at all the <u>democrat</u> he <u>wants to appear</u> to be now.[2] We live in great suspense in Belgium, where speedy evacuation is the only security. Every day brings new victories—we have got on beyond Roulers, Cortemarcq etc. What next!

FRIDAY, OCTOBER 18

1539th day of War.

Hurrah! We are back in Ostend, Tourcoing, Roubaix, Lille, Douai, Roulers, Lichtervelde, Menin, Wervicq, etc. etc. etc. The general opinion is that the German answer we are awaiting to Wilson's last stiff note will be very much as we want it & as it can't help being on account of our great successes & their great retreat on all sides. Austria is promising to do grand things for her different peoples.

Saw to-day in Avenues Van Bever & Prince d'Orange,[3] Bavarian cavalry & men, en route for the "East", the horses were grazing, the men hanging about, they are billetted in different villas—some saluted me as I passed. We haven't yet received the little lot we have been threatened with, but I suppose we shan't escape.

I wonder where King Albert is just now; we hear he has been slightly wounded. I long to be a week or two older, I think something final must happen before the end of the month.

SATURDAY, OCTOBER 19

I had lunch to-day next to the Dutch Minister, M. van Vollenhoven. He & the Marquis de Villalobar had been yesterday, with Von der Lancken & other Germans, in German motor-cars, to Tournai, Denain & Valenciennes. The Germans' reason for taking them quite near to the line of fire, was to show them the situation of the civilians who had preferred not to be evacuated. They are in perpetual danger from the Allies' bombardment, & several are killed daily, in spite of their living in

---

[2] Allied distrust of Maximilian von Baden, who belonged, after all, to a German ruling family, was deepened by the publication, in October 1918, of a personal letter Max had written in early 1918, critical of "parliamentarisation" and of the Reichstag's July 1917 endorsement of negotiated peace.

[3] Lanes in the Forest of Soignes close to La Fougeraie.

their cellars, but now the Germans won't allow them to go away, saying it is against the rules of war to evacuate those who could tell exactly what the position of war is in their locality. At Denain, where bombs were falling all around, the Germans wanted to send Vollenhoven & the Marquis with white flags to explain the case to the Allies, but the Marquis argued it might be represented by the allies as a step in favour of the Germans, so they didn't go. Bruges, (thank God) is free at last of the Boches! Also Courtrai, & the towns visited by Villalobar & Vollenhoven yesterday will very soon fall. It is <u>felt</u> by all that Germany's answer will be absolute submission to all we exact. 5 German carts, 10 horses & men *Bavarians* arrived at the Fougeraie this morning, & more are expected. They are all lodging in the stables & orangerie. The men did not know in what part of Belgium they were, but told the coachmen they came from Flanders (Grammont [Geraardsbergen]), & are en route for Louvain, Tirlemont, Liège &—Germany; that they & their officers are tired to death of the war. They are quite polite, take off their caps as we pass, & look "gentle, obedient, docile & mild." We may presume we have helped to make them so.

... The German residents here are suddenly "going home for a holiday". Theophile's German lodger went off the other day in a hurry; probably they have been advised to get away before complications arise. Vollenhoven received 2 "urgent" passports to be signed for Holland, but as they were for "Activist Flamingants" he refused to sign them. I commended him for this & hoped he would "keep it up." No country wants those traitors, & he said he knows arrangements have been made for them to be "executed" by the Belgian populace.... [I]f it were done legally it would make martyrs of them for those of their own treacherous set, & that would not do.[4] ...

SUNDAY, OCTOBER 20

No news yet this morning of the German answer, which is rumoured to be "all we want," but something exciting at Church. From the pulpit, at every mass was read a letter from Cardinal Mercier, stating that on Thursday last, 17th inst [of this month], he received the visit of a German functionary, sent him by Governor von Falkenhausen & <u>by Berlin</u>. He brought to the Cardinal the letter of which the following text was read to us: "We have the greatest veneration for your Eminence, & knowing him to be the ruling power in Belgium just now, we announce that (to-morrow) on Oct 21st all Belgian political prisoners not in the Étape, will be released, & those that are in Germany will be set free as soon as the evacuation commences. After living 4 years in Belgium we are glad to render homage to the great qualities of patriotism etc of

[4] Many activists made their way to the Netherlands. Those who remained did not suffer personal injuries during the explosion of popular violence that followed the departure of the German troops, but angry mobs did attack activists' property.

the Belgians."⁵ . . . This is quite sensational & exceedingly significant just now. What next! And what a change of demeanour towards the Cardinal & the Belgians!!!

Baron Coppée, who lunched here, told us different things about the Germans' great cruelty when they fought in his park in 1914. They shot 2 of his game keepers in bringing wood to make a fire.⁶ M. Coppée also said that 10 years ago, during a friendly conversation he was having with a German officer, the latter expressed a hope of never having to go to war, because the awful atrocities they were taught & compelled to commit were beyond any horrors one could imagine—this proved true in 1914—what an account they will still have to render for their treatment of Belgium & the north of France since 1914. Germans have been going about, trying to make eye witnesses make false statements to exonerate the criminals, but fortunately haven't made many of them retract their first & true versions.⁷ This evening sensational news: the German answer to Wilson (which it seems will be most conciliatory) is delayed on account of an arrangement to be made for Belgium to have the left shore of the Scheldt, & Denmark to get back something of Schleswig-Holstein. . . .

MONDAY, OCTOBER 21

This morning we heard that the Germans were out of Ghent yesterday morning, but from communiqués in this evening's *Belgischer Kurier* it doesn't seem true, for they speak of fighting about Ursel & at Deynze!!! God spare dear Mary & all her family at Oydonck, & may the children not be terrified! . . . All the afternoon loud explosions were heard, not very distant either; we think it must be bridges, railways, stations etc, being destroyed by the Germans, to hinder our pursuit.

We are all beginning to think of the Belgian & the Allies' flags to decorate our houses, but there is no material to be had to make them; I hear people are speedily having their sheets dyed for this purpose & I hope that by paying well, we shall be able to make a good show.⁸ How I should love to be in Bruges with the Allies! What joy everyone must be in after 4 years of persecution by the Germans. How happy many people are to-night, to have back their poor prisoners, & all the boys who were caught when trying to pass the frontier. . . . In to-day's *Belgique*, there is an order of Falkenhausen to set free all prisoners made by the German military. How

---

⁵ Ferdinand Mayence, *La correspondence de S.E. le Cardinal Mercier avec le gouvernement-général allemand pendant l'occupation 1914–1918* (Brussels-Paris: Albert Dewit-Gabalda, 1919), 433; on the political context of this letter, Ilse Meseberg-Haubold, *Der Widerstand Kardinal Merciers gegen die deutsche Besetzung Belgiens 1914–1918: ein Beitrag zur politischen Rolle des Katholizismus im ersten Weltkrieg* (Frankfurt am Main-Bern: Peter Lang, 1982), 165.

⁶ Mining magnate Évence Coppée whose Ardennes estate saw heavy fighting in August 1914.

⁷ This is correct regarding the "atrocities" of 1914: John Horne and Alan Kramer, *German Atrocities 1914: A History of Denial* (New Haven: Yale University Press, 2001).

⁸ Finding fabric for flags was "the question of the day!" Gille et al., *Cinquante mois d'occupation allemande*, 4:346 (October 15, 1918).

Hindenburg & all the militarists must be in a rage to see their Prussian militarism trampled on so thoroughly already, thanks to the perseverance of the Entente.

WEDNESDAY, OCTOBER 23

Yesterday, all day, all night & to-day we hear the cannon as we never heard it before, it makes everything rattle. Yesterday & again now there are separate explosions; we wonder what is being blown up; we thought it might be the Braine-le-Comte tunnel because the explosions lasted hours. No news yet except appreciations of different papers on the German reply to Wilson, & we are now expecting his, which it is thought may be definite. I think of my dear friends on the Lys & Schelt, where there is terrible fighting all these days. God save them!

FRIDAY OCTOBER 25

Xmas two months hence! Will there be peace on earth to men of good will? Wilson's reply read this morning. Everyone is optimistic & thinks the Boches will give in, & that they have been holding out "pour la forme." [for form's sake] I am very distressed about the fierce fighting between Waereghem & Deynze, & so anxious about the Boulez, & all the 't Kint family, & no less about dear Valérie for the line is nearing Ghent from Somerghem & Deynze.... We hear the king & queen of the Belgians were in Bruges in an open motor, & wonder if they remain there.

How I envy them all there the first sight & welcome of our brave men. Aeroplanes passing here all the time, shooting still heard. We hope to get back from the Boches every farthing they cost Belgium—the private fines (there will be the 3 thousand marks for Micha's antiflamingante manifestation, 60 m. that Mme W. had to pay for bearing a harmless note etc etc) & pensions for all the invalid soldiers, money to repurchase wool for our mattresses & copper & brass utensils etc etc. I am longing to see our linen properly washed, with real soap, & looking clean; now & all the four years it has come back from the laundry as soiled as when it went, & greyer each time, it quite disgusts me, and I am so impatient to get new clean clothes. No end of Spanish grippe [influenza], Pavlick & Serge are paying their tribute, & I also, slightly. I called on the Rinquets this afternoon, poor Ellen had been making enquiries yesterday about her soldier sons, fortunately no bad news, may God spare them to the end! Dick wrote me on the 11th inst [of this month], I got the card yesterday, he had heard from Edith, she has been to Paris for a week, but hadn't heard yet when her fiancé might land in France. Unfortunately we can't communicate any longer with poor Sidonie in Antwerp, latter being in the Étape since the 19th. inst [of this month]; I am so sorry for her, but hope it won't be for long, & that freedom will shortly be rendered to all Belgium. Wonderful sign of the Boche times in Belgium.... They had taken

Mme W.'s fine new Minerva motor car, a fortnight ago, without paying—& it has been quietly sent home thanks to the friendly interference of the Dutch minister M. van Vollenhoven.

SATURDAY, OCTOBER 26

I haven't been to town this last week so have been spared the painful sight of the arrival or passing of refugees from Flanders & all the other parts where fighting is now going on, but they are coming in crowds, on foot, in carts, some with what they have saved of their belongings, a heartrending sight. . . .

I have had a notice from the Ixelles Administration that an English soldier[9] is to be buried to-morrow, from the Military Hospital, at 3.15 pm. I am so sorry I can't go this time, but think there may be several people, it being on Sunday afternoon. May the poor fellow rest in peace!

. . . Another "sign of the times": yesterday Mme W. was driving up to the German motor-car dépôt at the Cinquantenaire, to cut through as usual, *found* it was *partly* barred, & a sentinel informed her there was no thoroughfare any longer. She answered him in German that we no longer put up with nonsense of that kind, & told the coachman to drive on, which he did, the sentinel satisfying himself with merely shrugging his shoulders.

How altered the Boches are in so many ways, even here, since they've started democracy. The price of meat has fallen greatly, 13 fs a kilo what was recently 23, & several other articles on the same scale.

MONDAY, OCTOBER 28

To-morrow we leave the Fougeraie—this time, let us hope, the last during the war, it is already the 5th departure "en guerre." I went to see the poor Clarisse nuns, at Mme F. W's [Madame Frantz Wittouck's] villa, at Boitsfort. They were at Métay near Le Câteau, till Oct 12th; the English at a few meters from them. They had been forgotten, in a cellar, therefore contrary to regulations were helped by the Germans, to leave the fire line during the night. Four of their old infirm nuns had to be carried out of it, in a sort of canvas cloth, held by the corners, like they use for the wounded. They did 6 kilometers on foot, through fallen & falling bombs; some of the Germans who were helping them were struck down, they saw many killed & wounded lying about. Finally they found conveyances, & were taken to a train at Maubeuge, whence they arrived in Brussels last Wednesday. They told me that some of the civilians were allowed to go towards the English lines, when they were in a village that was about

---

9 Private W. A. Stallwood of the Machine Gun Corps.

to be taken by latter, but in that case the refugees were not allowed to take anything of their belongings with them, & one of the nuns saw a scene where the Boche soldiers got furious, & flung away all the people's luggage.

Ludendorf [*sic*] has resigned. . . . What next! We are hourly expecting to know the Allies' conditions of armistice. . . . This morning 7 to 800 *miserable sick* horses, led by 2 to 3 hundred Germans, with carts, provisions, furniture, went up the Ch^ssée de la Hulpe, towards Groenendael race-course, where they are to spend the night. They are en route for Liège—Germany. How different they are leaving, to what they were arriving four years ago, in their vain glory!!! The fall of militarism is so evident, even in all we see here.

WEDNESDAY, OCTOBER 30

We left the Fougeraie yesterday, in the loveliest autumn weather; it continues; the right kind for a grand cleaning of Belgium after 4 years of grey Boches. I heard several bits of authentic good news on arriving. When the Bruges Conseil Communal was holding its 1st assembly after the departure of the Germans, rumors were heard on the Square below, & his majesty King Albert walked in, fell into the arms of good old Burgomaster Visart & there was a scene of joyful patriotism that will be recorded in history. How I envy those who were present!!!

As soon as the barbed wire was cut between the north of Flanders & Holland the *wealthy* American, Mrs. Kirk (mother of Mrs. Ruddock) who lives at the Hague with her son who is Attaché at the American Legation, rushed into Flanders in her motor & made a long distribution of money to the poor. (Another one to be envied!)

Last Saturday, the d'Arenberg Palace & all the adjoining houses belonging to the Duke d'Arenberg were sold to the town of Brussels for a mere song, 7½ million francs, the property is worth at least the double, but the d'Arenbergs who can't live here any more, were anxious, I suppose to settle their affairs before the general departure of the Boches.[10]

Theophile's lodger has returned from Germany, nearly starved, says we know nothing here of the misery & excitement of the German people, who seem on the verge of revolution at the prospect of having to pay war indemnities for perhaps a century. To-day the separation between Austria & Germany is complete, former hoping for more favourable conditions of peace than will be granted to Germany. Mme Wittouck went this afternoon, to see if she could do anything for the thousand Russian prisoners that are at Uccle.[11] Their German guardians would not let her approach them, or

---

[10] Gille et al., *Cinquante mois d'occupation allemande*, 4:368–369 (October 26, 1918).

[11] On October 28, 1918, several hundred Russian POWs were brought to a camp in Uccle; civilians, shocked at their mistreatment, gave them food. Charles Tytgat, *Bruxelles sous la botte allemande, de la déclaration de guerre de la Roumanie à la délivrance. Journal d'un journaliste* (Brussels: Imprimerie scientifique Charles Bulens & Cie, 1919), 518–520.

distribute clothes she had brought for them. She is trying to get the "Administration Communale" to provide them with a good meal a day, that she will pay for.

Last week, there were over 200 English Tommies *prisoners* at the farm at Petit Bigard for one night, but they are well equipped & warmly clad by our government. Refugees coming in constantly, & so many dying. Great mortality in every class of society, from infections grippe, dysentery, pneumonia, & numbers of young people are carried off. Priests, doctors & infirmarians can't suffice for the numerous cases; I suppose there is a general break down, after 4 years of suffering & privations of all kinds.

FRIDAY, NOVEMBER 1, ALL SAINTS.

To-day I had a great surprise—dear Anna Boulez arrived. . . . She drove her mother from Zulte, (Flanders) to Brussels, stayed a week en route at Synghem [Zingem, south of Ghent], one night at [illegible], which she left yesterday at 10 am & got to the Basilique at 3 pm. Père Guinet took them to a Clinique, where they can live quietly in awaiting events. Poor Anna & poor Mme Boulez! Anna says she can never express all she has suffered during these 4 years. . . . They were 3 days & nights in the cellars at Zulte, then ordered out by the Germans & she decided to go to Brussels. Since then, their villa & all the surrounding houses, the church & part of Waereghem, all has been destroyed, but all that is now in the Allies' hands. She told me heartbreaking tales of what she saw. People dying all along the roads; hundreds of refugees spending the night in churches, three women prematurely confined the same night in one of them; a boy she knows & his father were in a cellar, the father died & for 3 days the boy remained with the corpse, & hurried out to bury it in the garden as soon as the firing ceased a little. The Germans have no more men, no wall of men to oppose to ours, but just a few to serve their artillery. . . .

All the left side of the Lys, she says, is in our power. She brought away the family silver, 50 kilos, & buried it, with business papers, at Synghem. She says the family is quite ruined, but I cheered her with the news that the Boches will have to make it all good.

Before her eyes, a German officer took away all her bedroom furniture & knick-knacks. It is posted up everywhere in the "ligne de feu" [firing-line] that the military are allowed to take away anything they desire, & may not be opposed by the inhabitants. Anna bought a calf & a pig to feed her family & the needy, & had to help a German kill the animals & cut them up. She is indeed a brave, plucky woman! She wonders where the rest of the family fled to. . . . Terrible events in Austria— the Tcheque-Slovacs have the upper hand over the German Austrians. Brussels is crammed with refugees, especially men from 17 to 35 years of age, that are sent out of all the localities that the Allies are nearing. 100.000 have thus been moved on, but now the Germans say they can't move any more & want to make an agreement that if they let them stay in their town & villages, they must agree not to join the

Allies' armies when they enter!!! . . . that is for mere form's sake on the Boches' part, & because they are no longer masters of the situation, quite nonsense to talk of such an agreement!!!

Last Friday there was a 2nd train to Holland for the English, & I wasn't warned, nor could I have communicated with Sidonie on account of Antwerp being in the Étape. What <u>will</u> poor Dick think on seeing that second arrival of women in Holland, & not his wife. . . . [N]<u>ow</u> M. Kattendyke says there is question of the Germans allowing the English women to go freely into Holland. I've tried to make Sidonie understand by a "Carte d'Affaires" [Business card] sent her to-day, but I fear it won't get through. I went yesterday to the "Comité National" about getting 27 blankets for the poor French Clarisse nuns at Boitsfort, & hope to succeed.

SUNDAY, NOVEMBER 3

I went yesterday to see Mme Boulez & Anna, Poor Mme B in such distress, quite overwhelmed by the agonies she has gone through these last 4 years. I pity her with all my heart, she & Anna are real martyrs of the war. I hope the C's will invite them to stay with them, for it is too cold where they are, the Clinique hasn't coal to heat the house, & there are no fireplaces. I shall fortunately be able to place the good old pony that brought them to Brussels. Who could have ever imagined that I should see those dear old friends in <u>such</u> woeful circumstances! They told me heart-rending tales of their life at Waereghem & Zulte, under the Germans. The Allies are now there & Oydonck must also be out of danger. This evening's paper says the Germans have retreated upon Ghent. . . . What can that mean for dear Valérie & Emma! God grant they may be safe & free from terror. The German staff officers at Synghem told Anna all the bridges at Ghent were mined & that there would be fighting there, but I don't believe it. To-day we read the Kaiser's declaration of being the "Serviteur" of the people & democracy!!! I think he would gain in dignity by abdicating instead of pretending he has gone over to ultra modern democratic ideas. We are still impatiently awaiting our conditions of the armistice. Cannon <u>so loud</u>, even in town & in spite of trams etc. . . .

TUESDAY, NOVEMBER 5

1555th day of War.

I went yesterday to M. Kattendyke about Sidonie's departure for Holland; he assures me the Germans are arranging for all the women & children to leave, in fact all those who receive relief are compelled to, or else the relief is stopped, except in certain cases to be appreciated by the Dutch Legation for the British government, so I hope Sidonie will be off soon.

It is supposed that after retiring from Ghent, the Germans will defend themselves a little on the Dendre. The head officer of the staff at Synghem, told Anna that their last defence would be on the Scheldt. Cannon loud again to-day, & last evening, about 9 o'clock, 3 of the Allies' aeroplanes were bombarded, in Brussels, it was noisy, but didn't last long. To-day, the news of Austria's acceptation of all our conditions. When are those for the Boches going to be published! In yesterday evening's *Belgischer Kurier*, there was an appeal to all German civilians in Brussels to make arrangements to quit the town by Nov 6th, the German authorities not being responsible, after that date, for their getting away with their luggage....

FRIDAY, NOVEMBER 8

We are living on our nerves at high pressure, expecting every moment to hear the armistice is signed and ... on what conditions.... A German paper to-day gave the Socialists' ultimatum to the Kaiser, to abdicate by to-morrow, at noon. This afternoon, German papers were thrown from an Allies' aeroplane, bearing some message to the German soldiers here, I saw someone who had seen the papers fall, but hadn't been able to secure one. All day long, there are German convoys, quite lamentable, passing on our Boulevard & *on all the roads around Brussels* going Eastwards; cannon, horses, carts full of all sorts of things being saved in the nick of time. I saw Maria Schöller who happened to be at Antwerp when the Germans were retreating from the coast & West Flanders—all the town was out to see the sight of the armies passing the Scheldt from East Flanders into Antwerp, on rafts & boats. Anna Boulez told me yesterday, how the grand stallion Balsamon, was taken by force *by the Boches* from M. Ribaucourt's stables at Zulte, knocked down by a motor when on the road a few minutes & mortally injured, its thigh was broken—80 thousand fs.[12] More for the Germans to make good to us. Anna resisted the German gendarme who summoned her to give up the horse—he called her no end of insulting names, but she didn't give in & said she would not countenance the robbery. When she went to the Commandanture to put in her complaint, they said they merely wanted to save the horse from the bombs!!! Everyone is excited about preparing the Allies' flags, all the accessories are coming out in the shop windows, but there is a great dearth of material—many people are having their last sheets dyed for flags.

Anna told me that the Belgian flag is hoisted as soon as the Germans are hunted out of every locality, even when there is only a distance of 200 meters between our lines & theirs, & that makes them mad, they turn round & try to fire at our colours.

---

[12] Count de Ribaucourt, a French textile magnate, founded a racehorse stable at Zulte; in 1912, he built the Villa Salomé (named after a horse), where the Boulezes resided after being forced out of Waregem.

SATURDAY, NOVEMBER 9

1559th day of war.

A year ago to-day poor M. Wittouck died. R.I.P. We had a beautiful anniversary service for him. How much happier we should have been if he were with us to see the end of the war!

At last! The Kaiser has abdicated & the Kronprinz has renounced the throne! The Marquis who was here this morning said: "Il est mort, enterré et sent déjà mauvais." [He is dead and buried and has started to smell bad already.] Bavaria has proclaimed the Republic. The Germans have to give their answer to our conditions of armistice by Monday at 11 pm. I hope they will anticipate, so as to save the most lives possible.

Cannon loud & windows rattling all last night, and the same to-night, even nearer, & we see the fire from the cannon in the sky in the east. I pray Ghent may be spared, but heavy firing is taking place not far off. Aeroplanes (Allies') flying frequently during the day & bombarded by the German guns in Brussels. When will the last shot be fired!!!

1560th and last? day of War

SUNDAY, NOVEMBER 10

A glorious fine day, all quiet in the morning after last night's shooting & terrible explosions about 3 a.m. I went to see Anna & her mother at Koekelberg. About 3 pm, great movement & excitement on the Boulevards, shooting at aeroplanes, people running & saying the Germans were making a revolution. Such was the case; soldiers on motor-cars making speeches, hoisting red flags & also the English & American I was told, disarming the officers who passed & in Avenue Louise there were some wounded. I went out at 4.30 with Isie, to go to the Grand Benediction for the A.D. [Assistance Discrète] at Ste. Gudule. The German soldiers were flying around in motors, had opened the Park, in which we walked a moment, so as to be able to say we did so on the famous 10th of Nov. 1918.[13] All the sentinels had been done away with, we walked up the R. de la Loi to the Ministères, saw motor cars with soldiers arriving all the time. I think they were rallying there. All the big military men have vanished & the soldiers are doing as they like. They hoisted the red flag on the Ministères, plucked off their German imperial insignia from caps & uniforms & threw them on the ground. The people went groping for them as "souvenirs." The *Belgischer Kurier* of 4 pm gave the conditions of the Armistice, but we don't know officially if they have been accepted, but don't doubt they will be. Between 8 & 8.30, terrible shooting as if at aeroplanes, but it is thought it was only a sham on the part of the Boches

[13] The Park in central Brussels had been closed to civilians for four years.

(non revolutionary??) to frighten the people. In any case we heard the cannon very loud & near, & saw the fire during dinner.

Anna told me <u>all</u> the trees in her part of Flanders have been felled, by the Germans & the Belgians, the latter using them for fuel. The effect of the horizon quite open is strange, she could count 17 church steeples from the tower of their villa at Zulte, though since the fighting there, many have disappeared, that of Waereghem amongst others.

I came back with the "famous" plan[14] in my pocket, quite an interesting German document to keep as an historical souvenir. . . . Mme W. went to Louvain to-day with Vollenhoven, in his motor. She says the "revolution" there was much more serious than here; there was firing in the streets, the soldiers stopped them several times, wanting to take the motor, but refrained, as it was the Dutch minister's. A German soldier desirous of getting to Brussels quickly merely travelled back with them on the foot-board & was polite—did not want to sit inside with them or *simply* turn them out as a Russian Bolchevist would certainly have done. We are anxious about what may ensue. . . . there is not *sufficient* police, no established authority here just now, capable of controlling the masses; it would be well if Burgomaster Max returned at once from his captivity in Germany, he would be able to control the populace. I wonder if we shall be having Americans or English as a police force, in awaiting the Germans have disappeared & the Belgians can appear in grand style.

Isie & I had the same feeling at St. Gudule this evening, that it is a blessing the fine church is intact, & a miracle indeed that those of Bruges did not suffer more during the long time they were in danger.

Interesting days ahead! God grant they may be peaceful!

MONDAY, NOVEMBER 11

1561st and <u>Last</u> day of War.

The German answer to the Armistice was due to-day at 11 a.m. We suppose it is "yes," though we've no <u>official</u> notification; if yes, fighting was to cease at 5 pm. & we've heard no guns to-day from the front, though there has been shooting by a certain party of German soldiers at the Gare du Nord, at those who are too revolutionary. They say several Belgian civilians have been killed & wounded. . . . On going out to 8 mass, I was very affected by the sight of 3 Belgian flags hoisted on the B^d. On my return, ½ an hour later, I counted about twelve, & now bunting is displayed everywhere, flags on most of the houses. Mme W. & several other people have not hoisted theirs, as they consider it "not the thing" to do, as long as the revolutionary Germans are running about with their red flags. I don't quite admit that point of view, but of course there are 2 sides to the question.

---

[14] Apparently a German plan of an attack at Zulte, given to MT by Anna Boulez.

Villalobar & Vollenhoven consider the situation as <u>very</u> precarious, some Belgian socialists having manifested against the king, & former, on the quiet, has dispatched a private messenger to King Albert, saying he should arrive as soon as possible, or the revolutionary movement may spread amongst the Belgians. I consider that if the armistice is signed, we should have powerful military Allies' forces here <u>at once</u>, to keep the Germans & our socialists in order, & make the former realize that we master the situation & "boss the show" now & for ever. . . . Adieu Germans, not au revoir! . . .

We had an assembly at the A.D. [Assistance Discrète] this morning; I am deputed, with others to collect at the door at Ste Gudule, next Friday, at the Te Deum for the King's feast. I shall ask for "le sou de la victoire pour les pauvres," [a victory penny for the poor] & hope we shall do well.

This evening Mme Poncin wrote me asking me to see 3 badly wounded (English) soldiers at the military hospital to-morrow & to take them little comforts. I hope to be admitted. Serge went down town at 4 pm to see what was happening, & had to run & take shelter in a house, from Germans in a cart, shooting as they drove along, in order to clear the streets. He says lots of windows are broken down there & there have been many people wounded.

TUESDAY, NOVEMBER 12

So yesterday, the 1561st day of War was the last, the armistice being signed at 11.50 [*sic*], & no more fighting 6 hours after. It was a day of unrest down town, some civilians having attacked Germans at the Gare du Nord; Germans of different parties shot at each other & the German revolutionists were about all day, & to-day also with their red flags.

Mr Saura of the Spanish commission & Paul Emile Janson who were sent to King Albert saw him at Bruges; he was in good health & spirits, & his army also.[15] Police military forces will be here by Saturday (I hope for Friday, the King's feast) & the Royal Family are to return on Tuesday, but I imagine they may anticipate to give us a surprise. Ladies are planning to decorate the Queen's apartment with mauve, white & yellow flowers. The new Germans have dispatched a motor to Germany, to bring back Burgomaster Max. All the burgomasters of the grand Bruxelles [greater Brussels] have made a lively appeal to the people to remain calm, & to put up their bunting & flags only when they see the national flag on the Town Hall, so the many that were out already have been taken down.

I had a great happiness this morning—M. Kattendyke wrote me that Sidonie & Bobby got to Rotterdam on Nov. 1st. & joined Dick at Scheveningue. Thank God! . . .

---

[15] At Loppem near Bruges, King Albert met with a delegation of Belgian politicians (including the socialist leader Eduard Anseele) to declare universal male suffrage immediately upon liberation. Subsequent attempts to introduce votes for women, however, failed.

After much struggling with the soldiers at the door of the military hospital I was taken to the ward where there are 8 English Tommies, a Russian & a Belgian; 3 Tommies in a very bad state & all of them completely neglected—no care, no nursing, next to no food, dirt & squalor, in fact the sight of their misery continues to haunt me. I gave them sugar & jam & a guinea for cigarettes they can buy from the sentinel. I went to Father Lecourt & Mr Gahan to tell them to go to see them also, & they were going to do so at once. I shall make another attempt on Thursday. I hope these poor fellows will soon be in the hands of our own nurses & doctors. How many could have easily been saved by proper care & nursing!

The ex-Kaiser is hiding in Holland, in hopes that a counter-revolution will restore him to the throne. Rupprecht de Bavière was too scared to spend Sunday night in Mévius's house, place Stephanie, so spent it at Villalobar's.[16] All the great militarists are quite cowed even by the little bit of revolution we have here. The general of the staff at Petit Bigard had sentinels all round him on Sunday night, & finally consented to hoist the red flag when going away. The soldiers simply make them submit, nevertheless there is of course, as usual, a counter-current of those who remain faithful to the old army, & they quarrel amongst themselves.

Each night we eagerly look forward to the events of the next day, it is an interesting time to live just now. I wonder if Melle Bolo remembers how, already in 1914 she & I had decreed that our chastisement for German Imperialism was to make a small republic of Prussia! How chimerical it seemed then, we even laughed at our own audacity, & yet it has come true!!!!

A year to-day we buried M. Wittouck R.I.P. How I deplore he is not here now!

WEDNESDAY, NOVEMBER 13

All the Allies who were prisoners have been set free by the Germans, & are all about the town being helped by everyone & taken into houses till arrangements can be made for sending them home. A band of Russians were brought here to-day at noon, Mme W. accepted 5, they are at our No. 20, and delighted with their clean comfortable beds & quarters, they have roughed it terribly all though the war, & only in Bavaria met with the same treatment as here. I took them some sugar when they were in bed, they are very grateful & kiss our hand as gracefully as our society men.

The Germans are passing through in continental convoys, evacuating as quickly as possible. I saw some to-day, they were trying to keep up appearances & singing snatches of songs now & then. There is, to me, something pathetic, in the sight of the

---

[16] Baron Gustave de Mévius, a Catholic senator. On Rupprecht's fears for his safety, Gille et al., *Cinquante mois d'occupation allemande*, 4:390 (November 8, 1918); Michael Amara and Hubert Roland, eds., *Gouverner en Belgique occupée: Oscar von der Lancken-Wakenitz—Rapports d'activité 1915–1918. Édition critique* (Brussels-Bern: P.I.E.-Peter Lang, 2004), 391–392.

vanquished enemy returning so humiliated (which they deserved). How different to the troops we saw invading us in 1914! On the whole, the Belgians behave very well, look at them as they pass & don't provoke them in any way, but at the Bourse, near the Gare du Nord, & in different places, there are German Maxim guns ready not only to keep the Belgians in order but also for the Revolutionaries to defend themselves against the men of the old régime.

I heard the English Tommies I saw yesterday at the Military Hospital were sent to the Ixelles Hospital, I must look them up there. Anna came to tea & told me the following story: When she was at Synghem, Prince Rupprecht de Bavière was in a house a few minutes from Alfred Amelot's,[17] & she saw him constantly walking about with the General, whose plan of the attack at Zulte she appropriated, the Staff of 22 officers who were in Alfred's house while she & her mother were there. One day Alfred's cook told her to go & see what was taking place in the kitchen. There were 9 German cooks & helps, one of them was rolling a fillet of beef upon the dirty floor & then making a dog lick it before cooking it. That he said was out of hatred for their chiefs; he spoke French well, & told Anna that he & his comrades were each to kill an appointed officer when the time came. . . .

An officer then entered the kitchen, & the men took the usual military attitude of deep respect. Anna told them afterwards that they were vile hypocrites, they replied the alternative was death, but that their time would come. That was during the week from Oct. 20th to 28th. . . . The time came a few days later when the Revolution broke out in Germany & here last Sunday Nov. 10th, the night that Rupprecht out of fear, spent at the Marquis de Villalobar's.

THURSDAY, NOVEMBER 14

. . . The Marquis de Villalobar told us of his meeting with the King & Queen yesterday at Ghent; both passed a review, on horseback, at the Place d'Armes, looking so well & happy, & Prince Léopold has become a tall distinguished lad. Frantic enthusiasm! Mary d'Alcantara espied the Marquis at a window of the Club on Place D'Armes, & got herself pulled up, her brother Juan pushing her up behind. Just like her! Full of go as ever. The Marquis says the king will only arrive in state next Friday to-morrow week, all has to be cleaned & got ready in the Palace & everywhere. The Royal Cortège will not, we fear, pass before our house, the King wishing to show himself first to the people down town in the popular districts.

I shook hands with & talked to two Tommies in the street, a Canadian & a Londoner, fine bright young fellows. I went to St. Peter's hospital & had our sick Russian Philip Tiausoff taken there by D[r]'s orders. All the hospitals are full of the Allies' sick prisoners, set free yesterday.

[17] Alfred Amelot, a Liberal politician, estate-owner, and burgomaster of Zingem.

Please God we may do better for them than the Germans did. I must find out the boys I went to see last Tuesday. Several Belgian soldiers have been seen in their uniforms, having walked from Ghent to see their family. A poor woman, in the street, told me how her brother turned up to-day, & her joy . . . she was ill in bed & was cured at once. She had thought him dead, never having heard from him since he went to war. The Te Deum for the king's fête to-morrow is postponed, a wise measure, in order to keep the people from manifestations while the Boches are still here. They continue to pass "lamentably" such an impressing sight! Read to-day how the Kaiser went from Spa, through Visé to Holland, it seems just retribution, Visé was the first town he destroyed & the last he will ever see in Belgium.[18] They say now that Fritz Hohenzollern is not murdered by the sentinel at the frontier.[19]

All the German states have become Republics—Melle Bolo & I only suggested it for Prussia![20] I am glad that Lloyd George spoke as he did in announcing the armistice in the House of Commons, & that his idea of going "to thank God humbly" for victory at St. Margaret's Church was complied with. May this act of religion be an example to France! Foch will be happy God was thus publicly recognized as the giver of victory, he the apostle of the Sacred Heart. . . .

FRIDAY, NOVEMBER 15

To-day, in my visits in the slums I was very struck by the absence of Germans who were still so numerous in the trams & everywhere yesterday. I only met one between this & the Rue Haute, & then only 2 more parties of 2 & 4. The streets really appeared all the cleaner for their absence. I met & spoke with several bands of our Tommies amongst whom one Scotsman in a kilt, a nice young New Zealander. I walked a little with them. They are so refreshing in looks & manner, after the horrid greys of 4 years standing. It is said no more Boches may be seen here after 4 am to-morrow; they are still passing in convoys while I write.

Much noise of cannon & explosions & maxim guns again; we presume that, contrary to the stipulation of the armistice, the Boches are destroying their ammunition somewhere. The Fords called this evening, Alec told me his communiqués speak of terrible cruelties at Deynze, just before the Boches cleared out, they shot about 54 civilians.[21] . . .

[18] During the invasion, units of Königsberg Pioneers had burned and pillaged the border town of Visé, expelled women and children, deported men to Germany, and killed twenty-three inhabitants.

[19] The German crown prince was rumored to have been killed at the German-Dutch border.

[20] Between November 7 and 23, the royal rulers of all of the German states abdicated.

[21] From October 18 until November 2, the town of Deinze saw heavy fighting because the German Fourth Army wanted to hold on to this strategic railway hub. Parts of the town were

MONDAY, NOVEMBER 18

What glorious days!

On Saturday Micha & I spent the afternoon at the Hôpital St. Pierre, visiting the English & Russian freed prisoners. In the evening three Tommies, who had escaped from their camp in Westphalia, rang at our bell & were brought in, looking like scarecrows.

They had been tramping & hiding 4 months! A party of 8 when they escaped, 2 were shot, 2 wounded & one lost en route & George Robertson, waiter, 40 years old, William Joyner, London 27, married, 2 children, John Clarke, 21 jockey Newmarket. We sent them to the baths, fed dressed & made them comfortable, & are placing them in friends' houses, as we have already our Russians.[22]

This morning I took them to Rue du Chêne & spoke to the English Colonel & officers working there, trying to settle for the numerous prisoners that were freed in or near Brussels.[23]

On Saturday, while I was busy with my Tommies, in came Maud Bainbridge, in her nurse's uniform, fresh from the front, with 2 decorations, heroically earned. She had motored in from Bruges for a look at us, she has been a heroine & deserves a great deal from Belgium; she nursed Belgians & French worst wounded men all the time, & retreated & advanced with the front. She looks "grand" in her uniform; I had the pleasure of having her & Isie to tea together.

Pavlick & Micha went to Berchem St. Agathe yesterday to see our different men, coming in gradually. They witnessed an aeroplane coming down, went & spoke to the two American officers who drove??? it & brought them home to dinner.

Such splendid types of Yankees, gentlemen [MT lists names and addresses ...] They were most interesting, and quite delightful, & will take letters for us to Calais in their aeroplanes & post them there, no post going yet here, so I wrote to Edith & Carrie & let Isie write also.

The German soldiers pillaged their own stores, & sold all sorts of things for a mere song to the people who were in contact with them.

There was alas! in spite of the great joy, much sadness in many homes. Trains of German ammunition in the stations of Schaerbeek & the Midi exploded & caused much loss of life; so much that the papers (now we have already the old Belgian ones & some new national ones) don't speak much of the victims & the havoc caused. The cause is not yet known; but people incline to believe that it is German treachery

---

destroyed; at least one hundred civilians were killed by artillery. But no source mentions any execution of civilians by the German military.

[22] In October and November 1918, many POWs, whether escapees or freed men, sought assistance because no provisions had been made to repatriate them.

[23] The British military had set up a temporary bureau in Rue du Chêne in central Brussels.

& revenge.[24] The traitor Belgian journalists, accapareurs [hoarders] etc are being arrested & will get their due.

TUESDAY, NOVEMBER 19

I don't remember if I mentioned, that on Sunday, as I was going to Koekelberg to see Anna & her mother, between 9 & 10 o'clock, no flags were yet out, but when I returned at 12, the streets were splendidly decorated, the Burgomaster Max having returned to the Town-Hall. To-day more soldiers have returned, great enthusiasm to greet them.

I went with our Russians to the University to get their bread tickets & inscription to receive 3 fs 75 every 2 days.

I saw our two charming American Lieutenants, they were not able to fly off to Calais, weather being too misty, so I gave them another letter for Freda [Sanders], Mary Burman & Louie Anderson, they will probably go to-morrow, & my friends will soon get my letters.

SUNDAY, DECEMBER 15

Poor old Diary, how I have neglected thee, since the coming of better days!!! But what a number of "imprévus" [unexpected things] each day brought, to accomplish for others!

Well the King & Royal Family had a splendid reception; likewise all the Allies' troops marching through to Germany. We saw specially many French. We made comparisons with the Boches when they marched in in August 1914. What glorious days these are! Lots of British & Americans everywhere. Several theatrical companies of soldiers have been giving public performances of what they played at the front. I took Isie to "Pinafore" by the Canadians.[25] Latter gave a dinner to a crowd of girls last Monday, & a ball afterwards to a greater number, in the Salle de Fêtes of the Egmont Palace ex d'Arenberg.[26] I hear that C.[tsse] Paulo de B. [Borchgrave] who had the organizing of the affair, didn't invite the English Legation (Lady Villiers) or any of the English colony—hence great criticism.

The first letter I had from England was from dear Freda [Sanders] of Nov 12th, reached me on the 23rd, & others have been coming since. Such joy, after a barrier of our 4 years.

---

[24] Explosions of munitions trains in Brussels stations killed fifteen civilians and wounded thirty-six. Civilians accused the German military of having booby-trapped trains, but no order to do so could be found.

[25] The Gilbert & Sullivan operetta H.M.S. Pinafore.

[26] The Duke of Arenberg's urban palace, now sold to the City of Brussels.

Such a grand, noble, though distressing letter from Captain Anderson, poor Louie dead of a broken heart, & the 3 sons & son-in-law killed at war.[27] His letter might indeed be entitled: "The price England paid for victory."

I have had a lot to do for English & Russian prisoners; saw former several times at Hospital St. Jean, & assisted at the last departure of English ambulances for Ath.

Mr Theophile Liefmans told us *at Koekelbergh* tragic stories of the Boches' unnecessary cruelties of the last days; many civilians were asphyxiated "on purpose" while hiding in their cellars, especially at Avelghem, where there were about 1500 victims.[28]

This the Boches will have to account for. We hear how they constantly crucified their prisoners, provoked cruel explosions etc etc, in fact so much goes to make us loathe their conduct more & more. . . .

I remember how often I had to hide this Diary, each time Boches were sighted coming into the house for perquisitions; it would have been bad for me had it fallen into their hands.

I don't yet quite realize we are free at last.

No means of travelling, even to Ghent; the rare trains crawl, take sometimes 30 hours, being constantly shunted.

I am trying to get a seat in a closed motor for Ghent. People get to Paris thus: in motor from here to Lille, a thousand fs for the 4 seats, & thence by train to Paris. The only means of getting here by train from France is round by Boulogne, Calais, Dunkerke [*sic*] & through the Yser country. . . .

The shop-keepers who traded kindly with the Germans, have had their shop & windows smashed & goods plundered—the La Faire comestible shop, Rue de Namur, the 2 grand & "expensive" pork-butchers & the pastry-cook at Porte de Namur, & others of course in other neighbourhoods. Wygaerts at B.^d Anspach etc etc.[29] . . .

Dick in London, disappointed at not getting occupation & having no friends there. I never understood his "idée fixe" [obsession] of going there at this bad season.

WEDNESDAY, DECEMBER 18

There was a grand reception & speeches yesterday at the "Chambre des Représentants" [House of Representatives] in honour of Brand Whitlock, the

---

[27] Louie Gertrude Anderson died on November 2, 1917.

[28] The town of Avelgem was heavily bombed during the liberation offensive (the British reached the town on October 22). Inhabitants fled; hundreds died of influenza or artillery fire en route. Of those who stayed, many were killed hiding in their cellars, though not the 1,200 Thorp referred to; nor is there any indication that the Germans locked civilians in cellars, as had happened in several places in 1914. Théophile Liefmans was a local brewery heir and aviator.

[29] At war's end, furious crowds attacked businesses owned by people accused of having traded with the Germans. Much damage was done before police intervened. One of the targets was the Grands Magasins Victor Wygaerts on Boulevard Anspach.

Marquis de Villalobar & Van Vollenhoven. Several speeches, but Whitlock's was splendid, a real model, grand thoughts nobly expressed & gratifying all round without too much "incense."[30]

To-day I received 2 post-cards from William—one posted at Capetown on Oct. 4th 1914, on his way home from Europe, the other posted at Adelaide on Dec. 24 1914, from an anxious brother. How anxious he must often have been since, poor fellow, when reading of the Boches' unheard of cruelty in so many instances.[31] . . .

There are 3 English soldiers & 2 officers living next door but one to us. I spoke to two of them this morning, & aired my desire to get to Ghent in a motor or a lorry—the officer says he won't forget me or rather my demand. . . . It is good to get in touch once more with all those I love. . . .

XMAS EVE

Peace on Earth! May all my dear ones & I enjoy that peace the world can neither give or take away! How different our feelings at this midnight mass will be to those of the last four. May God have mercy on all the victims of the war, alive and dead.

The last few nights I've been sleeping on my wool mattress, that has come out of his hiding-place—how much more cumfy than oat husks! It is so good to see all our & Allies' soldiers about, & visiting S^{te}. Gudule & the monuments, after the galling times we had seeing the Boches do the same. I often pass a few words with the soldiers; the other day in the tram, a young Canadian told me he had come in, from Rixensart, for the officers' Xmas mass, he was in quest of a goose, but poultry is scarce & if obtainable, very expensive, there has been no food for poultry.

On Dec. 31st the 4th Canadian Division give a ball at the Town Hall, they say the Prince of Wales is to be present. . . .

XMAS NIGHT

. . . At 4 pm, nearly a hundred British soldiers, billeted round about the Fougeraie, were to assemble in the kitchen at the Fougeraie for their Xmas dinner. I happened to talk to two of them in a tram, & they told me the menu was to be: turkey, Xmas pudding, beer & rhum. They decorated the kitchen with evergreens, I regretted I hadn't the time to go & have a peek at them during their feast.

There are thousands of English in the outskirts of Brussels, Ellen Rinquet has 10 to lodge in her little house. I heard that a number of motor cars had come from

[30] Whitlock's speech received thunderous applause; he called it "the most remarkable day of my life." Allan Nevins, ed., *The Letters and Journal of Brand Whitlock* (New York: D. Appleton Century Company, 1936), 538–540.

[31] MT's half-brother.

Boulogne or Calais, crammed with Xmas cheer for all the soldiers. What a relief they can enjoy their Xmas knowing the war is over. . . .

FRIDAY, DECEMBER 27

Isie finally got a seat in a military car & went off to Bruges yesterday morning. I hope she won't catch cold or be laid up with rheumatism. The boys also started for Ostend, & to-day is the worst possible weather for their first day's tramp to the trenches, cold rain & wind. I hope Pavlick won't be laid up; I can't help apprehending it. My trip to Ghent quite fell through alas! I saw dear May Bullen last evening, she arrived from Le Hâvre on Saturday, 40 hours train journey snail's pace & hours to wait in different stations, 2 nights in the train, 6 persons per compartment!!! She saw the devastation of Flanders, as one does coming from Dunkirk to Bruges. She told me a dreadful tragedy—a cousin of hers had 11 sons & a daughter. The 11 sons died at war . . . on hearing of the deaths of the 11th, the father dropped down dead. What a subject for a tragic author! Wilson is expected in Brussels next week. No revival yet whatever in business, nothing more to be bought in the shops than a month ago, & there will not be, as long as trains can't bring us anything.

MONDAY, DECEMBER 30

Dear Bainy[32] dropped in last evening, came from Vinckem, in an ambulance car, & stays till Wednesday. She told me a lot more about her experiences as War-nurse; she has really been most brave & valiant, the only woman at the advanced posts, & often under fire. The life is a hard one, admits of no comforts whatever, she could not undress even sometimes for several days together.

I was down town to-day, & went to see Tietz's[33] premises converted into a fine Y.M.C.A. home for all the Allied soldiers. It looks very spacious, 2 thousand beds, open night & day. I am so glad they have at last a place where they can turn in with pleasure. Boots still 125 fs a pair in ordinary stuff & only a leather tip. . . .

A copy-book that used to cost a penny, now 1 f 25. We've had news from the boys touring on the battle-field, mud & slosh & swamp everywhere. All foreigners, even the Allies, have to declare themselves & show their papers at the Town-Hall, so I have that "corvée" to get over. Very bad news from Mme Schmourlo at Riga; the

---

[32] Maud Bainbridge.

[33] On November 10, 1918, the Grands Magasins Léonard Tietz, a department store in central Brussels partly owned by German nationals, was placed under sequestration order by the Belgian State.

Bolchevists took away 6 thousand of the 9 thousand roubles she left Petrograd with; took away her pearl-necklace; her husband was forced to sell his over-coat; she & the children are living miserably at Riga; the money Mme W. tries to send can't reach her; all the former Society people of Petrograd are ruined, & trying to earn their food in the lowliest manner.[34]

God grant we may be spared <u>such</u> a revolution.

1919

WEDNESDAY, JANUARY 1

God grant this year may make us all "better", & make us forget the four last! It opens with a bright sunny little frost, quite a treat after so many damp dull days.

Mrs. O'Connor was in the Gare du Nord yesterday at 5 a.m. to see a friend off to England via Gand-Bruges-Bologne, & will never forget the sight she saw.

About 30 open goods & cattle trucks, <u>packed</u> with <u>patient</u>, well dressed passengers, standing up; the train was to leave at 6. a.m. And most of the people had <u>spent the night</u> in the station to secure this very "indifferent" standing-space.

There was one carriage at the end of the train, packed with Tommies for Boulogne, & very diplomatically she got them to adopt her friend as their "sister." They smuggled her into the carriage & promised to see her safely to Boulogne. . . .

We lunched to-day at Petit Bigard with the Marquis de Villalobar, General Leman, his daughter & son. The Marquis promised to take me in his motor to Ghent the first time it goes that way. General Leman had just returned from Bruges, where he made a stay of a few weeks. He told me Bruges is not very much damaged, but all the outlying German military works were splendidly aimed at by the English artillery.

He looks very old & ill, though only 66; he had his feet badly hurt during the siege of the Forts at Liège, he has lost several toes, & going to lose another, suffers from diabetes. His daughter is naturally very proud of him.[35] They have been staying a long time at Petit Bigard. Their house at Liège was of course entirely plundered by the Boches. The Canadians' ball at the Hôtel de Ville on New Years' Eve was a great success, & different little hops are taking place for the Allies' officers. They say the Queen doesn't quite approve, on account of so many deaths in quantities of families, & that is why she & the king & their children are spending the Xmas holidays quietly at La Panne.

---

[34] The Schmourlo family (occasionally written as "de Schmourlo"), Russian aristocrats.

[35] The Belgian General Gérard Leman commanded the Liège forts in August 1914 and offered fierce resistance before being captured. In 1917, he was released from war imprisonment because of bad health and spent the rest of the war in Switzerland. He returned to a hero's welcome in November 1918.

The Prince of Wales is staying at C^tsse. John d'Oultremont's place at Ham-sur-Heure, & motors in to Brussels constantly. He was at the Canadian's ball. They say he likes a bit of fun & only the new fangled dances, (which I & many others think horrid) such as the Fox-trot, & all the other animal steps which I consider not only ungraceful but disgraceful.

We have good news every day from the boys, on their trips to the battle-fields. They are having some good experiences of make-shifts in the way of food & lodging, (do them good!) are very impressed by the horror of all they see, & meet some very jolly English, Americans & Australians.

WEDNESDAY, JANUARY 8

Pavlick & Micha came back from their trip to the battlefields, very impressed by all they saw; everything was interesting; great desolation everywhere; many corpses & dead horses lying about. They brought back as many mementoes as they could carry, belts of English cartridges that were lying near a skeleton in a trench hut. There are great quantities of unexploded ammunition everywhere, cannon & guns, in fact all that was left behind by our troops rushing on victoriously.

Ostend is not as much damaged as I feared; the houses on the sea-front are still there, Micha brought me a nice little birthday present from Ostend, he says things are cheaper there than here; from La Panne he brought me something that pleased me immensely, a cake of Pears soap, he only paid 2 fs for it, it is not to be found here, & if it were, would be at least 6 fs, like the other decent soap! ... Everyone in Belgium is dissatisfied because business doesn't look up at all, the government is blamed for not letting in goods that certain tradespeople have waiting for them over the frontiers—I can't understand the pretext which is that certain merchants may not be favoured with detriment to others. It is to be hoped each day will now some, what [sic] alleviate the straits we still live in. Mme W. has had worse & worse news of the state of her family in Russia, especially of the distress of her sister who has reached Riga, & can't come on here. I have written for her to our minister here, Sir Francis Villiers, to beg for British interference for her to enable her to reach some Dutch port, by English boat, thence come on to Brussels.

All the post-offices here are closed to-day, the employés are on strike & they have put up a poster demanding the resignation of their chief at the general P. [Post] office, a Mr Dohet, whom they accuse of having served them ill with the Germans & having caused several to be deported to Germany.

SUNDAY, JANUARY 12

Poor old diary, it is terribly neglected. I have so much to do & just now propaganda for Women's votes is in hand.[36] Last Thursday went to the Town-Hall & got my

---

[36] The Union Patriotique des femmes belges was waging a campaign for women's suffrage.

provisional "permis de séjour." [residence permit] Every stranger, even Allies, have had to report themselves their parents' & grand-parents' age, dates of births, deaths etc, all that in order to know who is in this country.

Saw Marie Cazé this morning, back from her 10 days in Paris. She had no luck on the railway, 22 hours each way, having to be shunted for hours to let pass 1500 of the engines that the Boches had to send us. She says there are 3 million over population in Paris just now, mostly from the devastated districts, everything much less dear than here, fresh eggs 70 c, here 1 f 20, good boots 52 fs here, bad ones 150 fs & more. The English officers are giving dances in many of the country houses where they are living; the Duke of Athlone, & the prince of Wales accept invitations also, former was last Thursday at the C^mtsse Aug. d'Ursel's latter was "empêché" [prevented] at the last moment.

... At last, I hope to go by train to Ghent to see dear Valérie, next Thursday, about 3½ hours journey instead of barely one, but now there are some closed carriages. I am longing to see her again....

THURSDAY, JANUARY 16

Just had a card from dear Carrie, written 13th inst [of this month], (very quick) & by the same post, one from Anna Boulez, Waereghem, of Jan 12th! Nothing from Edith since Dec 19th, am so anxious.

Mme Schmourlo telegraphed yesterday she had arrived at Copenhagen, so we hope she will soon be here. I had a letter from Private Webb, Sidcup, one of the English Tommies I saw in the hospital here—quite nice to be remembered.

Epilogue: "Quite Nice to Be Remembered"

"I had a letter from Private Webb, Sidcup, one of the English Tommies I saw in the hospital here—quite nice to be remembered."[1] So ends the diary of Mary Thorp on January 12, 1919. It seems a fitting conclusion for a woman's chronicle of war that lingers so often on her thoughts of others. Throughout the diary, Thorp visits, she corresponds, she frets, and she prays, not just for her friends and family, but also for the unknown victims of war. Energetic, stoic, oriented toward others, deeply religious, imbued with a sense of duty and mission, and proud of her status as an Englishwoman abroad, Thorp's worldview is firmly framed in the kind of nineteenth-century Englishness that was celebrated in middle-brow and uplifting literature.

Her diary also reflects the experience of life in an occupied city in wartime. Accompanied as she is by constant rumors and the background of cannon, Thorp negotiates the cityscape as a woman, a foreigner, a resident, a worker, and a volunteer. She observes <u>and</u> participates, always recognizing the precarious position in which she finds herself. On December 15, 1918, she finally allows herself to reflect on the end of the war. Freedom means a return to normalcy and the possibility of being reunited with friends and family. The last few entries of her diary suggest a lightening of her spirit and raised hopes for the future.

Mary's postwar life is a bit of a mystery, although we know she remained with the Wittouck household. She was, in all probability, a companion to Madame Wittouck, who died in 1928. In 1930, she was still registered as living with the family. But such family documents as survive do not bear any traces of her—let alone shed light on what she might have thought of some momentous developments. In July 1940, her youngest former charge, Serge Wittouck, aged thirty-six, died in murky circumstances in Manila. He had been prospecting for oil in Portuguese East Timor on behalf of the Japanese government.[2] During the Second World War, the occupation authorities turned the Wittoucks out of the Fougeraie to allow the Belgian Fascist leader Léon Degrelle to set up court there.[3] By then, Thorp no longer lived at the château, but she lived close by in Uccle, in a residence that the family had procured for her; they had also provided her with a pension.[4] If she kept a second war diary during the Nazi occupation, it has not been discovered; she still had her First World War diary with her, and on one occasion, in April 1941, even annotated it.[5] It is difficult not to speculate how she would have chronicled this second occupation experience. Mary Thorp died in Uccle, Belgium, on December 2, 1945.[6]

NOTES

1. MT (Mary Thorp), January 12, 1919.

2. He directed the Manila-based Allied Mining Corporation, a front for Japanese interests. Tim Charlton, "History of Petroleum Exploration in Timor-Leste," http://www.tim-charlton.co.uk/other-projects/timor-leste-history-of-oil-exploration; Robert Lee, "Crisis in a Backwater: 1941 in Portuguese Timor," *Lusotopie* 7 (2000), theme issue *Lusophonies asiatiques, Asiatiques en lusophonies*, 175–189; Glyn Stone, *The Oldest Ally: Britain and the Portuguese Connection, 1936–1941* (Martlesham, Suffolk: Boydell and Brewer, 1994), 183–186. See also the entry "East Timor" in Xiaobing Li and Michael Molina, *Oil: A Cultural and Geographic Encyclopedia of Black Gold* (Santa Barbara, CA: ABC-CLIO, 2014), 495–497.

3. Paul Delandsheere and Alphonse Ooms, *La Belgique sous les Nazis* (Brussels: L'Édition Universelle), 4:206 (July 24, 1944). See also Charles d'Ydewalle, *La cour et la ville 1934–1940* (Brussels: Éditions libres, 1945), 59–60.

4. Mr. Éric Wittouck, personal communication, with thanks. Thorp's last address was an apartment at Avenue de Fré 2 in Uccle. Belgium, State Archives, Foreigners' file 470286 (Mary Thorp).

5. MT, November 22, 1916.

6. Belgium, State Archives, Foreigners' file 470286 (Mary Thorp).

ACKNOWLEDGMENTS

Giving context and meaning to a document that is a hundred years old is not a simple task. We would like to acknowledge our debt to those scholars and librarians who helped us obtain the diary, find documentary evidence about Thorp's life, and re-create her world. Thanks to the In Flanders Field Documentation Center and its whole staff, who care for the original diary and who alerted us to its existence. Particular thanks go to Dominiek Dendooven. Other libraries and resources include the British Library, the Brussels and Bruges City Archives, the Belgian State Archives in Brussels, the Kensington local library, the Library of Congress, the Merrill-Cazier Library, and the Family History Library in Salt Lake City (and associated databases). Both of us owe a debt to our respective institutions, The Pennsylvania State University and Utah State University, for access to their resources.

In contextualizing some of the people and places in the diary, historians such as Emmanuel Debruyne, Alison Fell, Michael Khodarkovsky, Patrick McDevitt, and Tom Westerman were most helpful. Mr. Éric Wittouck, grandson of Thorp's employers, generously allowed Sophie to visit him at the family home in Uccle, Brussels, and provided ample access to photographs, family albums, and Thorp's teaching notebooks. Mr. Wittouck also answered questions about the history of the family, their business, their residences, and their memories of Mary Thorp. We are most grateful to him.

A delightful part of working on the diary is that we worked on this together. And that we could rely on wonderful staff, undergraduates, and graduate students at Utah State and Penn State. Enthusiastic thanks go to Olga Casaretti, Mathias Fuelling, Monica Ingold, Cody Patton, and Katrina Eckel, who, in addition to transcribing the diary, used it in a thoughtful master's thesis. Finally, we would like to express our gratitude to Nancy Toff and Elda Granata at Oxford University Press for their work in bringing the diary to print.

Tammy would also like to thank her husband, Todd Shirley, for traveling to Ieper and listening to tales of Mary Thorp. Sophie thanks *her* husband, Ronnie Hsia, and her children, Mathilde and Eduard; she also wishes to thank Michaël Amara, Jan D'Hondt, and Jean Houssiau, for archivists are a girl's best friend.

SELECTED BIBLIOGRAPHY

Alvarez, David. "A German Agent at the Vatican: The Gerlach Affair." *Intelligence and National Security* 11 (1996): 345–356.

Amara, Michael, and Hubert Roland, eds. *Gouverner en Belgique occupée: Oscar von der Lancken-Wakenitz—Rapports d'activité 1915–1918. Édition critique.* Brussels-Bern: P.I.E.-Peter Lang, 2004.

Anderson, Nancy F. "The 'Marriage with a Deceased Wife's Sister Bill' Controversy: Incest Anxiety and the Defense of Family Purity in Victorian England." *Journal of British Studies* 21 (1982): 67–86.

Archidiocèse de Malines-Bruxelles, ed. *Pèlerinage à Lourdes 1964–2014.* http://www.catho-bruxelles.be/IMG/pdf/dossier_de_presse_lourdes.fr.final.pdf.

Beckett, Ian F. W. *The Great War.* 2nd ed. Harlow: Pearson, 2007.

Behrman, Cynthia Fansler. "The Annual Blister: A Sidelight on Victorian Social and Parliamentary History." *Victorian Studies* 11 (1968): 483–502.

Benn, Gottfried. "Wie Miss Cavell erschossen wurde." In *Gesammelte Werke*, vol. 4, *Autobiographische und vermischte Schriften*, edited by Dieter Wellershoff, 194–201. Wiesbaden: Limes, 1961.

Bertrams, Kenneth et al. *Solvay: History of a Multinational Family Firm.* Cambridge: Cambridge University Press, 2014.

Boiteau, A. *Velaines dans le passé. Histoire du village qui vous a vus naître, grandir et qui garde le souvenir de nos aïeux.* Tournai: self-published, 1988.

Bolotenko, Bolotenko. "Wartime Explosions in Archangel, 1916–1917: 'Bakaritsa Is Burning'; 'Ekonomiia Is Now a Wasteland.'" *Northern Mariner/le marin du nord* 21, no. 4 (October 2011): 377–405. http://www.cnrsscrn.org/northern_mariner/vol21/tnm_21_377-405.pdf.

Broughton, Trev, and Ruth Symes, eds. *The Governess: An Anthology.* New York: St. Martin's, 1997.

Bunkers Suzanne L., and Cynthia A. Huff. "Issues in Studying Women's Diaries: A Theoretical and Critical Introduction." In *Inscribing the Daily: Critical Essays on Women's Diaries*, edited by Bunkers and Huff, 1–22. Amherst: University of Massachusetts Press, 1996.

Chamberlin, William H. *The Russian Revolution.* Vol. 1. Princeton, NJ: Princeton University Press, 2014.

Chickering, Roger. *The Great War and Urban Life in Germany: Freiburg, 1914–1918.* Cambridge: Cambridge University Press, 2007.

Corbett, Mary Jean. "Husband, Wife, and Sister: Remaking the Early Victorian Family." *Victorian Literature and Culture* 35 (2007): 1–19.

Davis, Belinda. *Home Fires Burning. Food, Politics, and Everyday Life in World War I.* Chapel Hill: University of North Carolina Press, 1992.

Debruyne, Emmauel. "La deuxième section et le renseignement militaire en Belgique occupée, 1914–1918." In *1915–2015: Het verhaal van de Belgische militaire inlichtingen- en veiligheidsdienst/ L'histoire du service de renseignement et de sécurité belge*, edited by Marc Cools et al., 129–154 Antwerp: Maklu Publishers, 2015.

Debruyne, Emmanuel. *Le réseau Cavell: des femmes et des hommes en résistance*. Brussels: Racine, 2016.

Debruyne, Emmanuel, and Jehanne Paternostre. *La résistance au quotidien 1914–1918: témoignages inédits*. Brussels: Racine, 2009.

Debruyne, Emmanuel, and Laurence van Ypersele. *De la guerre de l'ombre aux ombres de la guerre. L'espionnage en Belgique durant la guerre 1914–1918. Histoire et mémoire*. Brussels: Labor, 2004.

Debruyne, Emmanuel, and Laurence Van Ypersele. *Je serai fusillé demain. Les dernières lettres des patriotes belges et français fusillés par l'occupant. 1914–1918*. Brussels: Racine, 2011.

Decock, Pierre. "Sadi Kirschen." *Nouvelle Biographie Nationale*. Vol. 1. Brussels: Académie Royale des Sciences, des Lettres et des Beaux-Arts de Belgique, 1988.

Delplancq, Thierry. "Une chasse aux 'oisifs': Les déportations de civils à Bruxelles en 1917." *Bruxelles et la vie urbaine*, special issue of *Archives et Bibliothèques de Belgique* 64 (2001): 513–539.

Delplancq, Thierry. "Des civils dans la guerre. Une approche du sort des évacués français en Belgique, 1917–1918." In *Liber Amicorum Jacques-Henri Lefèbvre*, edited by Jacques Henri Lefèbvre, 71–80. La Louvière: Centre de Recherches et de Documentation Régionales, 2001.

De Schaepdrijver, Sophie. *Bastion: Occupied Bruges in the First World War*. Veurne: Hannibal, 2014.

De Schaepdrijver, Sophie. *La Belgique et la Première Guerre Mondiale*. Brussels-Bern: P.I.E.-Peter Lang, 2004.

De Schaepdrijver, Sophie. "A Civilian War Effort: The *Comité National de Secours et d'Alimentation* in Occupied Belgium, 1914–1918." In *Remembering Herbert Hoover and the Commission for Relief in Belgium: Proceedings of the Seminar Held at the University Foundation on October 4, 2006*. Brussels: Fondation Universitaire, 2007, 24–37.

De Schaepdrijver, Sophie. "L'Europe occupée en 1915: entre violence et exploitation." In *Vers la guerre totale: le tournant de 1914–1915*, edited by John Horne, 121–151. Paris: Tallandier, 2010.

De Schaepdrijver, Sophie. *Gabrielle Petit: The Death and Life of a Female Spy in the First World War*. London: Bloomsbury Academic, 2015.

De Schaepdrijver, Sophie. "Measuring Lost Time: Civilian Diaries under Military Occupation." In *Inside World War One? Egodocuments and the Experience of War*, edited by Richard Bessel and Dorothee Wierling. Oxford: Oxford University Press, forthcoming.

De Schaepdrijver, Sophie. "Occupation, Propaganda, and the Idea of Belgium." In *European Culture in the Great War: The Arts, Entertainment, and Propaganda, 1914–1918*, edited by Aviel Roshwald and Richard Stites, 267–294. Cambridge: Cambridge University Press, 1999.

De Schaepdrijver, Sophie. "An Outsider Inside: The Occupation Diary of Georges Eekhoud." In *Une guerre totale? La Belgique dans la Première Guerre mondiale*, edited by Serge Jaumain et al., 79–96. Brussels: Archives Générales du Royaume, 2005.

De Schaepdrijver, Sophie. "Patriotic Distance." *1914–1918 Online: International Encyclopedia of the First World War*, 2015. http://encyclopedia.1914-1918-online.net/article/patriotic_distance.

De Schaepdrijver, Sophie. "Populations under Occupation." In *Cambridge History of the First World War*, vol. 3, edited by Jay Winter, 476–504 Cambridge: Cambridge University Press, 2013.

De Schaepdrijver, Sophie. *"We Who Are So Cosmopolitan": The War Diary of Constance Graeffe, 1914–1915*. Brussels: Archives Générales du Royaume, 2008.

De Schaepdrijver, Sophie, and Emmanuel Debruyne. "*Sursum Corda*: The Underground Press in Occupied Belgium, 1914–1918." *First World War Studies* 4 (2013): 23–38.

Detournay, Céline. *La Grande Guerre sous le regard de l'élite tournaisienne occupée: contribution à la culture de guerre*. Brussels: Archives Générales du Royaume, 2003.

De Volder, Jan. *Benoît XV et la Belgique*. Brussels: Brepols, 1999.

de Weerdt, Denise. *De vrouwen van de Eerste Wereldoorlog*. Gent: Stichting Mens en Kultuur, n.d. [1990].

d'Udekem d'Acoz, Marie-Pierre. *Voor koning en Vaderland. De Belgische Adel in het Verzet.* Tielt: Lannoo, 2003.

Frevert, Ute. *Arbeiterfrauen in der Kriegsgesellschaft: Beruf, Familie und Politik im Ersten Weltkrieg.* Göttingen: Vandenhoeck & Ruprecht, 1989.

Gille, Louis, Alphonse Ooms, and Paul Delandsheere. *Cinquante mois d'occupation allemande.* 4 vols. Brussels: Albert Dewit, 1919.

Grayzel, Susan R. *At Home and under Fire: Air Raids and Culture in Britain from the Great War to the Blitz.* Cambridge: Cambridge University Press, 2012.

Gubin, Éliane. "La grande ville, un lieu féminin. L'exemple de Bruxelles avant 1914." In *La ville et les femmes en Belgique,* edited by Éliane Gubin and Jean-Pierre Nandrin, 77–96. Brussels: Publications des Facultés universitaires Saint-Louis, 1993.

Gubin, Éliane, and Valérie Piette. "Les employées à Bruxelles (XIXe s.–1960) ou la victoire de la travailleuse indésirable." In *Femmes et villes,* edited by Sylvette Denèfle, 379–398. Tours: Presses Universitaires François-Rabelais, 2004.

Gubin, Éliane et al. *Dictionnaire des femmes belges, XIX et XX siècles.* Brussels: Racine, 2006.

Haag, Henri. *Le comte Charles de Broqueville, Ministre d'Etat, et les luttes pour le pouvoir (1910–1940).* Vol. 2. Louvain-la-Neuve-Brussels: Collège Erasme-Nauwelaerts, 1990.

Hanna, Martha. "War Letters: Communication between Front and Home Front." *1914–1918 Online: International Encyclopedia of the First World War,* 2014. http://encyclopedia.1914-1918-online.net/article/patriotic_distance.

Healy, Maureen. *Vienna and the Fall of the Habsburg Empire: Total War and Everyday Life in World War I.* Cambridge: Cambridge University Press, 2004.

Heilbrun, Carolyn G. *Writing a Woman's Life.* New York: Ballantine Books, 1988.

Henry, Albert. *Le ravitaillement de la Belgique pendant l'occupation allemande.* Paris-New Haven: PUF–Yale University Press, 1924.

Herwig, Holger. *The First World War: Germany and Austria-Hungary, 1914–1918.* London: Bloomsbury, 2014.

Hiltermann, Rainer. "Midi à quatorze heures: la résistance des Belges à l'heure allemande et l'heure d'été (1914–1918)." *Militaria Belgica,* 2014: 151–172.

Hogan, Rebecca. "Engendered Autobiographies: The Diary as a Feminine Form." *Prose Studies* 14 (1992).

Hughes, Kathryn. *The Victorian Governess.* London: Hambledon Press, 1993.

Hull, Isabel V. *Absolute Destruction: Military Culture and the Practices of War in Imperial Germany.* Ithaca, NY: Cornell University Press, 2005.

Jeffery, Keith. *1916: A Global History.* London: Bloomsbury, 2015.

Jessen, Olaf. *Die Moltkes: Biographie einer Familie.* München: C. H. Beck, 2011.

Jones, Heather. *Violence against Prisoners of War in the First World War: Britain, France and Germany, 1914–1920.* New York: Cambridge University Press, 2011.

Jünger, Ernst. *Feldpostbriefe an die Familie, 1915–1918.* Stuttgart: Klett-Cotta, 2014.

Karau, Mark. *Wielding the Dagger: The MarineKorps Flandern and the German War Effort, 1914–1918.* Santa Barbara, CA: Praeger, 2003.

Kauffman, Jesse. *Elusive Alliance: The German Occupation of Poland in World War I.* Cambridge, MA: Harvard University Press, 2015.

Kenny, Michael. *The Politics of English Nationhood.* Oxford: Oxford University Press, 2014.

Khodarkovsky, Michael. *Bitter Choices: Loyalty and Betrayal in the Russian Conquest of the North Caucasus.* Ithaca, NY: Cornell University Press, 2011.

Khodarkovsky, Michael. *Where Two Worlds Met: The Russian State and the Kalmyk Nomads, 1600–1771.* Ithaca, NY: Cornell University Press, 1992.

Kirschen, Étienne Sadi. *Autobiographie d'un mandarin.* Brussels: Vander, 1988.

Kitchen, Martin. *The Silent Dictatorship: The Politics of the German High Command under Hindenburg and Ludendorff, 1916–1918.* London: Croom Helm, 1976.

Knezevic, Jovana. "The Austro-Hungarian Occupation of Belgrade during the First World War: Battles at the Home Front." PhD diss., Yale University, 2006.

Knox, Alfred. "V. A. Sukhomlinov." *Slavonic Review* 5 (1926): 148–152.

Köhler, Ludwig Von. *Die Staatsverwaltung der besetzten Gebiete.* Vol. 1: *Belgien.* Stuttgart: Deutsche Verlags-Anstalt, 1927.

Little, Branden. "Band of Crusaders: American Humanitarians, the Great War, and the Remaking of the World." PhD diss., University of California, 2009.

Mahaim, Ernest. *Le secours de chômage en Belgique pendant l'occupation allemande.* Paris-New Haven: PUF–Yale University Press, n.d. [1926].

Mahaim, Ernest, ed. *La Belgique restaurée: étude sociologique.* Brussels: Maurice Lamertin, 1926.

Majerus, Benoît. *Occupation et logiques policières. La police bruxelloise en 1914–1918 et 1940–1945.* Brussels: Académie Royale de Belgique, 2007.

May, Trevor. *Gondolas and Growlers: The History of the London Horse Cab.* Stroud: Alan Sutton, 1995.

Mayence, Ferdinand. *La correspondance de S.E. le Cardinal Mercier avec le gouvernement-général allemand pendant l'occupation 1914–1918.* Brussels-Paris: Albert Dewit-Gabalda, 1919.

McMeekin, Sean. *The Ottoman Endgame.* New York: Penguin, 2015.

Meseberg-Haubold, Ilse. *Der Widerstand Kardinal Merciers gegen die deutsche Besetzung Belgiens 1914-1918: ein Beitrag zur politischen Rolle des Katholizismus im ersten Weltkrieg.* Frankfurt am Main-Bern: Peter Lang, 1982.

Mick, Christoph. "1918: Endgame." In *The Cambridge History of the First World War*, vol. 1, *Global War*, edited by Jay Winter, 133–171. Cambridge: Cambridge University Press, 2014.

Nash, George H. *The Life of Herbert Hoover, Part II: The Humanitarian 1914–1917.* New York: Norton, 1988.

Nath, Giselle. *Brood willen we hebben! Honger, sociale politiek en protest tijdens de Eerste Wereldoorlog in België.* Antwerp: Manteau, 2013.

Neumann, Helga. *Maximilian Harden (1861–1927): ein unerschrockener deutsch-jüdischer Kritiker und Publizist.* Würzburg: Königshausen & Neumann, 2003.

Nevins, Allan, ed. *The Letters and Journals of Brand Whitlock.* New York: Appleton-Century, 1936.

Nivet, Philippe. *La France occupée.* Paris: Armand Colin, 2014.

Ó'Síocháin, Séamus. *Roger Casement: Imperialist, Rebel, Revolutionary.* Dublin: Lilliput Press, 2011.

Passelecq, Fernand. *Déportation et travail forcé des ouvriers et de la population civile de la Belgique occupée (1916–1918).* Paris: Presses Universitaires de France, 1928.

Piette, Valérie. *Domestiques et servantes: Des vies sous condition.* Bruxelles: Académie Royale de Belgique, 2000.

Pire, Fl. (Abbé). *Histoire de la Congrégation des Aumôniers du Travail, missionnaires des ouvriers, depuis la fondation jusqu'à Novembre 1918.* Charleroi: Imprimerie Collins, 1942.

Pirenne, Henri. *Belgium and the First World War.* Wesley Chapel, FL: Brabant Press, 2014.

Pirenne, Jacques, and Maurice Vauthier. *La législation et l'administration allemandes en Belgique.* Paris: Les Presses Universitaires de France, [1925].

Proctor, Tammy M. *Civilians in a World at War, 1914–1918.* New York: New York University Press, 2010.

Proctor, Tammy M. *Female Intelligence: Women and Espionage in the First World War.* New York: New York University Press, 2003.

Proctor, Tammy M. "Missing in Action: Belgian Civilians and the First World War." *Revue Belge d'histoire contemporaine* 35 (2005): 547–572.

Proctor, Tammy M. "Les politiques de la pomme de terre pendant la Grande Guerre en Europe." In *La Pomme de terre de la Renaissance au XXIe siècle*, edited by Marc de Ferrière le Vayer and Jean-Pierre Williot, 297–310. Rennes: Presses Universitaires de Rennes, 2011.

Ranieri, Liane. *Emile Francqui ou l'intelligence créatrice (1863–1935).* Paris-Gembloux: Duculot, 1985.

Reed-Lewis, William. *Bruges: An English Guide.* Bruges: English Printing Works, 1895.

Roshwald, Aviel. *Ethnic Nationalism and the Fall of Empires: Central Europe, the Middle East, and Russia, 1914–1923*. London: Routledge, 2001.

Rousseaux, Xavier, and Laurence Van Ypersele. "Leaving the War: Popular Violence and Judicial Repression of 'Unpatriotic' Behaviour in Belgium (1918–1921)." *European Review of History* 12, no. 1 (March 2005): 3–22.

Ryheul, Johann. *MarineKorps Flandern 1914–1918*. Hamburg: Mittler und Sohn, 1997.

Scholliers, Peter, and Frank Daelemans. "Standards of Living and Standards of Health in Wartime Belgium." In *The Upheaval of War: Family, Work and Welfare in Europe, 1914–1918*, edited by Richard Wall and Jay Winter, 139–158. Cambridge: Cambridge University Press, 1988.

Stibbe, Matthew. *British Civilian Internees in Germany: The Ruhleben Camp, 1914–18*. Manchester: Manchester University Press, 2008.

Summers, Anne. "Public Functions, Private Premises: Female Professional Identity and the Domestic Service Paradigm in Britain, c. 1850–1930." In *Borderlines: Gender and Identities in War and Peace, 1870–1930*, edited by Billie Melman, 352–376. New York: Routledge, 1998.

Tallier, Pierre-Alain. "'Bruxelles brûle-t-il?' Les explosions de trains de munitions dans les gares bruxelloises en novembre 1918." In *Bruxelles en 14–18: la guerre au quotidien*, edited by Serge Jaumain and Valérie Piette. Brussels, theme issue of *Les Cahiers de la Fonderie* 32 (2005): 28–33.

Tallier, Pierre-Alain, and Sven Carnel. *Inventaire des archives de l'Aide au Village. Oeuvre des Petits Villageois, 1914–1921*. Brussels: Archives Générales du Royaume, 2007.

Thiel, Jens. *Menschenbassin Belgien: Anwerbung, Deportation und Zwangsarbeit im Ersten Weltkrieg*. Essen: Klartext Verlag, 2007.

Thielemans, Marie-Rose. *Albert I: carnets et correspondance de guerre 1914–1918*. Paris-Louvain-la-Neuve: Duculot, 1991.

Turvey, Ralph. "Horse Traction in Victorian London." *Journal of Transport History* 26 (2005): 38–59.

Tytgat, Charles. *Bruxelles sous la botte allemande, de la déclaration de guerre de la Roumanie à la délivrance. Journal d'un journaliste*. Brussels: Imprimerie scientifique Charles Bulens & Cie, 1919.

van Biervliet, Lori. "'Dear Old Bruges': The English Colony in Bruges in the Nineteenth Century." *The Low Countries: Arts and Society in Flanders and the Netherlands* 6 (1998): 52–59.

Van Bosstraeten, Truus. *Bezet maar beschermd. België en de markies van Villalobar tijdens de Eerste Wereldoorlog*. Leuven: Acco, 2008.

Van Craenenbroeck, Yves. "L'Empereur et l'Abbesse. Une visite étonnante à l'Abbaye de Maredret le 23 juin 1916." Maredret, 2015. http://www.maredret.be/patrimoine/patrimoinehistorique/histoire/premiereguerremondiale_1914_1918/annales/lempereuretlabbesse/l_empereur_et_l_abbesse_yves_van_cranenbroeck.pdf.

Van den Abeele, Andries. "Een discrete Engelse aanwezigheid: Uithangborden in het negentiende-eeuwse Brugge." *Biekorf* (1980): 423–425. http://users.skynet.be/sb176943/AndriesVandenAbeele/engelse_aanw_in_brugge.htm.

Van San, Piet, ed. *La correspondance des Belges pendant la première guerre mondiale*. Brussels: Archives Générales du Royaume, 1999.

van Vollenhoven, M. W. R. *Memoires, beschouwingen, belevenissen, reizen en anecdoten door Dr. M.W.R. van Vollenhoven*. Amsterdam: Elsevier, 1948.

Westbrook, Shelby F. *Bolo Pacha: A Forgotten Story about Men & Women Who Made History in WWI*. Bloomington, IN: Trafford, 2009.

Westerman, Thomas. "Rough and Ready Relief: American Identity, Humanitarian Experience, and the Commission for Relief in Belgium, 1914–1917." PhD diss., University of Connecticut, 2014.

Whitlock, Brand. *Belgium: A Personal Narrative*. Vol. 1. New York: D. Appleton, 1919.

Wierling, Dorothee. *Eine Familie im Krieg: Leben, Sterben und Schreiben 1914–1918*. Göttingen: Wallstein Verlag, 2013.

Williamson, John G. *Karl Helfferich, 1872–1924: Economist, Financier, Politician*. Princeton, NJ: Princeton University Press, 2015.

Winter, Jay, and Jean-Louis Robert, eds. *Capital Cities at War: Paris, London, Berlin 1914–1919.* Vol. 1. Cambridge: Cambridge University Press, 1999.

Winter, Jay, and Jean-Louis Robert, eds. *Capital Cities at War: Paris, London, Berlin 1914–1919.* Vol. 2. Cambridge: Cambridge University Press, 2007.Zilch, Reinhold. *Okkupation und Währung im Ersten Weltkrieg. Die Deutsche Besatzungspolitik in Belgien und Russisch-Polen, 1914–1918.* Goldbach: Keip 1994.

INDEX